The
Minimal
Family

The
Minimal
Family

JAN E. DIZARD
and
HOWARD GADLIN

The University of Massachusetts Press
AMHERST

ISBN 0–87023–728–4

A Kailyard Book
Set in Baskerville by Graphic Composition, Inc.
Printed and bound by Thomson-Shore, Inc.

Library of Congress Cataloging-in-Publication Data
Dizard, Jan E.,1940–
   The minimal family / Jan E. Dizard and Howard Gadlin.
      p.   cm.
   Includes bibliographical references (p.   ).
   ISBN0-87023–728–4(alk. paper)
   1.Family—United States. I. Gadlin, Howard. II. Title.
HQ536.D59   1990   90–1081
305.85'0973–dc20   cip

British Library Cataloguing in Publication data are available.

Contents

Preface

The Minimal Family arose from an argument that began between the two of us over fifteen years ago. While we both agreed that the family was being steadily weakened, principally by the ways the economy erodes family solidarity, we disagreed about the significance of the change. Jan saw it as a mixed blessing at best. The change was bringing about greater equality between husband and wife; however, the basis of this equality had less to do with venerable forms of egalitarianism than it did with the reduction of men and women to self-interested economic agents. The decline of the family, from this vantage point, is lamentable. The lament, though, can only evoke nostalgia for a former golden age of family living, an idealization for which Jan had no appetite.

Howard avoided this dilemma by adopting the position that the demise of the family is largely to the good. Both the ideal and the reality of the family carry so many encumbrances on individual freedom and growth that they are insupportable. Even more important, as its conservative defenders insist, the family is a bulwark of the social order. Were the social order just and humane, then the family might be defensible. But clearly our social order can hardly be described as either just or humane. The family, Howard insisted, plays a pivotal role in perpetuating inequalities of class, race, and gender. In short, Howard argued that the family is both psychologically and socially repressive. So fundamental a disagreement is not the most promising basis for collaborative writing. Collaboration is hard enough to sustain, even when authors are in complete agreement about what they are writing. We decided to defy the odds because each of us found ourselves increasingly dissatisfied with the flood of writing on the family and, though it was hard to acknowledge at first, increasingly unhappy with our own stances.

The writing, as might be imagined, did not proceed smoothly. We each drafted sections that neither of us found satisfactory. We fought, and more than once accused the other of long lists of unpardonable ideological rigidities and only somewhat shorter lists of more personal failings. Had ours been a marriage, it certainly would not have survived. Luckily, we were "only" friends. We persisted, as it were, for better or worse. And as we alternately argued and fell silent, we gradually began to glimpse the possibility of a resolution.

We had been laboring with conceptions of how private and public life were related that no longer made sense. Our mutual distrust of the state, combined with our critique of commodity capitalism, had kept us tied to the alternatives of fanciful celebration of familism and equally fanciful hope for a proliferation of defamilized free spirits. What we had been overlooking was the elemental fact that the people whose lives we were trying to describe were by no means passive. If the family was eroding, it was because it no longer met people's needs, not merely because the economy required people to become more grasping or preoccupied with themselves. By the same token, we could not deny that family decline had failed to create the dynamic, emancipated personalities that the death of the family might have led one to expect. In their attempts to fashion better lives—or at least adequate lives—for themselves, ordinary people were changing the meaning of "family," and they were also implicitly changing the relationship between private life and public life.

Since the time when we began arguing and writing, many

books have been written on the fate of the contemporary family.
We looked upon this steady flow of books with decided ambivalence. We often quietly hoped that someone else would write the
book we were trying to write and get us off the hook. Even
though many of the books were stunning—and very helpful to
us—those that aimed at a general interpretation for the most
part reproduced one or the other side of our initial divergence.
They either deplored decline or discovered virtue in the latest
trend. Why should it be so hard to break away from these unsatisfactory alternatives?

As we were in that final stages of readying *The Minimal Family*
for the typesetter, a book appeared and caused us momentary
panic. In *Whose Keeper: Social Science and Moral Obligation* (Berkeley: University of California Press, 1989), Alan Wolfe raises precisely the questions that lay at the heart of our concerns: What
are private, family responsibilities and what should we rightfully
expect from the worlds of work and public policy? Wolfe even
comes close to using the phrase "public familism" that we
adopted early on in our work when he refers to Scandinavian
social policies as constituting a "public family." But for all the
shared assumptions between his work and ours, Wolfe cannot
let go of the idea that the family is simply being swamped by a
tide of economic self-interest and that even enlightened public
policy robs people of their spunk and independence.

He writes:

> [T]he weakening of the boundary between family and the market
> has real benefits, especially for women. These benefits are so im-
> portant, moreover, that most people, including this author, believe
> that we should not, even if we could, "go back" to the family struc-
> ture of the 1950s. . . . Yet one ought also to recognize that, along
> with the greater freedom of choice associated with market inter-
> vention into the family, it is more likely that consideration of self-
> interest associated with the economy will serve as moral codes
> within the family than that the family will serve as a moral world
> capable of influencing behavior in the economy (54).

Though Wolfe applauds increased gender equality, he records grave misgivings about the long-term consequences of
families' reliance on the state for the provision of many services

that were once the sole prerogative of the family. Wolfe suggests ". . . that as intimate ties weaken, so will distant ones, thus undermining the very moral strengths the welfare state has shown" (142). In other words, when people no longer rely directly upon one another they will cease being active citizens except when their own immediate comforts are threatened. There is much in contemporary social life, and even more in contemporary political life, that corroborates Wolfe's concerns. The rise of the right, most notably in the United States and the United Kingdom, but with visibility even in Scandinavia, can be seen in the terms Wolfe sets forth. In particular, the extent of opposition to new taxes seems to support Wolfe's contention. But without public familism, there is no apparent substitute for the traditional family. Wolfe, and the rest of us, appear trapped between an insupportable tradition and an equally insupportable individualism that is too easily manipulated by market forces.

Our argument is that the result is more complex than most seem willing to grant. To be sure, much that has changed has changed because an economy driven by profit-seeking has required it. However, people have neither easily nor fully accommodated to these imperatives. Moreover, as they wrestle with the changes experienced by their families, they are creating new needs that by no means fit easily into the agenda of industrial and commercial elites. In short, however much we share Wolfe's anxieties, our reading of how increasing numbers of people juggle the need for intimacy, the requirements of the workplace, and the temptations of consumer capitalism suggests that we are in the midst of a significant redrawing of the boundaries between public and private domains.

Two things are at issue. Having largely reshaped private life to accord with the requirements of an expanding industrial and commercial order, people are now beginning to demand that the economy be reoriented toward easing the pressures on their private lives. At the same time, there has also been steadily mounting pressure on both the state and employers to provide the social supports that traditionally have been associated with familial obligation. This shift is what we are calling the move toward public familism—shifting the premises of public policy and the marketplace from a preoccupation with accumulation

and narrowly defined efficiency to a sensitivity to the diversity
of life-styles and rhythms of private life.

We do not know whether these boundary changes will make
people passive, willing to be cared for, and reluctant to stand up
for principle for fear of being inconvenienced. There certainly
is a risk. But those who claim a benevolent employer or a welfare
state is destructive of hardy individualism and political independence have to contend with some uncomfortable facts. Paternal-
ist employers have rarely held workers in thrall for long. And as
we write this preface, millions of East Europeans are exerting
themselves in behalf of freedom. Some are fleeing to the West
but many more, at least for now, are demonstrating on behalf of
democratizing reforms at home. The capacity to resist, to speak
the truth, and to defend individual conscience and dignity is not
so easily extinguished.

Being taken care of need not induce passivity. If there is a
lesson in our analysis, it is that being taken care of and treated
decently ought to be a right. Like all rights, it has to be fought
for and, once secured, continually defended. Surely, there will
be periods of acquiescence and quietude, but fears that this will
be permanent are, we think, seriously misplaced.

Neither people's private lives nor the state will ever be fully
satisfactory or adequately responsive to the full range of individual and collective needs, if only because these needs will invariably change over time. As a result, we can expect continued,
albeit intermittent, conflict and flux as people strive to forge decent lives for themselves. No matter how diverse the definitions
of a decent life may be, all will require substantially increased
solicitude and flexibility from the public arena. Public familism,
in this context, is not a fixed agenda. Rather, it is more a sensibility, a set of expectations about how we should be treated and
how we should understand the inevitable dependencies and obligations that give shape and meaning to our lives.

We incurred many obligations in the course of bringing *The
Minimal Family* to fruition. Deborah Gewertz and Frederick Er-
rington gave us the first critical reading of our manuscript. Both
their critique and their encouragement came at a moment when
our uncertainty and self-doubt had peaked. Without their support, many more years might have passed before we finished.

Bill and Zelda Gamson, Bob Ross, Milton Cantor, Bruce Laurie, Donald Pitkin, David Wellman, Jim Youniss, and George Levinger all read earlier versions of the manuscript and gave us invaluable suggestions for ways to improve it. Jerry Himmelstein and Alan Babb were both steady supports and willing sounding boards as we began to test and refine our ideas. Betty Steele, Margaret Ferro, Paul Chapin, and Craig Garnett, the bedrock of Amherst College's fine computer center, made our move into the world of word processing as smooth and reassuring as it could have been. Their resourcefulness and good humor saved us untold numbers of hours, not to mention sanity itself. Ronald Pipkin was also generous with his expertise and experience in helping us exploit the intricacies of WordPerfect.

Rebecca Davison and Susan Mesner, aka Kailyard Associates of Montpelier, never lost interest or confidence in this project. It is fair to say that whatever clarity the manuscript exhibits is the result of their labors. It is also fair to say that without their persistence, we may never have persevered. At a late stage in the progress of the manuscript, Rosanna Hertz and Bruce Wilcox, the former as a reviewer and the latter as publisher, each generously provided us with many helpful ideas for revision.

Each of us, of course, has his own personal debts to acknowledge. Robin Dizard was, as much as anyone, responsible for Jan's contribution, not by being an editor, or typist, or long-suffering wife but rather by being herself. Robin demonstrated that it is possible to be autonomous and dependent, loving and self-possessed: this made the project, even in its earliest and most abstract versions, seem practical and compelling. Jesse and Seth Dizard made Jan continually aware of how dependency and love can be both emancipating and constraining. They have been patient teachers.

The graduate students in the Psychology Department at the University of Massachusetts encouraged Howard's forays beyond the boundaries of psychology. Howard's daughters, Mari and Jennifer, have kept him honest—insuring that his critique of the family neither overlooked its many pleasures nor oversimplified its many complexities. And finally, Brenda Hanning restored Howard's belief in the possibility of an intimacy that is both deeply satisfying and enduring.

Our individual and collective debt to all the above named is large, lightened, to be sure, by the prospect of association that will extend well beyond the preoccupations of readying *The Minimal Family* for publication.

The
Minimal
Family

1

The Emergence of the
Modern Family

TOWARD THE END OF APRIL, 1985, two young brothers, one twenty-two months, the other three and one-half years old, were placed in a foster home in the Highland Park section of Roxbury, a neighborhood in Boston. The children had been placed in foster care because they were thought to be at risk of being battered in their own parents' home. Indeed, their biological mother had approved of the placement. The placement had been arranged under the aegis of the Massachusetts Department of Social Services (DSS), which oversees foster care in the state. DSS, an agency formally charged with preserving and rebuilding families, had estimated that it needed at least 25 percent more homes to provide adequate care for the 6,000 children in need of foster care. Although foster families receive a modest allowance ($7 a day for childen under twelve, $10 for older children) to help cover expenses, foster homes are not easily found. Foster families must be deemed able to provide a "safe, nurturing, and stable family environment" and to have an "absence of physical, mental, and emotional impairments."

The foster parents, one a senior investigator for discrimination with the Boston Fair Housing Commission, the other a professional nutritionist, hoped that the foster care arrangement would be the first step toward a permanent adoption. They had been together as a couple for ten years and very much wanted to raise children. They had gone through a detailed eleven month long investigation to assess their suitability as foster parents. They had also been given letters of support from their respective ministers, a Unitarian pastor and a Catholic priest. Once approved, they had participated in a six week foster parent training program.

Two weeks after the brothers had arrived, the *Boston Globe* (9 May 1985) ran a story about neighborhood reaction to their foster care placement. While such placements are not usually newsworthy, the brothers had attracted attention because their foster parents were a homosexual couple, Donald Babetts, thirty-six, and David Jean, thirty-one. When contacted by a *Globe* reporter, a spokesperson for DSS said the placement had been based on the "clinical decisions of our professional staff." Later that same day, DSS removed the children from their foster home and placed them in a temporary home. A DSS statement about the action said, "We have decided it is clinically not in these children's best interest to remain in their current placement, and we are changing that placement today." In their own statement, Babetts and Jean said, "We wish to make it clear that we believe the removal of the boys from our home was not in their best interest. To see them leave us—angry, confused, and in tears, was one of the most difficult moments of our lives."

Both the initial foster placement with the gay couple and the subsequent revocation of that placement evoked strong feelings and controversy. Ben Haith, a community activist in the Highland Park neighborhood, was quoted as saying about the placement, "I'm completely opposed to it. I see it ultimately as a breakdown of the society and its values and morals." Jeff Lewis, of the National Gay Task Force, said that Massachusetts " . . . is denying the fact that a gay couple can create a loving family and a loving environment for children, and that is unfortunate for the children and for the couples who want to be parents."

Two weeks after the controversy erupted, the Massachusetts Department of Human Services announced a new policy guiding foster care placements. Anyone applying to be a foster parent is to be asked his or her sexual preference. Massachusetts thus became the first state in the country to inquire of the sexual preference of potential foster parents. While there were only a few states with policies explicitly prohibiting discrimination in foster placements and adoption, there were almost no states with laws or standards that barred homosexuals from being approved as foster parents. In its new guidelines, Massachusetts pledged itself to seek to place children "only in traditional family settings . . . that is, with relatives or in families with married couples, preferably with parenting experience and time available to care for foster children." Governor Michael Dukakis denied that the new policy constituted discrimination against homosexuals. He is reported to have said, "We're not talking about sexual preference here, we're talking about what is in the best interest of the children . . . . I think that's what the vast majority of people in this country believe. I believe it."[1] The plight of Donald Babetts and David Jean and the two boys who were being bounced from home to home reveals vividly the several strands of contemporary confusion and anguish about the family. Most obviously, there is the matter of what constitutes a family. Since the Massachusetts foster care ruling, courts in other jurisdictions have also contended with this matter. In one recent case, the New York Court of Appeals ruled that tenancy in a rent controlled apartment could legitimately pass to the gay lover of a deceased leaseholder under provisions that protect family members from eviction. Writing for the majority, Judge Titone observed that " . . . a more realistic, and certainly equally valid, view of a family includes two adult lifetime partners whose relationship is long-term and characterized by an emotional and financial commitment and interdependence."[2] While narrowly specifying the context as one involving evictions, Judge Titone's opinion clearly signals the shift that is occurring in the ways we think about family.[3]

Related to questions of definition are uncertainties about the criteria by which we judge what constitutes a "safe, nurturing, and stable family environment," and the suitability of people to parent. Our nation's high divorce rate alone makes stability an unreliable indicator of parenting adequacy, even with people who are in all other regards completely conventional. And the regular appearance of stories detailing physical and sexual abuse within families that seemingly meet all the criteria of "normal" create doubts about our ability to assess the safety and nurturance of a household merely from the outward appearances of those who would be parents. If we consider the multitude of ways in which people themselves understand their commitments to one another and the meanings they give to the living arrangements they construct, it is no longer possible to declare with confidence that a family consists of husband, wife, and their child(ren). Such a definition excludes the nearly 25 percent of American households that are headed by a single parent. It also excludes homosexual couples as well as heterosexual couples who have not married. And of course it excludes those who have chosen to live communally as well as those who prefer to live alone. Taken together, it is probable that close to a third of all American households are now occupied by people who are not a family in any ordinary or conventional sense.

The definitional quandary arises out of profound—and to some, profoundly threatening—changes that seem to have suddenly swept over us. Dramatic increases in divorce, equally dramatic relaxation of cultural prohibitions against unmarried cohabitation and homosexuality, and a steadily growing disinclination to marry (or remarry) have rapidly led to variations in intimate relations that, together, have produced a genuine confusion over what kinds of relationships can legitimately be regarded as constituting a family.

The issue is not merely definitional, however. What is at stake, though it is almost never put this way, is who shall be the bearers of familism. By "familism" we mean a reciprocal sense of commitment, sharing, cooperation, and intimacy that is taken as defining the bonds between family members. These bonds represent the more or less unconstrained acknowledgement of both material and emotional dependency and obligation. They put legitimate claims on one's own material and emotional resources and put forth a set of "loving obligations" that entitles members of the family to expect warmth and support from fellow family members. In addition, these bonds are assumed to be deeper and more lasting than those that exist in other, nonfamilial relationships. Familism embraces solicitude, unconditional love, personal loyalty, and willingness to sacrifice for others. Familism makes the home a base to which you can always return when your independent endeavors fail or prove unsatisfactory. In December 1986, when a mercenary supporter of the Contras in Nicaragua was captured by the Sandinistas, his brother, a liberal congressman and a staunch opponent of aid to the Contras, urged the Sandinistas to release his brother. The congressman explained, though an explanation was scarcely needed, that whatever their differences they were still brothers. The press corps saw no need to pursue the matter.

Familism not only describes key aspects of the relationships among family members, it also differentiates between relationships among family members and relationships with others. At least since the early nineteenth century, American society has contrasted the way one feels and acts toward members of one's family with the ways one feels and acts toward those outside the family circle. Most Americans are so accustomed to distinguishing between family and nonfamily relationships that the difference seems a natural one to them. But while the significance of family ties has long been acknowledged, the distinct separation of family and public spheres is a relatively new distinction.[4]

In colonial America, as the historian John Demos has shown, it was expected that all relationships, familial or other, be directed by the same "guiding values and inner purposes. . . . [T]he family and the wider community [were] joined in a relation of profound reciprocity; one might almost say they [were] continuous with one another."[5] The way one learned to act toward others in the family was seen as the model for acting in the community generally. Indeed, such thinking was the basis for the belief that the family is the building block of society, a belief that remains pervasive to the point of being a cliche. But as familism was progressively squeezed out of public life by the spread of marketplace rationality, a trend we shall examine in some detail later, familism came to be associated almost exclusively with the family. The world outside the home might be uncaring, immoral, and viciously competitive, but the family at least was a place where cooperativeness, mutual concern, and morality could safely reside. So long as this seemed true, the conviction that the family could be a restraining or a civilizing force could be clung to.

To the extent that people have come to associate familism exclusively with the family, many see alternatives to the conventional family as threatening. Diversity feeds the fear that as individual families founder, the society is weakened. Mary Jo Bane, a leading sociological analyst of the family, has argued that this fear is exaggerated: the vast majority of American men and women marry and have children. And though divorce rates are at or near historic highs, the rate of marital dissolution from all sources (including death of spouse) is not significantly higher than it was in the nineteenth century (when there were few divorces and many deaths, especially among women of childbearing age).[6] But those, like Bane, who contend that there is no particular crisis in family relations miss a crucial point: our desire to *form* families may remain strong, and in that sense the abstract idea of the family may be secure, but our capacity to sustain real families, and with them a sense of familism, is clearly questionable.[7]

In this sense, the crisis of the family is less about the trials and tribulations of individual families, or even the form the family takes, than it is about the steadily shrinking range of social contexts that call forth our capacities to cooperate, love, and make sacrifices for one another. If families, conventionally conceived, cannot be depended upon to nurture familism, where might familism be fostered? Questions such as this have aroused more anxiety than they have produced answers. The result has been a constant nagging sense of tension, a sense that things are not quite right, even though most people report that their own lives are not particularly unsatisfying or perturbed. It is important to recognize that a wide range of people, from reactionary defenders of old-fashioned patriarchy to radical critics of the structured inequalities of American life, have shared this concern and come to the defense of the family, warning of the consequences of its decline. But what unites these proponents of sharply conflicting social programs and political positions is a shared sense of the importance of familism. This is not to say, however, that proponents of each of these political viewpoints value familism for the same reasons. Conservatives emphasize the loyalties and respect for authority that familism can entail, while more progressive thinkers value the way unconditional love and family loyalty provide a psychological basis for independent critical thinking and resistance to authority. For each of these positions, familism is the basis of hopeful responses to the most threatening or objectionable features of contemporary society.

This widespread concern that families may no longer be generating familism as a counterweight to the egoism, avarice, and detachment that so commonly prevail in our workplaces, emporia, and in our interactions with agencies of government, makes all the more paradoxical the denial of family status to people who wish to raise children as an expression of their commitment to each other and the next generation. On the one hand, unconventional families are accused of threatening the values and commitments for which families stand. On the other hand, when they attempt to demonstrate those very same commitments and values, they are denied the opportunity to incorporate them into their lives. For most Americans, familism and the conventional family are so strongly associated that efforts to infuse nontraditional living arrangements with the values and commitments of familism seem like yet another assault on the already fragile family. Thus cohabitation, communal and group living arrangements, and homosexual couples, no matter how deep and conventional the sentiments and commitments that bind them, are judged by many as a threat to the very idea of family.

The Emotional Ties That Bind

The sense of crisis that has suffused virtually all contemporary discussions of the family is part of a longstanding American tradition that can be traced as far back as the decades just prior to the American War of Independence. The political turbulence of those years, marked by confident talk of freedoms, inalienable rights, and democracy, had unmistakable reverberations in domestic life, particularly in the relationships between parents and children. At issue, on the surface, was the growing insistence

that young men and women have greater freedom in choosing
their own spouse as well as more latitude in determining when
it was appropriate to marry. Both in England and the colonies,
parental control over mate selection had been easing gradually.
But, as is so often the case, the steady erosion of a social pattern
makes the residual manifestations of it all the more odious for
those pursuing change. As a custom nears extinction, protest
over it grows more vocal and urgent. To a degree that would
shock those who wish to think of our forebears as paragons of
virtue, this youthful assertion of independence was signaled by
a rapid rise in premarital conceptions. Reticent and imperious
parents were being confronted, if you will, with a *fetus accompli*.
In some New England towns, as many as 15 percent of all brides
were pregnant well before their wedding day.[8] This rebellious-
ness, and the breakdown in moral order it was presumed to indicate, fed the waves of religious revival that swept the newly
independent nation in the first third of the nineteenth century.
The Second Great Awakening, as this period of religious fervor
came to be called, bore down heavily on the presumed erosion
of moral conduct and scored the permissiveness that had allegedly become widespread.[9]

As important as this moral indignation was, the sense of alarm
sprang from deeper, more complex developments. Parental authority, potently symbolized in parents' control of the mate selection process, represented more than meddling in the affairs
of children. Parental power traditionally embraced a wide range
of claims on couples, not simply during courtship or at the point
of the decision to marry, but throughout married life. Involved
were such economic considerations as who would help work the
land or manage the herd, who would remain at or near the parents' home to assist them should they grow infirm, and so on.
Moreover, parental claims also represented ties that bound the
couple to a network of kinfolk who were, typically, economically
as well as emotionally interdependent. This elaborate web of
claims greatly circumscribed the couple, implicating them in numerous reciprocal obligations. The net effect was an emphasis
on the bonds between the couple and others in the network of
kin and diminished importance of the bonds between husband
and wife. Thus, the challenge to parental authority as regards

mate selection was also a challenge to what had been the customary balance between kinfolk and the nuclear family.[10]

Many young people were, in effect, acting upon a set of expectations for family life that revolved around the desire for greater intimacy and affection between husband and wife, and between parents and their young offspring. Marriage, they were asserting, should be based on romantic attachment, not on the basis of how well the prospective mates met parents' needs. When parents controlled mate selection, they chose largely on the basis of the qualities of a prospective mate's family: Was he or she from "good stock," from a family that could be depended upon or that would present some advantage for one's own family? This is not the stuff of romance. It is simply another way of expressing the dominance of the larger family system over the couple. The couple's interests, whatever they might be, were presumed to coincide with those of their kin group and, should the two diverge, the kin group took precedence. To wish for a romantic aspect was to question the subordination of the couple to the larger kin network.[11]

Historian Lawrence Stone insists that this emphasis on emotional bonds between husband and wife sets the modern family off from its predecessors.[12] The modern family is expected to be emotionally self-sufficient. Traditional households, even when they were commonly home only to a nuclear family, were expected to be permeable: kin were accommodated. By contrast, the modern nuclear family is distinctly more autonomous, set apart from kin and the networks they formed. It is not that relatives become totally irrelevant: they simply become peripheral.

Correlatively, the bonds between nuclear family members grow more intense, far more emotional. In traditional households relationships between spouses and between parents and children were not necessarily affectionate. Indeed, love and affection were long regarded as a silly, if not dangerously fragile, basis for marriage. But as traditional family arrangements slowly dissolved, love became the preeminent basis for marriage. The young wanted to marry those they cared for, not necessarily those who would best fulfill the obligations and duties of family life. The modern family came to have an emotional economy of its own, a set of relationships predicated on the romantic attachment of husband and wife and their affection for their children. The maintenance of this emotional economy necessarily reduced the intensity of their involvement with others, especially kin.

By the late eighteenth century, this change was apparent but by no means unambiguously secure. In part, though the reasons for this are still unclear, the earliest expressions of the change seem to have been limited to England and, via the English settlers, the New World. The European continent, not to mention the rest of the world, was to remain bound to traditional forms of family life well into the nineteenth century and beyond. Even in England and the American colonies, the modern family's arrival was uneven. Its first appearance, according to the research of Stone, was made among the English elite in the mid-seventeenth century.[13] Two interrelated changes began and became mutually reinforcing. First, there was a marked rise in the affect between husbands and wives and between them and their children. Before the mid-1600s, it was customary for the elite to send their children away at birth to be cared for by a retainer. Only after weaning, some eighteen months to two years after birth, did the son or daughter of the elite enter the parental home. Needless to say, this early and prolonged separation was not conducive to high levels of emotional involvement. But by the end of the seventeenth century, this practice was being sharply attacked and was in decline.

Second, swaddling of infants also began to be met with widespread disfavor by the seventeenth century. Doctors and other domestic advice givers urged that infants be more lightly dressed that they might move their limbs and better be cuddled and comforted by their mother. Swaddling was an ancient device for managing infants in a context in which the caretaker had many tasks and could not be bothered by the insistent demands an unfettered infant would impose. The demise of swaddling not only signaled a heightened regard for the person of the infant and an enlarged sense of the infant's need for freer expression, it also signified a greater emphasis on the role of the wife as mother. Other household tasks receded in importance and childcare began to assume a prominence in the mother's life that is now commonplace. As the role of the mother began to be

elevated and infused with sentiment, a parallel sentimentalization was occurring in the relationship between husband and
wife.

According to Stone, new ideals of intimacy and privacy for
the couple began to be articulated, and emphasis on duty to one
another was gradually supplanted by an emphasis on love for
one another. The couple, as an entity, slowly disengaged from
the web of kin that had long been the predominant locus of
loyalty for husband and wife. Gradually, the couple emerged as
the principal object of attachment, and the larger world of kin
and associates was set apart, ultimately even against, the conjugal pair. Stone calls this emergent family arrangement "companionate marriage," adopting a usage that was made popular in
the United States by the sociologist Ernest W. Burgess.[14] Though
Burgess was referring to a family form he identified as coming
into prevalence in the twentieth century in the United States, his
description bears striking resemblance to the family norms that
Stone discovers among the English elite by the late eighteenth
century. These norms focused on the expectation that the
couple would be emotionally self-contained, the attractions of
love and friendship between husband and wife far outweighing
the sense of obligation either might feel toward relatives or
friends.

This emphasis on the emotional bonds between husband and
wife went hand in hand with a growing emphasis on love, personal attraction, and compatibility as a basis for mate selection.
The greater solicitude that parents began to show their children, from infancy onward, obviously contributed to the gradual enlargement of parental accession to the wishes of their children in mate selection as well. Romantic attraction as a prelude
to marriage, and the expectation that love and affection would
continue to grow and deepen after marriage, also carried the
implication that the formal hierarchy in the household, a hierarchy that demanded deference to the husband, also gradually
began giving way to more egalitarian modes in family life. Husbands and wives were becoming companions, lovers, and partners in an emotional enterprise.

It bears repeating, before we proceed, that these changes in
family life were by no means unfolding as coherently as we are

making it seem here. The historical sequence, if there be such in this matter, was most irregular. As we read the record, we have found it helpful to imagine a number of developments occurring simultaneously but semiautonomously. At first, few grasped the full implications of what were seen and experienced as independent developments. Some could endorse certain of the changes and incorporate them into their family life; other changes were rejected as too radical a departure from tradition or too threatening to their social position. Moreover, as the several strands of change advanced and began to converge, broader implications became apparent and, for some, abhorrent. One particularly vivid example of this tangled process may suffice for our purposes.

In the very beginning of industrialism in England, when the first textile mills appeared, the assumptions that governed the recruitment of labor were assumptions rooted in traditional society, a society in which the family was the basic unit of production and family organization was also labor force organization. Thus, in the earliest days of the factory, entire families would be employed. The male head of household was, in effect, a working foreman hired to do a certain job for which he would enlist and supervise the labors of his wife and children.[15] Factory work was not welcomed by many, but in its early stages, at least, it was not particularly disruptive of longstanding traditions of family life and authority. But as this traditional model of the family grew weaker among the elite, the elite came to see another sort of advantage in the changing family. Instead of hiring only family heads, employers began to hire individuals as individuals, not as members of family units. The result was to undermine the authority of the husband-father and, at the same time, drive wages down. There were, no doubt, terrible motives at work in this. But the evident cupidity of employers was possible because the traditional family, which had protected factory hands from some kinds of abuses, was no longer in favor. The protests of workers whose standards of living were being driven down, along with their dignity as householders and family heads, fell on deaf, or at least unsympathetic, ears, in part because the norms the protesters appealed to were no longer widely shared. Workers' attempts to smash machinery and burn down factories were as much defenses of traditional norms as they were harbingers of a new class consciousness.

What we see in this instance is not only how the broader implications of family change occasioned considerable dislocation and protest but also how the sentimentalizing of nuclear family relations went along with the draining of sentiment from other sorts of bonds, including the paternalistic bonds that had existed between the elite and the working class. The world outside the household gradually was becoming differentiated from the world of the home. At home, one came to expect love and consideration. Away from home, self-interest became the prevailing motif, the governing principle. The circle of people to whom one felt obligated and for whom one was responsible was shrinking, and conceptions of morality and justice were shifting from a basis in community and family to a basis in individuals themselves. These interwoven changes had the effect of gradually constricting familism to the domain of the family. And as the family itself grew smaller, familism, too, seemed to diminish. Let us examine this more closely, shifting our attention from England to the American colonies, especially New England.

Constricting Familism

The settlers who removed to the New World needed a stern faith in order to persevere in the face of the rigors that greeted them. After a debilitating Atlantic passage, they had to contend with a harsh climate and a land that was only slightly less difficult to clear than to coax into fecundity. These rigors obliged the new arrivals to draw upon the resources of the group rather than depend solely upon their families to see them through. Indeed, their interpretation of the Bible made the relationship between the community and individual families a particularly close one.[16] It was the proper role of the community, operating through the congregation and through civil agencies, to strengthen the moral and social cohesion of the family. The husband-wife bond, ideally to be arrived at prayerfully with the guidance of God, the Father, as well as with the guidance and approval of fathers, was an important bond but not unbreakable should the community decide that the union was incapable of sustaining a well-ordered religious household. Love and affection, it was assumed, would best develop and be nourished in orderly, observant homes.

In many respects, the Puritans were a bundle of contradictions. The bundle began to unravel before too many generations grew to maturity in the colonies. They carried both the old and the new within them and had no way of reconciling the call of obligation and the pull of the heart except through unremitting religiosity. Even in the short run, this intense religiosity was impossible to sustain. The Puritans insisted upon devotion to kin, including the kin acquired through marriage. Samuel Sewall, a prominent early Bostonian, records in his diary his correspondence with literally hundreds of kinfolk, reporting on news of the family on this side of the ocean and eagerly asking of news from the other side. Moreover, he relies on kinsmen in England to help him make business contacts and to vouchsafe his honor and trustworthiness. In spite of the difficulties of sustaining such a correspondence, he took it upon himself as part of his duty and reproached himself when he let his correspondence falter.[17] This loyalty to and embeddedness in kin obligations is anything but modern.

But Sewall's diary also records involvement with members of his immediate family that are distinctly modern. Unlike the accounts of callousness that seem to have prevailed earlier, he records profound and touching grief at the loss of a child. And though his efforts at consoling his daughters and sons in their sicknesses and confusions seem awkward at best and counterproductive at worst, it is nonetheless clear that he takes, as we would now say, "parenting" most seriously. One can see beneath the language of religious duty and piety a growing sensitivity to the particular needs of children who are assumed to be distinct individuals with distinctly discrete needs.

If tradition and modernity dwelt within Samuel Sewall, so too did they reside in the community itself. In the Puritans' conception of the social order, the family was the fundamental building block upon which all else rested. Sound families would produce sound, well-ordered communities that, in turn, would perpetuate sound families. Sadly, all families were not sound. As a result, the Puritan community, through church and courts, was an interventionist force in family life. Not content to rely on the strength of kinship bonds to keep individual families in line, the power of the community was enlisted to enforce traditional norms, especially those buttressing the prerogatives of the male head. For example, the colonists carried on with inheritance patterns that kept sons closely bound to their fathers. As a result, men were well into their twenties before taking a bride, and many waited until they were thirty or more years old before marrying. Communities passed numerous laws that regulated family life and kept continuity with tradition.[18]

But even the vigorous moral vigilance of the early settlers was not up to the task of stemming the tide of sentiment. In fact, as was disturbingly apparent on the eve of the War of Independence, the very successes of the colonists helped to set loose the desires for greater personal freedom, including freedom from parental authority. As settlements grew and became secure, it became apparent that the new continent offered a staggering abundance of land. To be sure, putting the land to use for grazing and crops often presented formidable challenges and risks, but population pressures and the difficulties posed by multiple claims on inheritance pressed colonists to spread inland, away from the coastal settlements. Though this process was governed by Royal deeds and the controls of tradition, access to land, the material underpinning of parental authority, was inexorably shifting the balance toward greater autonomy for children. The effect, expressed over the course of several generations, was to give sons (and their prospective brides) greater latitude in determining for themselves when and whom they would marry.

Solidification of the settlements, coupled with fairly rapid population growth and dispersion of settlements, meant that commerce began to grow. Though needs were, by modern standards, rudimentary, and in spite of the fact that families continued to produce most of what they required for survival, the prospects for trade between settlements and for transatlantic commerce increased rapidly. Before long, the colonies were able to support a middle class—a class of people who did not need to produce for their own consumption—as well as a class of artisans. Settlements were becoming more diversified and complex. As they did, there were more and more opportunities for individuals to strike out on their own, more or less independent of parental wish. Family connections were by no means irrelevant, but they were no longer the only vehicle for social placement.

Young Ben Franklin, for example, set out for Philadelphia after finding little pleasure in pursuing the trade in which his older brother had become established. With no connections awaiting him, he nonetheless found himself a job in a print shop and from there began his most illustrious career, in spite of rather than with the assistance of kin.[19] To be sure, Franklin is in no way typical. Early on, it was only the atypical, the unusually talented or lucky or stubbornly independent, who took such autonomous moves. Most were still living close to the land and to the conditions of life and labor that made cleaving to kin materially necessary if not emotionally gratifying.

In this sense, though we think Stone correct to anchor the modern family's emergence in the emphasis on sentimental attachments within the nuclear family, the modern family is also indebted to the rise of a market economy. Without the market, which offers a means of exchanging goods and services independent of kinship, sentimental attachments would necessarily have remained heavily circumscribed by the need to maintain the cohesion of the kin network. By the same token, the separation of the nuclear family from the wider network of kin, such that it could establish its own emotional economy, depended upon the growth of community structures that could support and sustain this disengagement. Sentiment simply cannot stand by itself as a basis for family life.

The modern family, this is to say, reduces its ties to kin and focuses in on the needs of the nuclear family. Reduced dependency on kin requires extremes of self-sufficiency, emotional and material, that few can sustain. Alternatively, autonomy from kin can be sustained by reliance on impersonal networks of exchange, provided these networks are both varied and stable enough to be depended upon. However much people may have begun to want to follow their hearts in matters of family formation and relations among kin, the full expression of these aspirations awaited the moment when emotional autonomy could be roughly matched by material autonomy, by the capacity to support wife and children without heavy reliance on kin or traditional community networks. Personal obligations to people outside the immediate family circle had to be replaced by impersonal, diffuse obligations in order to free up the emotional reservoir from which the nuclear family would draw its cohesion.

The development of commerce made it possible for more and more people to act upon their desires for companionate marriage.[20] We cannot identify a date when these several and seemingly unrelated developments converged sufficiently to produce a stable basis for the modern family. Of course, the issue is not when the first modern couple emerges, nor even when isolated examples can be discovered. Rather, it is when such arrangements become generally available and accepted. This is obviously open to considerable debate. If by "general" one means the whole of a population, then the modern family's time has still not arrived. But by the early nineteenth century the modern nuclear family was well established in the urban middle class—the aggregate of shopkeepers, factory owners, doctors, lawyers, and ministers, as well as numbers of skilled artisans, many of whom would themselves go on to become tradesmen and factory owners.

Historians of the American family have now amassed considerable data on this stratum of the population, and much if not all of it clearly reveals the presence of those aspects of the modern family we have been discussing.[21] By the early nineteenth century, it seemed utterly uncontroversial, indeed, virtually commonplace, for the young to marry whom they chose so long as they could demonstrate to parents that they did so out of genuine love for one another. Of course, then as now, parents could try to veto a marriage that seemed inappropriate or outrageous, but they no longer had the automatic backing of the community in this and the young had recourse of their own.[22] But the diaries of young and adult alike reflect the broad acceptance, again at least in the middle class, of romantic love as the basis for a happy marriage and of the appropriateness of letting the young themselves determine the genuineness of their love. Indeed, it is important to remind ourselves that to take for granted the need for happiness in marriage, the need for emotional satisfaction gained from affection and intimacy, was itself constitutive of a tremendous change from the expectations in force only a few generations earlier.

No doubt part of the reason parents were willing to concede considerable freedom in mate selection to their children can be found in the significantly enlarged concern that parents showed for their children's happiness, in childhood as well as later in life. Again, diaries of the period, from both men and women, reveal an intense involvement in the emotional life of the child, in some instances almost to the point of obsession.

> Bronson Alcot, father of the famous author, records in his journal his reaction to the birth of his daughter, Anna, in 1831: "How delightful were the emotions produced by the first sounds of the infant's cry—making it seem that I was, indeed, a father! Joy, gratitude, hope and affection were all mingled in our feeling."[23]

> A woman worries in 1846: "I lay awake all night thinking I do not know what course to persue (sic) with our children. They need much more care than I can possibly bestow. . . ."

> A father writes to his son (24 years of age) in 1855: "We hope you will ever consider us your best friends, and as such freely and fully communicate with us at all times and on all subjects as you may desire."[24]

The contrast with traditional standards of emotional disengagement could not be more striking.

At this same juncture, we discover explicit changes in the ways middle-class men and women conceived of their marital roles.[25] In the increasing differentiation between home and community, between the public and private that constitutes another of the features of the emergence of the modern family, the wife comes to be the keeper of an increasingly idealized home. Entrusted with the family's virtue, she was the religious beacon and emotional helmsman. Her engagement in the public sphere was ideally limited to religious activities, churches having become the only public institution that retained any measure of continuity with familial values. In some circles at least, women came to be regarded as the force that cooled the passions awakened by the rapidly expanding stimulations of public life. Old moral conceptions were dissolving, and traditional notions of social place were being rapidly replaced with a freer, more relaxed sense of opportunity. Gone were the strictures of the Puritans and, in the larger cities at any rate, the sense of community norms was dissolving in a sea of anonymity. Self-control was an issue of considerable concern, and many looked to the home, particularly to the wife, for this control.[26]

For his part, the middle-class husband was to be enterprising and upwardly striving, ever alert to the opportunities that were assumed to be everywhere. Though the marketplace was volatile, to say the least, the net direction seemed ever upward: commerce was expanding, both in terms of volume of goods changing hands as well as in terms of the variety of goods and services entering the stream of commerce. The important feature of this trend, for our discussion, is that without a vigorous and growing economy, people have to rely upon kinfolk and other face-to-face dependencies. This is inimical to sustaining the delicate balance between intense emotional bonds and the acknowledgement of individuality that is the hallmark of the modern family. But a vigorous economy also requires at least some people to be vigorously engaged in it. Thus, the emergent norm for the male role in the modern family was to be the breadwinner. Men had long been regarded as the chief economic force in the family—the holder of title to lands, the person responsible for entering into contractual obligations, and the principal organizer of the labors of wife and children. This pattern, with modifications reflecting urban-rural differences as well as differences between the working class and the precarious middle class of small-scale shopkeepers and artisans who frequently employed family members at low or no wage in their efforts to gain a foothold on the ladder of success, continued well into the twentieth century. But for the growing ranks of the secure middle class, the husband quickly became the sole economic agent in the family.

Conclusion

In sum, by the mid-nineteenth century, the behavior and attitudes that form the ideal of the modern family began to cohere. As a complex series of social and economic developments converged and solidified, each separate strand reinforced the oth-

ers. Broadly speaking, this process consisted of two distinct developments. First, there was a change in expectations regarding
the character of family life.[27] A growing desire for intimacy and
affection within the nuclear family required a transformation in
the nature of the ties between the nuclear family and the larger
surround of kin and community. This gradually reduced the
emotional investment in extensive kin ties and increased the intensity of emotional ties within the nuclear family. But in order
for these changes to become stabilized and generalized, the
broader society had to undergo changes as well.

Second, the economy had to be vigorous and reliable enough
to make it possible for couples to bid for greater independence
and autonomy. As more and more of the population was drawn
into the expanding economy, both as wage or salaried workers
and as consumers, the numbers of people who could imagine
reducing their reliance on kin grew, and the opportunities for
greater emphasis on the nuclear family expanded. Over the
long run, the result was the desiccation of kinship as a vital force
in society. To be sure, most American families, even today, maintain more or less vital ties to close kin—parents, a favorite aunt
or uncle, brothers and sisters—and a considerable flow of
money and emotional support still travels along kinship paths.
But having said this, the fact still remains that it is the husband-
wife-children unit that is *the* family in our culture: its needs predominate, or are supposed to, and its *raison d'être* is autonomy,
emotional and financial. That relatively few have ever sustained
this ideal fully is not surprising: such self-enclosed autonomy, in
some sense epitomized in the honeymoon, is an unsustainable
ideal. But full realization is not the point. The important feature
of this is to see how the ideal, as an ideal, weakens traditional
bonds and places more emphasis on the narrower and largely
self-selected bonds of the modern era.

The ideal of the modern family can be sketched rather easily
but we do not want to leave the impression that such an arrangement ever predominated, even in the most conducive of settings. Just as traditional ideals gave rise to varieties of family
arrangement, varieties conditioned by variations in societies as
well as by the peculiarities of the people involved, so too has the
modern ideal encompassed a range of possibilities, some more

sharply disjunctive with the past than others. As we shall endeavor to make clear in succeeding chapters, the variety of specific forms of family organization, all of them informed by the ideals we have been discussing, make talk of *the* modern family difficult.

The modern family is, in fact, a number of different families. The specific form a given family takes is a function of what the individuals involved bring to their relationship, the sum of their convictions, their ethnic traditions, and their own, personal desires and aspirations. But these individual qualities do not exist in a vacuum. At any moment in time, society makes some relationships more likely or more durable, by virtue of the resources it makes available as well as the kinds of aspirations it encourages. In the chapters that follow, we shall describe the ways in which broad social changes have shaped the kinds of families our society has encouraged. To do this, we will show how the practical aspects of familism, for example, dependence on family members for mutual aid, have been transformed. We will also examine the ways in which the other pillar of familism—emotional dependency—has been transformed as well. Having seen how major aspects of familism have changed, we will then explore the ways contemporary Americans endeavor to shape their family lives. The emergent norms informing contemporary family life comprise what we will call the "minimal family." This family, in all its varieties, gives rise to the increasing concern for the fate of familism we noted at the outset of this chapter.

The longer story we relate in the following chapters can be summarized now in a preliminary way. The modern family is the result of the interplay between a growing economy that seeks to stimulate steadily expanding consumption and individuals whose personal lives are increasingly predicated upon egalitarian and democratic forms of interaction. The consequence of this interplay is movement toward family forms that stimulate further individuation and, in the long run, diminish the hold that family relationships have on individuals. This has meant, in turn, that many are left without the support, emotional and material, that customarily flowed from familial ties. The inevitable result is that other sources of succor are sought—material support is sought through private employers and from the state; emotional support, when not forthcoming from friends and workmates, is increasingly sought from professional counselors and therapists. But while this shift has been gathering momentum over the past two hundred years, we have continued to think of the family as the repository of the highest values the society could sustain. This belief has persisted despite the actual lived reality of family life.

The present crisis of the family, then, is part of a much broader crisis of the political economy and is likely to be resolved only when we confront the fact that families can no longer be expected to be the exclusive domain of familism. Indeed, we think that even traditional forms of family life are unable to sustain familism. We will further argue that to the extent that we wish to sustain the essential spirit of familism—that is, an emphasis on mutual aid rather than competition, mutual obligation rather than absolute independence, and emotional intimacy and affection rather than anonymous sensuality—we shall have to insist that our public lives, our lives at work, as consumers, and as citizens, more thoroughly encompass those values and patterns of interaction that have long been characteristic only of family life.

2

The Transformation of Dependency

THE RISE OF INDUSTRY and the spread of commerce gradually supplanted the dependencies that had, for millennia, framed the emotional basis of family life. The growth of markets competed directly with traditional patterns of exchange that were structured along kin lines. To be sure, well before the industrial revolution and prior to the Enlightenment's celebration of the individual, families were involved in market exchanges. But typically, these transactions were an adjunct to the primary means of securing a livelihood. Household production and exchanges between households linked by blood and marriage were the central loci of economic activity. As production shifted out of the household and into factories and workshops, more households needed to buy more of the goods required for daily life. As this happened, the nuclear family's energies increasingly came to be directed towards meeting its own needs rather than fulfilling obligations to an expansive array of kin.

Necessarily, these changes in economic activity and dependencies were associated with other changes in familial ties, among them changes in authority. Over time, the authority of older kinfolk came to be supplanted by the impersonal authority of the state. As with the rise of markets, this change was anything but orderly and unambiguously welcomed. Nevertheless, many came to prefer the impersonal authority of courts and governmental agencies to the arbitrary will of an elder. Impersonal authority gave more latitude, more room for persons and nuclear families to explore and develop distinctive qualities.

Though these changes are often referred to as part of the process of modernization, we must be careful to remember that the specific historical sequence by which rational bureaucratic authority and impersonal markets arise and come to dominate social life varies widely from one society to another. In fact, there is no sequence as such, only a more or less common starting point and a more or less similar result. Ties to kin weaken, face-to-face interdependencies are drastically reduced, and impersonal structures (markets and forms of political and administrative authority organized by the state) come increasingly to mediate between individuals and between small nuclear families. Nor are the effects of these changes the same for all. For some, this process was exhilarating. Freed from what Marx characterized as the odious weight of the traditions of "all the dead generations," some flourished. Whether measured in wealth, creativity, or simply the satisfaction that comes from preferring one's own mistakes to those of one's forebears, the increasing autonomy afforded by the eclipse of expansive familial obligations was genuinely emancipatory for many. But at any moment in time during this process, there were many for whom the emancipation was scarcely welcomed or comforting, much less exhilarating, who saw the new ways of ordering interaction and exchanges as liabilities. As a result, the break from the past was never a clean one: old and new ways continue to exist alongside one another in varying proportions down to the present. Only over a considerable expanse of time were the traditions of mutual aid overwhelmed and then replaced, to one degree or another, by other, nonfamilial, forms of succor—charity, public dole, and, ultimately, varieties of programs that we now know as the welfare state. Before we examine this process in greater detail, let us first briefly examine the origins of this process of transforming dependency.

Accumulation and the Vicissitudes of Mutual Aid

In order for the process of industrialism to begin, capital had to be diverted from the uses to which it had been traditionally put and directed toward investment in machines and materials used in the production of commodities. Essentially, this meant changing consumption patterns of the elite, the holders of the bulk of whatever surplus there was. Customarily, the upper classes consumed most of the surplus they garnered each year from taxes, tribute, and rents paid them. They spent the surplus in sumptuous living, commissioning monuments to themselves and their godly protectors, and on more earthly forms of protection: forts, armies, and weaponry. Generally speaking, such uses of surplus were unproductive. They gave rise to little new production and provided little incentive to initiate new or different cycles of investment. In order that the shift from immediate consumption to investment be made, a new discipline had to emerge: a culture that celebrated thrift, that decried extravagance, and made work a virtue rather than a curse. Greater emphasis on the nuclear family aided the middle classes in the mobilization and concentration of capital for investment rather than consumption purposes. For all but the aristocracy, traditional family networks were well suited to the dispersal but not the concentration of surplus. By legitimizing a heightened focus on the nuclear family, and by simultaneously sanctioning the reduction of obligations the nuclear family had to others, the middle classes made the family itself into an instrument of accumulation. But while the process of accumulation was supported by the increased autonomy of the middle-class nuclear family, it required something quite different from the families of the peasantry and the new ranks of proletarians.

Scholars still debate at what point industrialism began to improve the lot of common folk. Few would dispute that in the earliest stages of industrialization workers experienced a decline in standard of living: they had to work much harder and more steadily, and for their labors they rarely if ever received enough in return to buy what they had formerly provided for themselves from within the pre-industrial economy. Indeed, the rapid spread of child labor as well as the wage labor of married women indicates that the household economy was being thoroughly undermined.[1] The fruits of this low-wage labor went largely to the factory and mill owners who, in the aggregate, were utilizing the profits to enhance their own power as well as to enlarge the sphere of production. For those at or near the top of this accumulation process, the emergent ideals of companionate marriage and increased nuclear family autonomy must have appeared ever more compelling and reasonable. But for those at or near the bottom, the ideals, even if compelling, were anything but reasonable. Whatever semblance of order and solicitude there was in their lives was largely derived from their dependence on, not their freedom from, kin.

The disruption of the household economy and the imposition of wage labor had the effect of reducing, even obliterating, what autonomy these households had had. With wages held down, often at or below subsistence levels, and with employment itself episodically interrupted either by swings in the business cycle or by illness or injury, nuclear families were tenuous social units at best. At worst, as the numbers of vagrants, foundlings, and otherwise uprooted individuals in nineteenth century cities indicate, the nuclear family often collapsed under the weight of the burdens imposed by capital accumulation. In order to avoid collapse, many drew upon and invigorated the venerable networks of mutual aid provided by kinship ties. Early on, the people involved may have experienced little or no disjunction in all this: they were simply following age-old patterns of intrafamilial exchange. Economic circumstances supported traditional networks of interdependence well into the twentieth century, by which time, however, the ideals of the modern family had become widely disseminated. The result was an uneasy configuration of couples more or less desirous of autonomy who were nonetheless obliged by circumstances to remain heavily reliant on kin. In fact, the family traditions that people relied upon, their capacity to take solace from one another and to derive satisfaction from one another's company—in short, the willingness to live a life with little need for commodities—made the herculean task of accumulating capital possible. Had workers needed to purchase all that their family networks made available "free

of charge," there never would have been sufficient capital left
over to invest in new machines or factories.[2] In this sense, the
traditional family, even as it was slowly being transformed, sub-
sidized a considerable portion of the bill for industrialization.
By providing channels along which goods and services could
flow without the mediation of capital, family networks made it
possible for workers to endure the long hours and low wages
that contributed to growing profits.

But the very successes of accumulation depleted this endur-
ance. However comforting close-knit families might be, they
were no long-term substitute for higher wages, a humane work
day, and dignity in one's work. As industry grew and enveloped
more and more people in its rhythms, the family networks of
mutual aid became strained and overburdened. People were
forced to seek alternatives to the dependencies that had constituted traditional family-based social life. As reliance on kin
waned, there were increasing calls for programs and policies
that would enable people to stand on their own, not necessarily
because they disliked relying on kin and neighbors but rather
because those dependencies could not sustain them.

Meanwhile, those presiding over the design of the economy
had their own headaches. Having availed themselves of peoples'
capacities to rely upon familial mutual aid and having accumulated capital in part as a result of being able to keep wages low
and the workday long, industrialists now confronted a paradox:
an unprecedented capacity to produce commodities had been
achieved, but it was premised on the bulk of the population remaining content with low levels of consumption. Without rapid
expansion of markets for the products being churned out of the
nation's factories, the whole edifice would be jeopardized.[3]
Warnings of imminent collapse were being heard as early as the
1870s; in subsequent decades the rumblings grew louder. Fifteen of the last thirty years of the nineteenth century was spent
in economic depression. Each new downturn was deeper than
the last, and recovery came more slowly. The system that had
proved effective at accumulating the capital necessary for establishing an industrial system was foundering on its own bul-
warks—low wages and concomitant low levels of consumption.

Taken together, the collapse of familial mutual aid and the

paradox of accumulation kept American society in a constant
state of tumult that spanned the last third of the nineteenth century and virtually the entire first half of the twentieth century.
In this eighty-year period, the general outlines of the contemporary family grew sharper and more distinctive. Playing out
themes of autonomy and intimacy that had emerged long before, Americans were encouraged to reduce their reliance on
kin and depend, instead, on goods and services provided imper-
sonally, through public or privately organized means. By the late
1940s, large numbers of Americans were ready to make this
shift, ready to savor the promised delights of relative autonomy—or autonomy from relatives. With the way cleared by New
Deal legislation (notably social security, unemployment compensation, and disability insurance) and, after the war, provisions of
the G.I. Bill, a complex set of forces began accelerating the pace
of change. At the same time, change was diffused throughout
all strata of our society, change that continues to reverberate
down to the present. In order to appreciate the complexity and
magnitude of these changes, we need to look more closely at
both the collapse of mutual aid and the shift from an emphasis
on accumulation to an emphasis on consumption. We can then
examine the ways in which our current concerns for the fate of
family life have been shaped by changes in our economy and
political structure.

The Collapse of Mutual Aid

In the earliest stages of American industrialization, the workforce had one foot in the factory and the other in the field. One
of the principal sources of anxiety for mill owners was, in fact,
the undependability of the workforce—workers frequently
failed to show up for work, in part because they did not yet rely
exclusively on wages for their subsistence and in part because
they had other activities, productive or recreational, that were
as attractive or compelling to them as work.[4] The economists'
metaphor of elasticity captures the situation nicely. Many workers' need for work was elastic, variable over the course of any
given month or year. As a result, when factory work fell off, for

whatever reason, the resultant layoffs were not nearly as devastating as they would later become when most workers were wholly reliant on wage labor. Early on, laid off workers, in effect, returned to the still vigorous preindustrial economy based on subsistence farming.

There was also, obviously, a family dimension to this elasticity. Not everyone owned their own land, such that they could simply pick up a hoe when they pleased or when the factory suspended operations. More typically, erstwhile workers were absorbed into the nexus of the family economy, helping a father or uncle or brother till the soil, check the trap line, or whatever. Of course some were left high and dry by the earliest manifestations of the business cycle. These unfortunates were the basis of the lumpenproletariat ("the reserve army of the proletariat," as Marx put it) that grew in fits and starts with the advance of industry and the cash economy. The lumpenproletariat, above all, was marked by the fact that it had no alternative means of subsistence to that offered by the emergent market economy. When it failed them, they were obliged to make do in the interstices of society, drifting, never far from disreputability, and cut off from kinship networks that remained firmly anchored in the preindustrial subsistence economy to which their more fortunate workmates could turn.

Over time, as the modern sector of the economy grew, increasing numbers of people came to depend fully upon wage labor. For some, this came as the result of eliminating alternatives, either by virtue of migration or by virtue of emotional cleavage. Australian poet Henry Lawson captures the range of bridge burning in his poem "The Shame of Going Back."[5] In the poem, Lawson writes of proud people who are determined to make their own way in the world, only to find themselves cast upon the shoals of hard times. Rather than submit to the ignominy of returning to their starting point, Lawson asks us to appreciate the strength that their despair otherwise masks. Lawson writes:

> When you've come to make a fortune and you haven't
>   made your salt,
> And the reason for your failure isn't
>   anybody's fault—

When you haven't got a billet, and the times are
    very slack,
There is nothing that can spur you like the shame
    of going back;
      Crawling home with empty pockets,
      Going back hard up;
Oh! it's then you'll learn the meaning of humiliation's cup.

When the place and you are strangers and you
    struggle all alone,
And you have a mighty longing for the town where
    you are known;
When your clothes are very shabby and the future's
    very black,
There is nothing that can hurt you like the shame of
    going back.

When we've fought the battle bravely and
    are beaten to the wall,
'Tis the sneers of men, not conscience, that make
    cowards of us all;
And the while you are returning, oh! your brain is
    on the rack,
And your heart is in the shadow of the shame
    of going back.

When a beaten man's discovered with a bullet
    in his brain,
They post-mortem him, and try him, and they
    say he was insane;
But it very often happens that he'd lately
    got the sack,
And his onward move was owing to the shame
    of going back.

Ah! my friend, you call it nonsense, and your upper
    lip is curled,
I can see that you have never worked your passage
    through the world;
But when fortune rounds upon you and the rain is
    on the track,
You will learn the bitter meaning of the shame
    of going back;

> Going home with empty pockets,
> Going home hard-up;
> Oh, you'll taste the bitter poison in
> humiliation's cup.
> In humiliation's cup.

Bids for autonomy, Lawson teaches us, are precarious and emotionally loaded. They are more so when the institutional structures supporting claims to autonomy are, themselves, fragile. When reverses set in, some found that their network of kin was simply unable to reabsorb them. Much depended upon the particular characteristics of each network: How diversified was it? How integrated into the modern sector was it? How many households needed to be absorbed? How many were there to do the absorbing? Not everything hinged on there being some core of kin still tied to the land. As long as hard times did not equally disrupt all the elements of a kin grouping, those who were still working could be called upon to help those who weren't. Thus, in times of rising unemployment, households expanded to accommodate kinfolk who could no longer make it on their own. Then, as times improved, households contracted back toward the nuclear core. This accordion-like movement of households in response to economic cycles persists to our own day: in the most recent severe downturn of 1982–83, the number of households declined and the average size of households increased.[6]

By the late nineteenth century, each swing downward in the business cycle found more and more households confronting needy kinfolk. Space was made for an uncle in the already crowded beds of the family; the stewpot was watered to make it stretch to fill the additional bowls at the table. But the magnitude of need clearly overwhelmed the capacities of kin to respond. Traditional supplements to family-based mutual aid— charities and churches, guild associations and *landsmanschaften*—were also inundated. The brute fact that familial mutual aid was not equal to the tasks set it by industrialism helped lay the basis for a growing acceptance of new ideas about how the family ought to function in society—what its place was in the expanding array of modern institutions and what its obligations to members ought to be. If the family could not be depended upon for everything all of the time, what could it do—when, for whom, and for how long? And who or what should be available to augment or even supplant families should that become necessary? Some weighed into the discussion of these and related questions on the side of maintaining the family as it had been, seeing in the tumult of unemployment and family collapse the bracing struggle that Darwin had only recently discovered as the mechanism of improvement in the organic world. An inability to persevere, to keep the family intact, like unemployment itself, was judged a sign of inherent weakness. No correctives need be taken because the process would inevitably sort families and individuals out into the worthy and the unworthy. In the long run, the misery of the unworthy would be eased by the accomplishments of the worthy, to everyone's benefit. For conservatives, in other words, the evident stresses and strains on families were of little concern. The weak would succumb; the strong and innovative would succeed; and progress would be insured.[7]

As the economy careened from boom to bust, the stress on families began to show more and more clearly. The divorce rate began steadily climbing after the Civil War and the rate of its ascent also increased. In 1880, the divorce rate was approximately one divorce for every twenty marriages. By 1900, there was approximately one divorce for every twelve marriages, a 60 percent increase in twenty years.[8] Desertion was also becoming a problem, even within ethnic groups noted for the closeness of their families. For example, the Yiddish weekly *Vorwarts* had a regular column containing pictures or descriptions of husbands and fathers who had disappeared, leaving wife and children to cope as best they could. The numbers of children and young adolescents who roamed the city without apparent supervision or purpose save that of scavenging and raising hell steadily increased. Intrafamilial violence was reported with greater frequency; crime rates were rising. Conservatives called for tighter restrictions on divorce and tougher enforcement of laws holding parents responsible for the actions of their children. They also issued warnings against becoming soft-hearted, lest charitable impulses deflect the struggle for survival and interfere with the processes of natural selection.[9] Though the air was thick with ringing defenses of the family, with admonitions to tighten belts and pull together, to take responsibility for one's own fortunes and misfortunes and be prepared to assist those of your kinfolk who are in need, the realities of mounting suffering produced a growing clamor for supplements to or replacements of the traditional family-based system of mutual aid.

More people, both workers and middle-class reformers and radicals, began to insist that government take an active role in insuring the welfare of the population. Emergency relief, unemployment and disability insurance, and other "radical, socialistic" ideas became the rallying cries for many. In addition, agitation for a shorter work week and higher wages mixed with calls for an end to child labor and safer working conditions. While not all of these demands were explicitly linked to the collapse of familial mutual aid, it is clear that they were based on the recognition that it was cruel to expect workers' families to cope with the ravages of the industrial system on their own. New ways of sharing burdens and distributing gains would have to be instituted.

Other sources of agitation in this period were more directly linked to the stresses on the family in the face of the dislocations that industrial capitalism created. Feminism, which had been formally initiated in this country in the late 1840s, began to gather adherents in earnest in the last decades of the nineteenth century. Though the concerns of the early feminists had more to do with questions of equal rights for women and entertained serious reservations about the compatibility of marriage and equality, the movement was fed by women aroused and moved to activism around a wide array of so-called women's issues: temperance, birth control, home economics, child labor and protective legislation for women workers. As is so often the case in mass movements, the success of feminism hinged on its capacity to provide a link between diverse issues. Consequently, feminism's own goals narrowed to something that all could agree to work for: suffrage. In the process, much of feminism's initial radicalism was forced to the periphery of small sectarian groups just as the reforms that formed the substance of the women's movement came to be seen as reforms that would strengthen the family. But crucially, the reforms did not seek to resuscitate the networks of familial mutual aid so much as they sought to enhance each nuclear family's capacities to stand on its own.[10]

For many of the early feminists, and for many contemporary feminists as well, the insistence on equality meant the rejection of marriage, at least so long as marriage remained embedded in patriarchal traditions. Marriage, in this view, almost invariably meant that the wife became her husband's chattel, obliged by dint of custom and law to be her husband's helpmate: his cook, nurse, washerwoman, and vehicle for sexual pleasure. In return, the wife, if lucky, got a roof over her head, food—that she prepared—and the security that comes from being protected by a man. Even the ideal of companionate marriage, clearly an improvement over traditional arrangements, at best offered a problematic equality between spouses. At worst, the emotional equality at the core of companionate marriage was seen as sham equality, one that kept the wife subordinate even as it acknowledged her emotional needs. Equality meant autonomy for the more radical of the early feminists, not simply the same legal rights that men enjoyed. In this expanded sense, equality meant that women should be free to come and go as they please throughout all aspects of society, their gender encumbering them not at all. They should work alongside men—as women had for millennia—but not at men's bidding or sufferance. Only under such circumstances, when women no longer need the "protection" of a husband, could the ideal of companionate relations be met. Full equality between the sexes would free men and women of the compulsions of family life, conceivably making families stronger because they were freely entered into.[11]

At the time (indeed it is still the case today), this conception of equality, however compelling, had an unavoidably utopian cast, if only because it bore such scant relation to the conditions that most women and men confronted. Under the prevailing conditions, women were being shamelessly exploited in the labor force. Moreover, they were often in the labor force because their father's or husband's wages were insufficient or too irregular to support the family. The notion that women were being protected by and thus made self-effacingly dependent upon their husbands must have struck the majority of women of the day as something to envy rather than reject. In fact, even as the feminist movement gained adherents, other social movements were gathering momentum in efforts designed to enhance women's dependence on men. Temperance, the movement for protective legislation, and the home economics movement each shared space with feminism, as it were, and their fates were more than once entangled.

The temperance movement marshalled many arguments against drink, but the most effective was probably the one based on the plight of wife and children pathetically awaiting the arrival of husband-father who is busily drinking up his paycheck—heedless of the hunger, disease, and loneliness of those dependent upon him. Drink, they argued, led men astray and deflected their natural impulses to be the provider, thus violating the integrity of the family and the social order itself. If drink were banned, families would be able to make ends meet and the need to turn to others for assistance would thereby be greatly reduced. The new order, with its low wages and disruptive cycles of unemployment, was not the problem in the scenarios sketched by the Anti-Saloon League. The family was being undermined by demon rum.[12]

The temperance movement was attempting to recapture and restore the virtues that inhered in family, church, and neighborhood—the loci of traditional networks of solidarity and mutual aid. Its efforts, though successful in getting a constitutional amendment prohibiting the sale of alcohol, were in vain. Drink or not, the forms of mutual aid, togetherness, and interdependence rooted in stable kinship ties simply could not be rescued. Needless to say, the problem was not with alcohol. Some felt the problem was in the home itself: too many women did not know how to manage a home efficiently under modern conditions; the skills acquired at their mothers' sides were no longer suitable to the tasks of running a home. As a result of outmoded ideas and practices, wages were misallocated and proper nutrition was sacrificed to fads or to foods that were unhealthy. If women could be brought up to date through education, the swings in the business cycle would not have the devastating effects they had thus far produced and the family would be more stable and better able to adapt to changes in the economy.[13]

Attempts to modernize the home had begun before the Civil War, most notably with the writings of Harriet Beecher, but it was not until the 1880s and 1890s that the home economics movement crystallized a coherent view on the matter. With links to leading educators and to commercial food processors and other manufacturers interested in the home as a market, the home economics movement began to spread its gospel.[14]

The home, it was argued, needed to be *managed* rather than simply held together. At a time when more and more jobs were being formalized into professions by virtue of the steady injection of technical know-how, advocates of home economics argued that housewives/mothers should also be informed by the findings of science and the benefits of technology. Though distant from the radical feminist ideas of equality, the home economists did insist that women should bring to their "occupation" the same sort of rationality and openness to expert advice that their husbands brought to their occupations. In a very real sense, the home economists were seeking a replacement for the collapsing system of mutual aid by making the nuclear family more nearly autonomous and self-sufficient. Among the many accomplishments of the home economics movement was the successful effort to incorporate home economics in public school curricula across the nation. Young girls would learn in school that they could prepare themselves to be homemakers without relying on the advice of their mothers. Indeed, strong support for home economics came from those who were concerned that the tide of immigrants would perpetuate "unAmerican ways" unless children could be taught differently. In home economics classes, the daughters of immigrants learned that garlic was unhealthy, that milled and enriched flour was better than its less processed cousins, that a "dash of this and a pinch of that" was archaic compared to precise and standardized measures, and so on.[15] In effect, home economists were determined to stamp out the knowledge of "old wives," which is to say they were committed to weakening traditional family ties in favor of strengthening the integrity and self-sufficiency of the nuclear family.

The home economics movement focused on rational planning in the home—planning balanced meals, planning children's futures, planning the family's finances. The deepening collapse of the traditions of mutual aid also gave rise to advocates of another form of planning: family planning. The initial impetus for birth control, which was linked to a desire to see women as equals, came out of the feminist movement and, more particularly, out of the conjunction of feminism and socialism. In bringing under control the one certain thing that distinguished women—their exclusive ability to give birth—the whole array of derivative differences in the ways women and men were treated could be avoided. Radicals saw in birth control the emancipation of women as well as the emancipation of women's and men's sexuality. Over time, the base of support expanded to include people who saw in birth control a way to stem the rapid population increase among the poor and recent immigrants. Fears of being outbred by the "lower orders," whom the science of the day was "proving" to be genetically inferior to the middle and upper classes, as well as concern for the alarming array of miseries that attended unregulated fertility, gradually eclipsed the radical roots of the birth control movement. The result did not challenge conventional notions of family life and sexuality and instead produced a movement that upheld the virtues of the middle-class family ideal.[16]

In its early days, the birth control movement, led by Margaret Sanger, was hounded and harassed by the federal and many state governments. Sanger, in the eyes of most male legislators and judges, was promoting promiscuity as well as threatening the foundations of civilization itself: namely, motherhood and the family. Sanger's publications were seized by postal authorities under powers created by legislation specifically designed to stymie the dissemination of birth control information. It is likely that Sanger was indeed committed at one time to at least some of the radical goals, like free love, that were attributed to her. But it is also clear that her ideological commitments were secondary to her profound indignation at the needless grief and desperate misery that unregulated fertility visited upon women and the men who supported them. The avoidance of unwanted or unsupportable children became her single goal, and Sanger sought allies wherever they might be found, regardless of the broader agenda those allies were intent on promoting. Eugenicists were thus welcomed to the fold, even though Sanger hardly shared their theories of race suicide. Similarly, she distanced herself from her erstwhile comrades on the left in order to shed the opprobrium attached to the advocates of free love and equality between the sexes. But the crucial step in Sanger's campaign to make birth control an accepted feature of family life was her alliance with the medical profession. By making birth control a medical issue, something to be worked out between a woman and her doctor, Sanger and her medical supporters succeeded in defusing the opposition. Gradually, birth control, renamed family planning, became respectable. Though the full implications of family planning would await the discovery of the Pill in the early 1960s, the spreading knowledge that fertility could be regulated without resort to abstinence helped families reduce the number of children born and made many families more able to respond to both opportunity and adversity, thereby reducing the degree to which they required the support of traditional networks of mutual aid.

By itself, the collapse of mutual aid and the wide variety of responses this collapse elicited would have produced as many different family adaptations as it did different ideological viewpoints. The old ways were clearly being undermined, though they were by no means being happily relinquished, but no new possibilities were emerging with any force or clarity. People were, in effect, preparing for a change; they were exposed to many, and often conflicting, ideas about what was necessary or desirable long before any of the possibilities became seriously plausible. Though mutual aid patterns were under duress and unable to bear the weight, the alternatives to relying upon kin were slight and surrounded with the stigma of almshouses and disreputability.

Attempts at both rescue and reform flourished in the late nineteenth and early twentieth centuries precisely because the family was unable to meet the needs it was expected to meet. The source of this inability was, as we have already suggested, the economy. As the economy grew and productive capacity increased manyfold, consumers had to be found to absorb the expanding output. In the absence of customers, production would fall off, unemployment would begin to rise, and people would find themselves unable to meet even their most modest needs.

A new economy and a new, more streamlined family emerged together, if not quite hand-in-hand, in alternating waves of change and elaboration. The traditional family was poorly adapted to consumption: its *raison d'être* was rooted in sharing, hand-me-downing, and cooperative endeavor. The new mode, purchasing goods and services, required more emphasis on the nuclear pair and a heightened awareness of what the couple required for a fulfilling life. Gradually, longstanding admonitions to thrift gave way to inducements to buy and consume. Though the origins of the modern or companionate family antedated industrial capitalism by a century or more, the growth of industrial capitalism generalized the conditions that made the companionate ideal broadly attainable. With networks of mutual aid in disarray, and with wages still low and employment insecure, neither the companionate ideal nor consumer capitalism could prosper. But the linkage between the two, once made and institutionalized, meant the rapid expansion of both. It is to this relationship that we now turn.

Who Will Buy . . . ?

The contradiction within the economy between the need for consumers and the desire to keep wages low, thereby reducing most peoples' capacities to consume, seems both simple and self-evident, but it was not an idea that was widely accepted until quite recently.[17] There were many sources of resistance that had to be overcome before this new way of thinking could become compelling. Chief among these sources of resistance was the deep-seated belief that economic rationality and efficiency dictated that employers must keep wages down, along with any and all other ways of cutting costs. This commitment, one that is by no means absent from the minds of today's employers, virtually takes the form of a credo. Marx, the most astute critic of capitalism, understood the self-defeating character of this. He wrote:

> Although every capitalist demands that his workers should save, he means only *his own* workers, because they relate to him as workers; and by no means does this apply to the remainder of the work-

ers, because these relate to him as consumers. In spite of all the pious talk of frugality he therefore searches for all possible ways of stimulating them to consume, by making his commodities more attractive, by filling their ears with babble about new needs. It is precisely this side of the relationship between capital and labour which is an essential civilizing force, and on which the historic justification—but also the contemporary power—of capital is based [emphasis in original].[18]

But adherence to this narrow view cannot be seen merely as greed mixed with self-defeating stubbornness. By the time the problem of overproduction/underconsumption had ripened to the point of threatening general ruin, an entire culture had been constructed around the "natural" desire to keep wages low. At the core of this cultural system were celebrations of thrift and self-denial. Thrift and self-denial were virtues as much as they were necessities. To pay workers more than was required for them to lead a bracingly frugal life-style was not only foolish, insofar as it reduced one's own profits, but was also likely to upset the whole order by which hard work and thrift are rewarded—if not in this world then in the kingdom beyond. Indeed, there was no guarantee that workers whose checks were enlarged would in fact turn around and buy things. Practical experience and prevailing economic theory (not always coincident) taught that workers might well elect to simply work less, preferring leisure to higher levels of consumption. Thus it was that many were convinced that higher wages would lead almost directly to the dissolution of the moral and motivational fabric that made industrial capitalism possible. Unless something could be done to insure that higher wages would not be translated into reduced incentives to work, the industrial system would clearly not run smoothly, if at all. More importantly perhaps, there was reason to worry about the effects of enlarged appetites for consumption, particularly the possibility that expectations would rise faster than wages once the heavy restraints of thrift and self-denial were lifted.

From our vantage point in the late twentieth century, these concerns about the viability of a consumption-oriented capitalism must seem a mixture of quaint, absurd, and prescient. Such a shift may indeed have contributed to what some observers claim has been a steady decline in the work ethic, particularly noticeable and widely commented upon in the late sixties and early seventies. And there is no gainsaying the potential volatility that arises from wide discrepancies between expectations and capacities to meet those expectations.[19] Left to their own devices, given generations of accumulated custom and continual admonition to thrift, there is little reason to doubt that a sudden increase in wages in, say, 1910, would have produced more savings than consumption as well as an appreciable increase in leisure. What was needed, among other things, was some assurance that a general increase in wages would yield increased consumer demand, which would radiate out through the economy, producing new orders and thus new employment and new investment—in short new sources of profit and growth.

Two deeply interrelated factors were at work and made change slow at first—in effect, neither factor could budge without the other—and then, once begun, quite rapid. People had to be disabused of their commitments to thrift, on the one hand, and employers, on the other hand, had to be disabused of their commitment to an incentive structure built around low wages. People in general, obviously, could not abandon thrift in the absence of some reasonable certainty that their purchasing power would steadily expand. Employers would not abandon their commitment to low wages without some reasonable assurances that (1) other employers would follow suit and (2) consumer demand would in fact materialize and spur growth. Obviously, there could be no guarantees on these matters and so, amid much talk of the necessity for change, change itself was halting, tentative, and surrounded by increasingly polarized debate. Several kinds of innovations appeared, innovations whose full effects would await the watershed of the post-World War II decades.

The innovations clustered in three areas of large-scale institutional realignments: (1) attempts to stimulate consumer demand, principally through advertising and by the extension of consumer credit; (2) the beginnings of a social contract between employers and employees in which control over the work process—transferring or conceding to management traditional rights of laborers to organize their crafts and defend their skill hierarchies—was traded for wage increases and a shorter work-week; and (3) a growing reliance upon the federal government to regulate economic competition as well as to provide assistance to those individuals and families who were victims of industrial accidents, unemployment, or other circumstances that threat-ened to end their self-sufficiency. As we shall see, each of these new departures tended to reinforce the others and, together, they began to make it possible for some to significantly reduce their dependence upon family and neighborhood based net-works of mutual aid. But before we see how these developments merged and matured, let us examine each of the components briefly, beginning with advertising and consumer credit.

Conditioned by a long history of privation and subjected to frequent interruptions of income as a result of unemployment or illness, the U.S. population in the late nineteenth and early twentieth centuries was not seething to consume any but a rather prosaic and short list of commodities, mostly what could be reasonably thought of as staples. A certain amount of eco-nomic growth would result if everyone's basic needs were met, but the real promise of industrial expansion and higher profits had to come from the constant creation of new needs, needs for things that, if not luxuries, were nonetheless far from what then prevailed as the definition of "basic." Advertising played a cru-cial, perhaps even decisive, role in making people accustomed to satisfying their needs through consumption, and it legiti-mated a steady expansion of needs. Moreover, as Stuart Ewen and others have shown, over time advertising came more and more to play upon peoples' concerns about self-worth.[20] The re-sults, at least in the abstract, were an almost limitless frontier awaiting the inventive manufacturer and merchandiser.

More was involved than just hucksterism. After all, merchants and sharpsters had always appealed to vanity, greed, and all the other deadly but nonetheless irresistible sins. Informing both the advertisers and a steadily increasing proportion of the pop-ulation was a radically new sense of the self and a revised ori-entation toward change. The developing economy provided the metaphors for all domains of life. Character, understood as a set of integrated, relatively stable psychological traits established early in life, was gradually replaced by the notion of personality—a loosely interrelated constellation of traits that people could and did revise in response to altered circumstance and new experience. This new psychology was, of course, contested, both in academic circles and in popular culture, and even today it is by no means unassailable. But particularly for the new middle classes—those strata that began to emerge in the latter part of the nineteenth century around new and expanding professions and the occupations derived from the rapidly increasing need for coordination and management—the idea of a continually developing self struck a resonant chord. With nothing fixed or permanent, adaptability, flexibility, and openness became celebrated personal qualities. The healthy individual was open to personal development.

The embrace of new technologies, new modes of organizing human labor, and new products—in short, the embrace of *progress*—gradually became honored. The expression "newfangled" gradually lost its pejorative connotations—new was better; homemade was inferior to store bought. Buying products demonstrated not only economic solidity but also progressive character. Advertisers helped effect this shift at the same time that changing views of human development made it possible for the advertising industry to depict itself as an agent of higher social purpose rather than a manipulator in behalf of greed and deception. Advertising, it was claimed, was a profession, and like other professions it upheld ethical standards and played its part in the sweeping task of guiding the nation to a bright new future. This future was understood to be one in which science and technology, including the new sciences of social and psychological functioning, would replace tradition and superstition as bases of human conduct. Of course, businessmen may not have accepted or even cared a fig for this underlying rationale. What they confronted were bulging warehouses and periods of underutilized productive capacity. They needed customers. And so, by the early twentieth century they began to turn more and more consistently to advertising specialists. Money spent on advertising increased dramatically between 1900 and 1930, going from $200 million in 1900 to $2.6 *billion* by 1930.[21]

One major advertising theme, as we have already suggested,

was to validate the new, the heretofore untried, even the un-
imagined. "Revolutionary new" became a standard slogan and
people were urged to be pioneers of sorts by being among the
first to have this or that new commodity. Appeals to adventur-
ousness and status were complemented by suggestions that
some products could also offer independence. A new tractor
and its accompanying implements could do the work of many
hired hands (or sons) come harvest time. The refrigerator
ended the need for daily shopping, thus *freeing* the homemaker
for other things, things presumably more of her own choosing.
More and more commodities were spoken of as extensions—or,
better, as projections—of self, a self that was adaptable, innovative, exploratory, and autonomous; a self capable of making
intelligent choices unburdened by prejudices and habits inher-
ited from the past.

New consumer products centered on two consuming social
"units": the individual and the nuclear family. Wider arrays of
kin and neighbors figured in, if at all, only as an admiring audience. Consumption—the embrace of the new—was adver-
tised as making individuals independent of these more traditional associations. Sentimental ties could remain, but in the
world being ushered in, the thick webs of reciprocity and obligation that bound folks together and provided the social basis
for reproducing tradition were undermined. Homes, modern
homes that is, were to be self-contained, able to function with
little or no outside help, save that of experts in home economics,
childrearing, and other carriers of the new culture. For individuals, advertisers praised the virtues of an increasing array of
goods that carried with them statements of self-confidence, mas-
tery, and worldliness. Mass production now allowed fashion to
be within the reach of many, and advertisers lost no time in making it clear how important stylishness was to success—in career,
in social life, and in courtship and marriage. As social horizons
expanded well beyond the orbits of kin and neighbors, it became important to present one's self correctly, to manage, using
Erving Goffman's apt phrase, the "presentation of self" so as to
create the right impression.[22] Standards of personal hygiene
rose sharply as advertisers played upon the insecurities and
fears inevitably aroused when the comfortable realm of the fa-

miliar is left behind. Bad breath, body odor, unsightly blemishes or hair—all manner of intimate detail was the object of scrutiny and the occasion for intervention and modification with the help of toothpastes, deodorants, depilatories, and endless varieties of personal grooming aids. Though most of these commodities were, until recently, aimed at women, men were often the intended audience and, as bestowers of gifts, often the actual purchaser.

Advertising, of course, was not the sole source of this emergent culture. In fact, it was really only the popularizer of it. The inventiveness of what came to be known as Madison Avenue involved the ability to translate a set of assumptions about human nature and social organization that were being formulated in esoteric journals and select conferences by scholars, civic leaders, businessmen, and professionals, into popular imageries linked to particular commodities. In this sense, advertisers were promulgating a way of life as much as they were selling specific products.[23] The life that was being celebrated with increasing consistency and vigor through the early years of the twentieth century was based on the conception of the nuclear family as, in Christopher Lasch's words, a "haven in a heartless world."

Family life revolved around a home that was presented as a single family home—there might be guests in the home but no borders or nonnuclear family members were permanently resident. It ought to be spacious, both inside and out, the expanse of grass and shrubs between houses making clear the value placed on privacy and on the autonomy of the resident nuclear family. Each of the children ought to have their own bedroom and these rooms ought to be remote from the parents' bedroom. The kitchen should be equipped with the latest appliances that are both easy to work with and an encouragement to the homemaker to constantly improve meal preparation. Such a kitchen would be a "joy to work in." As Delores Hayden makes clear, this conception of house and family was a highly conscious one, and she traces its origins back to the domestic advice of Harriet Beecher.[24] In the 1920s, soon-to-be-president Herbert Hoover served as president of an association called Better Homes in America. According to Hayden, this organization was made up of several thousand local chapters "composed of manufacturers,

realtors, builders, and bankers" who were committed to "boost-
ing home ownership and consumption."[25] Selling homes, it was
clear, meant selling furniture, appliances, and myriad accoutre-
ments of autonomous nuclear family living. It also meant, in
effect, selling a style of family living.

The sales efforts we have been describing were the work of
both advertisers, with specific products in mind, and influential
public figures like Hoover who had more general aims. Though
specific causal links between advertising and behavior are notoriously hard to prove, it is clear that the rapidly accumulating
weight of sales pitches had only a limited result. To be sure, sales
of homes did rise, as did the sales of household appliances, autos, cosmetics, and processed foods, to mention only the most
obvious of the new commodities entering the stream of commerce. But the market was still quite constricted, limited to an
expanding but still small slice of the middle class. However compelling the message, the proponents of consumer-oriented industrialism could not overcome peoples' empty pocketbooks by
advertising. The image of spacious new homes in verdant suburbs may have spoken to the longings of those eking out an existence in crowded tenements, but like most other of their longings, this too would have to be set aside in the face of low wages
and uncertain employment.

Even among the ranks of the expanding middle class of professionals and managers, incomes were not necessarily large
enough to permit the life-styles that were being promoted. One
way to overcome this dilemma without confronting the issue of
wages and salaries was to offer credit and repayment schedules
that would allow the purchase price to be spread out over a period of time. People had, of course, long been borrowing money
or accepting goods that they agreed to pay for later. Typically,
these transactions occurred within family or friendship circles
or between a small local merchant and his steady clientele.
These loans were as much affirmations of solidarity as they were
strictly business transactions. Generally speaking, these extensions of credit were intended to help someone meet an emergency. This kind of credit buttresses a culture based on thrift
and self-denial because it links indebtedness to short-term exi-
gency and the provision of bare necessities. Something quite dif-

ferent was involved when General Motors first announced that it would let its dealers sell cars to customers who paid as little as one-third down and agreed to pay off the balance over the next two years. GM was intent on expanding the market for its automobiles, an approach directly at odds with buttressing commitments to thrift. In order to sell autos, GM had to undermine the culture that had for so long prescribed staying out of debt and restricting appetites to available income.

Earlier extensions of consumer credit dated back to the 1870s and 1880s. Both Singer sewing machines and McCormick harvesters were marketed on the installment plan. The attraction of the Singer machine was that it was durable, versatile, and could be produced in long runs, thereby reducing the cost of each unit. But long production runs meant heavy investments in inventory and this, in turn, required techniques to expand demand. The Singer Company's success turned as much on the organizational innovations that helped orchestrate aggressive sales with productive capacity as on the productive capacity itself.[26] Singer's innovation played upon the older forms of extending credit by personalizing the relationship between buyer and seller, by making the extension of credit an affirmation of trust, such that a failure to pay was unthinkable. But however traditional the context, the transaction itself was solidly modern. It was indeed ahead of its time. The idea, in spite of Singer's success with it, did not catch on, at least not until after World War I.

As already noted, General Motors is generally credited with introducing installment buying for nonessentials. Following World War I, GM began waging a many-sided battle with Ford for leadership of the auto industry. Ford Motors was arguably the most advanced from a production standpoint, but Henry Ford's ideas about marketing and consumer demand were very traditional. Alfred Sloan, the chief executive of GM, by contrast, saw the possibility of expanding demand for autos by continually making minor alterations in his cars. In direct contrast to Ford's famous sales pitch, "You can have any color you want so long as it's black," GM began to offer an array of colors and two-toned combinations. For Ford, the central goal had been to produce a product that met a need and to do so as inexpensively as possible. For GM, the central goal became meeting needs it had itself played a significant role in creating. The extension of credit was really an extension of GM's more general marketing strategy. As one might expect, Ford was dead set against the idea of consumer credit too. The result, clear by the end of the 1920s, was that Ford, once far and away the leading automaker, was permanently relegated to a distant second place, and the company averted complete collapse only by belatedly adopting GM's marketing strategies.[27]

Large department stores also began experimenting with offering charge accounts to their preferred customers. Slowly, inroads were made into the belief that only cash in hand allowed one the privilege of buying. Home ownership in this same period, the first three decades of the present century, expanded: by 1930, 46 percent of the nation's housing stock was owner occupied.[28] Correlatively, mortgage debt expanded significantly over this same period, rising from a total of just over $1 billion in 1890 to $6.8 billion in 1900 and $46.5 billion by 1929.[29] Part of this expansion in mortgage debt was the result of home builders and realtors pressuring state legislatures and the federal government to allow banks to lengthen the mortgage payback period. Longer mortgage periods meant smaller monthly payments and, thus, put homes within reach of more potential buyers. But for all the experimenting with credit, both short- and long-term, access to the consumer market remained narrow. Too few people had incomes that were high and reliable enough to qualify for home mortgages or for most installment purchases. In some instances, particularly with auto sales, dealers were so eager to sell they engaged in "creative" financial arrangements that brought disaster to many dealerships. Shady practices did not help to encourage people to abandon thrift. Nevertheless, it is conceivable that credit would have gone on steadily increasing, thereby stimulating demand and calling forth higher levels of production. But the stock market crash of 1929 and the ensuing years of depression stopped budding consumerism dead in its tracks. It was clear that advertising and credit, by themselves, were not equal to the task of transforming the economy and ushering in a new social order. Two other institutional changes were also required before the structure for this new order could gel. A new relationship between employer and employee had to emerge and, relatedly, a new relationship between state and society had to be forged.

By the early 1900s there were few observers who were not concerned about the long-run viability of the U.S. system. Radical agitation among workers as well as widespread concern and organizing around issues of housing, poverty, the franchise for women, and immigration all swirled around and were intensified by recurrent economic crises. Thus, by the turn of the century, many prominent citizens—leaders from business, holders of public office, editorialists and educators—had begun to modify the long prevailing orthodoxy that held that the economy should be left to its own devices. Competition, the key process that was supposed to provide automatic regulation and insure the most rational allocation of resources, ceased enjoying the uniform support that it had long held. Particularly striking was the change among leading industrialists of the day, those whom one would ordinarily presume to be strong advocates of the free market. Instead, talk turned on phrases such as "ruinous competition." [30]

Hostility to competition resulted, in part, from dramatic changes in the nature of economic organization after the Civil War. For reasons that need not concern us, the scale of enterprise grew enormously. [31] Whether through mergers, bankruptcies, or sheer growth, in sector after sector, the American economy came to be dominated by a relative handful of very large corporations. While the numbers of small mom-and-pop operations remained roughly stable, their share of the economic pie rapidly declined. Small firms could wage economic war on one another with relatively little general consequence, save the net effect of weeding out the incompetent or inefficient. This weeding out would cause no widespread calamity, or so it was assumed. But once the significant economic actors became gigantic, representing huge capital holdings and giving employment to large numbers of people, weeding out looked very different. The failure of one of these giants could indeed pose the prospect of widespread, if not general, ruin. Something had to be done to regulate competition to avoid subjecting the nation's economy to such sweeping dislocation.

Businessmen began experimenting on their own after the Civil War, privately agreeing among themselves to set prices or divide up markets so as to avoid the harshest outcomes of "ruinous competition." These arrangements all proved unsatisfactory, and many were found illegal. In any case, because they were informal, there was no mechanism to enforce the pacts. As a result, few lasted for long. In the face of failed private agreements, business sentiment began to shift toward governmental regulation, once the anathema of the business community. The age of laissez-faire was drawing to a close.

The process was a long and complex one and cannot be done justice here; only the most general features of what happened can be included. First, trade associations dominated by the largest corporations began lobbying Congress and state legislatures for what amounted to protective legislation. Sometimes a trade association would make common cause with consumer groups who were seeking protection from dangerous products or corrupt business practices. For example, many unsuspecting folks had bought life insurance from woefully undercapitalized insurance companies, companies unable to pay out the benefits they had led their customers to expect. Such practices were so rampant that the largest insurance companies worried lest their reputations be dragged down or, even more likely, that popular indignation would lead to reforms and regulations that would dramatically reduce their profitability. They became active on their own behalf, ultimately securing legislation establishing minimum levels of capitalization. Consumers were thus protected from fly-by-night insurance firms; at the same time, larger and well-established firms were protected from competition from new companies because the large capital requirements greatly reduced the ease of entry of new firms into the field.

Trade and professional associations grew rapidly and turned to the government for various kinds of licensing and other forms of protection for their particular economic activities. Other groups, like the National Association of Manufacturers, emerged to help insure that government actions would promote business interests beyond those of specific industries. At an even more general level, groups began to form around very broad reform agendas. One of the more notable of these was the National Civic Federation (NCF), founded in 1900 by Ralph M. Easley, a prominent civic leader from Chicago.[32] The membership of NCF included a significant number of the nation's leading industrialists, as well as many legislators, past presidents, and a variety of prominent writers and educators. The labor leader Samuel Gompers was also an active member. The NCF sponsored a number of blue-ribbon commissions charged with studying a wide range of social issues and proposed model legislation to promote reform. A number of such efforts resulted in legislation that helped to legitimize a more active role for the government in the economy.

Federal regulatory actions were not the only concern of the NCF and groups like it. More directly germane to our interest in the family was the fact that groups like the NCF began to lay the basis for what came to be known as the welfare state. Though implemention of various forms of welfare and social insurance, most notably social security and unemployment compensation, had to await the New Deal, the reform-minded among the elite were beginning to recognize that the government would have to take a much more active role in cushioning the impact of technological change and the business cycle if the economy was ever to avoid the sharp reversals that characterized the post-Civil War era. Without reforms, the more far-reaching and radical proposals that were being promulgated by the growing ranks of socialists and labor militants might come to dominate political discourse. Proposals for emergency relief, disability insurance, and unemployment compensation were couched in language that celebrated the traditional family, but the long-term consequences for family life would be to make nuclear family autonomy more prevalent. Patterns of mutual aid, already severely weakened, could be supplanted almost entirely if a family's living standard was protected from unemployment, accident, or illness. Resistance to welfare was still far too deeply rooted to allow significant reforms until the Great Depression forced the issue. But the work of groups like the NCF helped prepare the ground.

In effect, the NCF helped lay the basis for the liberal consensus that has prevailed from the mid-1930s until the election of Ronald Reagan in 1980. The key elements in this consensus were policies that promoted economic growth by means of broad-based cooperation between the federal government and the private sector designed to stimulate consumption and regulate competition. In order to help keep consumer demand strong and to minimize the disruptive potential of persistent poverty and unemployment, the federal government began to provide income supports, social security for the elderly, and general relief for the destitute.

One other crucial aspect of the consensus required a federal role as well: labor and management had to reach an accommodation to reduce the work week and raise wage levels. By the 1920s, each of these elements had achieved significant support among the nation's business and civic elite. In NCF conferences, committee hearings of liberal legislators, and the roundtable discussions among prominent academics and journalists, it was increasingly self-evident that these general policies were necessary to safeguard and strengthen the American economy and the social and political order on which it rested.

It was, however, one thing to reach this conclusion around a conference table and quite another matter to reach agreement on how and when specific policies and legislation should be enacted. As we have just noted, it took a long time to begin, in a serious way, instituting federal welfare programs, even though many prominent figures knew they were necessary and inevitable. Similarly, it had been clear for some time that low wages and long hours of work were retarding consumption and were an important source of instability. But individual industrialists were reluctant to be ahead of the pack for fear that if others did not follow suit, the pioneers would be dramatically disadvantaged. Some way had to be found to make the changes that seemed necessary apply across the board so that no particular firm or economic sector would be unduly handicapped. As with welfare legislation, the depression was pivotal. With the passage of the Wagner Act and the National Labor Relations Act (1936), trade unions were recognized, organizing began, and a process for a more or less orderly means of setting hours and wages was put in place.

Though the Great Depression was a watershed period in terms of establishing the political-economic basis for a dramatic shift away from the culture of mutual aid and thrift and toward a cultural emphasis on autonomy and consumption, the immediate impact of the depression was to reaffirm the traditions of family-based mutual aid. Though this tradition had grown progressively more threadbare through the early decades of the twentieth century, the calamity of the thirties required families to pull together. Not all of them could or would. For many, the failure to sustain themselves and their immediate, nuclear family was a crushing blow. Having labored to achieve a measure of independence from kinfolk, large numbers were suddenly faced with the necessity to renew bonds of dependency. Some went to pathetic lengths to keep up the facade of self-sufficiency. Caroline Bird reports that many unemployed men left their homes each weekday morning dressed for work and stayed away all day long as if they were at work, in order to keep up appearances.[33] Households that had grown accustomed to nuclear family living were suddenly forced to adjust to the daily presence of relatives. Guilt, anxiety, anger, and psychological depression all flourished.

Of course there were also many families who responded differently. Baake reports that many of the couples he studied grew emotionally closer and more affectionate.[34] And kinfolk were, for many, a steady source of comfort, optimism, and dignity. But however well these traditions served, it was also clear that frustrations were growing under the pressure of hardship and foreclosed prospects of greater personal independence. With the return of good times, Americans in unprecedented numbers established marriages that were predicated not upon the face-to-face dependencies of kin networks but rather upon the freedom and autonomy offered by a steadily increasing reliance on the marketplace.

Undoing the Ties that Bind

Early in 1949, a real estate office opened in Hicksville, New York. The office stood on land that, only a short time before, had been under active cultivation. For several days before the office's opening people had been lining up. By the end of the first day's business, $11 million dollars of housing had been sold.

The first of Bill Levitt's subdivisions was afloat.[35] Perhaps more than any other single event, the rush for suburban housing that began in the late 1940s and continued steadily through the next two decades signaled the sweeping transformation of dependency that had been building slowly but steadily for several centuries.

By the late forties, large numbers of Americans were eager to strike out on their own, free from the scrutiny of parents and unencumbered by the weight of familial obligations. What Levitt promised his eager customers, most of whom were young marrieds, was much more than affordable housing. He was also offering them the privacy to conduct themselves and to raise their children as they saw fit. He was selling a life-style as much as he was selling houses. At the core of this life-style was a conception of the family as a self-contained, self-sufficient unit whose central mission was to provide a neat, safe, easy to manage environment for the raising of children and the restoration of husband's spirits after the proverbial hard day at the office. The design of the houses and the layout of the subdivision itself made it clear that each nuclear family was assumed to be independent. Houses were small, but more importantly, the rooms were arranged in ways that made it clear that only parents and their children were to be at home here. Mothers-in-law or other kinfolk might visit, but stays would be short. The whole marketing strategy concentrated on the nuclear family, its upward mobility, and its independence.

Emotional ties to kin persisted, of course, but these ties were gradually weakened as they ceased being augmented by the daily visiting and heavy reliance on kin for a wide array of services that now were increasingly purchased or obtained through the plethora of voluntary organizations that sprang up in the new suburbs. It was largely wives who formed these associations, not only because they were at home most of the time but also because they bore the brunt of the separation from kin and the disruption of social ties that occurred when young families left their old neighborhoods for the suburbs. Voluntarism was animated, at least in part, by the need to replace the social functions of kin.[36] To be sure, as schedules grew more crowded, the sense of freedom and autonomy might well have evaporated. But for all the ritual complaining about being overburdened by meetings, the fact is that most suburbanites seem to have preferred networks of associations to networks of kin.

People did not move to the suburbs in order to join clubs, however. They moved, by all accounts, to find an agreeable location for sustaining a companionate marriage. They wanted privacy, not only for themselves in relation to their children but to avoid scrutiny of kinfolk. They wanted to pursue their own hobbies and interests rather than simply following in the footsteps of elders. They wanted to spend time with their children in ways that their parents, for the most part, had not. They wanted to lead their own lives. Observers of the 1950s often commented critically on the conformity of the new suburbanites, seeing in their similar preferences a cowardice, a fear of being different.[37] Though some of this timidity was (and still is) present, we think this critique misses an important point. Much of the similarity arises not out of cowardice but out of common needs and desires. People were not offended by the "little boxes" of suburbia, in part because the sameness was not appreciably different from the sameness of city apartment buildings and row houses, which they would have inhabited had there not been suburban development. But as important, the houses in fact met their needs as they understood them. They may not have desired sameness, but they had the same desires.

As we have seen, these desires were not new—they had begun to take form several hundred years earlier. What was new was the fact that for the first time in our history, unprecedentedly large numbers of people could realistically aspire to satisfying these desires. The post-World War II boom converted what had until then been at best an ideologically middle-class society into a society in which a majority of the population could in fact approximate many middle-class norms, including the norm of the companionate family. With dazzling rapidity, the American landscape was transformed as young adults poured out of the nation's cities as quickly as developers could put together subdivisions. By 1960, nearly three-quarters of the nation's housing stock was owner-occupied, single-family homes. The American

Dream—a home of one's own, a steady job, time to spend with
wife and children, in a word, independence—seemed within the
reach of almost everyone.[38]

The shift to the suburbs and the rapid spread of home ownership may have derived from longstanding aspirations but the
aspirations themselves were not a sufficient force to set the ball
rolling. Just as suburbanization captures nicely the culmination
of a long process of change in family life, so too does it capture
the maturing and coming together of the institutional forces
that were necessary for the companionate family to become *the*
American family. The American Dream was predicated on the
collaboration of the public and the private sector in behalf of
shifting our economic and social life from an accumulation footing to a consumption footing. Building on the foundation of
reforms of the Progressive Era and the New Deal, the post-
World War II decades were marked by a steady elaboration of
policies designed to stimulate consumer demand. Many of these
initiatives also had the effect, intended or otherwise, of enhancing the prospects for autonomy for nuclear families. The suburbs, this is to say, were the result of a long process of planning.
Had the process been self-conscious and deliberate, something
other than what we have now might have emerged. As it is, we
got both more and less than we bargained for.

At the end of World War II, the economy was roaring along,
fueled by wartime spending, full employment, and relatively
high private savings that derived from a combination of full employment and war-imposed rationing of consumer products.
For the first time in years, Americans had some money to spend.
But the impact of their spending binge after more than fifteen
years of austerity soon threatened to peter out. By the late
1940s, a new word was coined—"recession"—to describe a failure of the economy to grow. Policy makers and financial experts
had anticipated this and had been at work trying to devise strategies to sustain aggregate demand in the face of a rapid decline
in government orders once the war was over and savings were
depleted after the initial burst of consumer spending.

In order to keep the economy from sliding back toward
depression, consumption had to be sustained, new jobs had to
be created, and American industry had to be modernized. Each

one of these goals interacted with the others to form a system that meant that once started forward, momentum would gather, one development reinforcing the others.[39] In a sense, the starting push could be arbitrary, so long as it could be sold politically. What sold in the wake of World War II was aid to veterans. Two features of the G.I. Bill were of particular importance for their impact on the economy and on family life as well. First, the federal government announced that GI's who could qualify for admission could receive a stipend roughly equivalent to the costs of attending college or a university. If married, the stipend would reflect the needs of supporting dependents. Thousands upon thousands of young American veterans enrolled in higher education, many of them becoming the first in their family ever to have graduated from college. Secondly, veterans' benefits included federally guaranteed home mortgages at extremely low interest rates (typically under 5 percent) for approved housing. The long lines outside Bill Levitt's sales office in Hicksville were largely made up by ranks of veterans who qualified for the long-term mortgages and minimal downpayments that the G.I. Bill made available.

College education opened up many avenues of occupational choice to individual degree holders, making them attractive to mortgage and loan officers. The construction of housing for this newly forming market became an important aspect of the economy, generating employment directly and indirectly. In all likelihood, the indirect effects were greater than the direct ones. Suburbanites needed cars to get from home to work, to buy groceries, get children to the doctor or to music lessons, and to visit friends and associates. Cars needed highways, gasoline, and servicing, as well as insurance and repairs. And that has just the beginning of the wave of consumer demand that issued from the "simple" decision to buy one's own home: freezers, hedge trimmers, Rototillers, home entertainment devices—the list goes on. Each new gadget was a plus in the GNP accountings.

In the aggregate, this dramatic expansion in the ranks of the technically educated also helped provide the know-how that was required to innovate and modernize the economy. As productivity increased, the ranks of administrators, technicians, and professional and managerial employees swelled. Before long, com-

mentators were heralding the arrival of the affluent society. But
what went largely unacknowledged was the significant role the
government had played by underwriting the higher education
of virtually an entire generation and then making it nearly ef-
fortless for them to purchase their own homes. Though unin-
tended, the government in effect had adopted a family policy by
making it possible for the generation of World War II veterans
to form families of a distinctly autonomous sort. The federal
government was doing for veterans what their kin networks otherwise would have had to do, if they could: namely, help with an
education and with the expenses of setting up a household.
Clearly, the government was better at it than private networks
of mutual aid.

Moreover, the rapid spread of public and private health and
welfare benefits, whether administered through government or
by an employer, began to reduce significantly the extent to
which individuals were obliged to rely on kinfolk in time of
need. Social Security payments, especially if they were supplemented by private insurance or a pension, began to reduce the
degree to which aging parents had to rely upon their adult children to support them in their old age. Unemployment compensation, disability insurance, and health insurance greatly reduced the extent to which individuals had to turn to kin in
emergencies. Of course, people continued to visit relatives, to
assist one another in time of need, and to exchange goods and
services.[40] But the steady expansion of alternate sources of support clearly allowed more and more married couples to concentrate their energies and resources ever more exclusively on
themselves and their children.

For its part, the private sector was engaged in what can only
be called a sustained barrage of urgings to do just that: concentrate on one's own needs and wishes. The advertising industry
came into its own in the fifties and in the television set that was
fast becoming a household necessity, advertisers found a perfect
medium. Ever more sophisticated messages were beamed into a
widening circle of homes, setting standards for home care,
beauty, and life-style. The uniformities of the suburbs also contributed to the success of advertising. Cut off from old neighborhoods and stable kinship associations, each of which con-

veyed standards and tastes, new suburbanites were almost invariably uncertain about how to present themselves—how to decorate the home, bring up the children, entertain, and so on. These uncertainties were played upon and plied for all they were worth; and they were worth a lot.

In one of the more subtle and penetrating studies of the culture and life-styles in the new suburbs, John Seeley and his associates painstakingly examined the way "arbiters of taste" emerged from the sociopsychological vicissitudes of suburban life. People who were strangers to each other were thrown together in a milieu for which they had little preparation. Standards of behavior—in the broadest sense—were unclear. In the absence of a sense of security that would have made the ambiguity tolerable, people turned to experts. Some of these experts were indeed expert: doctors, psychologists, and designers, for example. But others were often salesmen pretending to expertise as part of a sales pitch. And even those among the advice givers who were not selling anything (except their services) were regularly willing to make claims for their particular opinions that far exceeded their technical knowledge. All claims, Seeley and associates argued, professional, commercial, and even political began to look and sound alike. Each urged consumption: consumption of new ideas, new strategies for childrearing, or new products.[41]

In effect, more and more Americans were marrying and setting up households under conditions that were ideally suited to an economy predicated upon the steady expansion of needs. Increasingly cut off from the stable networks of kin and neighborhood, the young couples in the new suburbs were relatively easy marks for the arbiters of taste and the creators of new needs.[42] The result was a rapid expansion of consumption. Products that were long thought to be luxuries became necessities, and services that were once embedded in household or intrafamilial exchanges increasingly became organized under the commodity form, generating whole new arenas of need. The fear that workers would treat increased wages as an invitation to reduce their hours of work was finally put to rest: it quickly became clear that increased earnings meant increased purchasing power. In fact, Americans could not earn enough money quickly

enough to meet their rising expectations. As a result, the thirst
for credit grew and with it the last vestiges of a culture predicated on the virtues of thrift and self-denial began to disappear.

As we have seen, consumer credit was experimented with well
before the 1950s, but it was not until the fifties that consumer
credit became fully accepted and widely diffused. A few numbers tell the story. Between 1947 and 1969, the average American family's disposable income increased fourfold: for every
after-tax dollar earned in 1947, the family had $4.00 in 1969.
During this same period, mortgage indebtedness increased
eleven-fold, nearly three times faster than disposable income;
and short-term consumer credit (revolving charges, auto loans,
credit card accounts) increased *sixteen-fold, four times faster than
incomes were expanding.*[43] In effect, the desire for greater autonomy from kin and for greater emotional self-sufficiency for the
nuclear family met the society's need for a rapid expansion in
consumer demand. Privately generated desires met publicly
whetted appetites, and the old dependencies on kin were rapidly being supplanted by a reliance on consumption. Put another way, face-to-face dependencies were being set aside in favor of impersonal dependencies. For the first time, large
numbers of people could seriously choose to extricate themselves from the encompassing fold of the family. Incomes were
rising, opportunities seemed plentiful, credit was expanding,
and a thriving consumer goods industry was inventively creating
products to meet needs people didn't even know they had.
Moreover, pension plans, social security, and an expanding array of federal and state programs were coming into existence so
that couples could realistically concentrate on their own needs
without undue concern that they might be called upon to help
support an aging parent or an unemployed or recently disabled
sibling.

Of course, not all Americans flocked to department stores and
charge accounts. For significant numbers, fears of economic disaster were not simply the reverberations of the thirties. They
were continuing realities. Though everyone benefitted from the
growth in the economy after World War II, these benefits were
by no means evenly distributed, nor were they uninterrupted.
While the growing ranks of college educated, white-collar work-

ers experienced a steady expansion of good fortune with little reason to worry about uncertainties, blue-collar workers still had to contend with bouts of unemployment and wage levels that, though they were rising, remained well below levels that permitted high levels of personal consumption. Indeed, one of the great challenges to the consumer products industry was to devise ways of encouraging people whose objective conditions still bore an uncomfortable resemblance to prewar circumstances to begin to think of themselves as participants in the new wave of consumption.

This challenge was met with the help of increasingly sophisticated social science and market research. These two forms of research were fused in what remains, in our view, one of the most insightful and subtle analyses of working-class culture done in postwar America, Rainwater, Coleman, and Handel's *Workingman's Wife*.[44] We will discuss the substance of this research in Chapter 4. What interests us here is the way this research came about and the uses for which it was intended. Burleigh B. Gardner, director of Social Research, Inc., the funding source for the study, minces no words in his introduction to *Workingman's Wife*. He begins:

> An increasingly important, and economically substantial segment of our society—the working class—has, in the past, received only glancing attention from most of the writers reporting on the American class system. Recently, however, the economic importance of this class is beginning to be recognized. The fact is that the members of the working class in America form a group of major importance to every company which seeks a mass market for its products or services. This group is of vital concern to every advertiser who uses the mass media, as it is the target of most of the advertising communications prepared by American advertising agencies. . . . It is the purpose of this book to set forth in some detail the life style of the working class family, and to provide some clues regarding how best to reach these people with advertising and sales messages (13).

This volume addressed two problems, according to Gardner. First, advertisers were ignorant of the working class and thus did not know how to reach them. Secondly, the working class itself had a problem that advertisers needed to "help" them with: workers and their wives did not realize that their days of scrounging and avoiding debt were over. Gardner quotes Arno Johnson, vice president and senior economist of J. Walter Thompson Company, a leading Madison Avenue firm:

> As these [working class] families move up from one income class to the next, they could represent substantially increased markets for goods, services, and investments if only they were to take on the habits and desires of the income group into which they move. This is true even though taxes and the cost of living have increased.
>
> But there are reasons why they don't take on these new habits automatically. Their whole previous lifetime training, in most cases, was built around a different concept of how to live. There is a major job for advertising and selling to change these concepts and educate our population to desire and work for the better standard of living their increased productive ability justifies—a change in line with the changes in income now available as *discretionary* spending power. Shortening the "habit lag" can make possible a rapid resumption of growth in our economy. . . . [emphasis in original].

Manufacturers and merchandisers had to be convinced that blue-collar workers were a large untapped market and that they were good credit risks. The working class needed to be convinced of this too. The advertising industry clearly rose to the challenge.

Conclusion

In the process we have just sketched, an elaborate array of policies and programs were adopted by both the private and public sectors that supplemented or extended the conditions conducive to the nuclear family that had begun to appear in the early twentieth century. Social security benefits began to rise, medicare and medicaid were instituted, unemployment compensation was extended to include higher benefits and longer periods of coverage. In the private sector, unions won improved health and welfare benefits accompanying the wage gains that generally attracted most attention at the time. In combination, all these initiatives produced enormous incentives to reduce reliance upon kin and to shift allegiance to the marketplace. Each need that was met through consumption rather than through intrafamilial exchange added to the GNP and the nation's official sense of well-being. Within a very short period of time, roughly the scope of one generation, significant numbers of Americans ceased expecting their children to care for them in their old age. Wanting neither to be a burden to their children nor to be burdened by their children, the rapidly expanding ranks of the nation's elderly relied instead on pensions and social security. When the business cycle dipped, people quickly came to expect that the government would protect their incomes until they were rehired or found a new job. Of course kinfolk were not eclipsed entirely. But the nature of the bonds and the ways those bonds were reaffirmed were changed decisively. For more and more Americans, the bonds between kin became weaker and far less extensive. Though kinfolk still assisted one another, the assistance was more and more a supplement, a gesture, which however deeply appreciated, was no longer crucial. Married couples could plan their future without feeling obliged to take into account the needs of parents, siblings, and more distant relatives. More and more they could concentrate on their own needs and desires. And as they did they discovered that those needs and desires steadily expanded.

As industrialism gained momentum, it necessarily had to undermine the bases of familial mutual aid. In order to produce the autonomy that a full-fledged market economy requires, both the public and private sectors had to adopt policies that would make it possible for people to reduce their embeddedness in kin networks, allowing them to be geographically and socially mobile and more receptive to the idea of meeting needs through markets rather than through intrafamilial exchanges. But these reforms only made the changes we have been describing possible. At the same time that broad changes in the economy and in the role of the state in the economy were taking place, the family itself was experiencing changes that produced a steadily expanding number of people who wanted autonomy from kin. It is to this internal family dynamic that we now turn.

3

Dependence, Authority, and the Desire for Autonomy

BY NOW IT SHOULD be clear that the traditional family was held together in multiple and mutually reinforcing ways. The importance of the family was heightened by the absence of any systematic and dependable alternative to the mutual aid that kinship provided. In effect, virtually every aspect of traditional society reinforced the supremacy of the family over the individual and the kin network over the nuclear family. Autonomy, whether for the individual or for the couple, was simply not a real possibility. For autonomy to flourish individuals must have choices. In traditional societies choices were few and far between.[1]

Parents were the principal and authoritative interpreters of the world for their children and generally possessed the skills, aptitudes, and know-how that children knew they needed to get on in the world. No matter how much children might have bridled at their parents' instruction (and the testimony of the millenia indicates that children regularly have resisted parental dictates), reality conspired to sustain parental authority. Parents' skills were undeniable, even if they were resented. Traditional societies offered the young few, if any, alternatives to parental guidance. Whatever the style of parent-child interaction, whether parents were authoritarian or permissive, stern and distant or gentle and warm, *they were authoritative*. Because this authoritativeness was grounded in the realities of daily life, the inevitable tensions between generations did not threaten the dissolution of family ties as some fear they do today. Father-son conflict, for example, played itself out along a very narrow path in traditional societies, a path at the end of which the son was reconciled to the father's wisdom. In whatever way the son may have struggled with his identification with his father, more likely than not he took on the essence of his father's skills, aptitudes, and values. He became his father's successor. If anything, young women were even more tightly bound to the lives of their mothers, with both childrearing and cultural expectations limiting the possibilities for autonomy. For boys and girls, then, the world they came to inhabit as adults closely resembled the world of their parents. Any centrifugal forces generated within the family were contained, or at least deflected.

As a consequence, traditional societies provided virtually no encouragement for what two analysts of the coming of modernity have called "the wish to be free."[2] Of course, the desire to be free was not absent in traditional societies; rather it was underdeveloped, bearing scant resemblance to the yearnings for independence that we recognize and have come to celebrate. For the most part, however, the appetite for autonomy was squelched, masked by traditional solutions to recurrent dilemmas and by the unavoidable necessity of relying upon kin. There was simply no social space in which autonomy could take root and flourish. Only with the erosion of parental authority and familial interdependence do we begin to encounter autonomy.

The Erosion of Authority

The dawning of the modern era began to unravel the culture and social structure that had bound kin to one another as tightly as it had bound one generation to the next. With the rise of industry and the gradual shift in the basis of wealth from the land to the ownership of capital, whole new repertoires of skills were called forth. For a time, these new skills coexisted with the older skills, but it was not long before the pace of change quickened, rendering obsolete the skills of adults long before they reached old age. Slowly at first, but with steadily accelerating momentum, parents ceased being the authoritative interpreters of the world for their children. The skills learned from parents were no longer the only skills, nor even the most important ones, needed to get on in the world. "Good parents" became the ones who could motivate their children to go outside the family to learn what would be needed to make a life. Children were still subordinate to adults, obviously, but as the circle of adults upon whom children depended grew, both in number and in variety, children no longer experienced the adult world as if having one voice. This new plurality of often inconsistent voices opened the prospect of choice for the young.

One aspect of this change is common to all societies undergoing industrialization and urbanization. In the shift from an agrarian to an industrial society, adults rooted in agrarian pursuits cannot guide those who seek a life for themselves in the factory or city. Quickly, children become more knowledgeable about the new social order than their parents. "How you gonna keep 'em down on the farm, now that they've seen Paree?" is a question that opens up the prospect of psychological distance far greater than the geographical distance between farm and city. The subordination of children to parents ceases to be supported by the parents' superior command of the culture. Parents begin to instruct less and less by doing and more and more by saying, "do as I say, not as I do." For the child, internalizing the parents' standards no longer serves as the basis for a later reconciliation to parental authority. Instead, it practically guarantees that the child will be divided psychologically between the old-fashioned ways of his or her family and contemporary notions of what is acceptable and proper. And for parents, children become more of a reminder of mortality; parents no longer believe they are reproducing themselves when they have children.

Discontinuity between generations becomes endemic. Technological displacement becomes a standard feature of modern societies. The spectre of having one's skills stripped of importance is a pervasive threat, affecting adults in all strata of the workforce. This threat extends to parental authority. Indeed, given the fact that more and more of the content of parents' culture is of dubious relevance to the lives of children, parental insistence on the *forms* of authoritativeness in their interaction with children does not make them authoritative; it merely makes them authoritarian. Over time, this authoritarianism gets harder and harder to sustain, precisely because it carries so little substance with it. Rapidly changing circumstances oblige the good parent to concede, more or less gracefully, his or her obsolescence.[3]

As we have sketched it thus far, this dynamic between generations applies generally to all societies undergoing the transformations of industrialism and economic growth associated with modernization. In the United States, the role of immigration in our nation's history adds a special dimension. From the first settlers onward, adults confronted the uncomfortable fact that their children were in many ways more knowledgeable about their new home than they were.[4] It was commonplace for children to teach their parents the English they would need to shop, find work, or carry on transactions with police, social workers, and other representatives of mainstream culture. The intense chauvinistic Americanization campaign begun in the late nineteenth century and sustained through the early decades of the twentieth century altered to the point of inverting the customary relationship between parents and children. In manifold ways, the systematic discrediting of ethnic cultures and languages drove a wedge between parents and children. The fact that this went on under official auspices and thus carried the full weight and blessing of the society as a whole clearly certified the children as culturally superior to their parents.

Needless to say, this "second generation phenomenon" was characterized by considerable guilt and ambivalence on the part of both parents and children. Parents, wanting the best for their children, were obliged to step aside. The less they insisted upon continuity, the more readily would their children become established and secure in the new world. Some ethnic groups were more vigorous than others in defending their culture and thus in preserving parental authority and kin solidarity. Italo-

Americans are a case in point. For a number of reasons that we need not go into here, the kin network remained a significant feature of family life over several generations for the majority of Italians.[5] The authority of parents remained high, if not entirely intact, and as a consequence, school dropout rates were persistently high among second and third generation Italo-Americans and occupational mobility was comparatively low. In a sense, Italo-Americans preserved the authority of parents by resisting the full force of the Americanization that went on in the nation's schools.[6]

Other groups who came to the United States seemed to accommodate more readily to the dominant culture. Jews, for example, utilized the schools and were highly mobile in the span of two and three generations. While family stability remained quite high, the hold of the kin network over the family and the authority of parents seemed distinctly lower than among Italo-Americans.[7]

These inevitable and important variations are, from our point of view, variations on a theme rather than different themes. To one degree or another, immigration served to reduce the status of parents vis-a-vis their children. If parents insisted on their children's obedience and respect, they flirted with disabling their children in the world in which they would live. The combined effects of immigration and rapid industrialization undercut the substantive basis on which parental authority rested.

This is precisely the bind of modern parenthood. All families are like immigrant families—torn between the desire to maintain the values and beliefs of the parents' generation and the desire to assimilate into or integrate with the mainstream culture. No parent wants to produce a misfit. To the extent that parents want their children to be happy or successful, they must direct the child toward the preferences of the larger society. Otherwise, they must be confident that they can prepare their children for participation in a subculture that can exist apart from or in opposition to the mainstream. Needless to say, the seductions and power of the dominant culture are difficult to escape.

By referring to these changes as a loss of authority, we do not mean to suggest that this loss should be interpreted as negative in the way, for example, a loss of health is. Nor do we mean to suggest, even implicitly, that the restoration of traditional parental authority would be an effective or desirable solution to the dilemmas that accompany the loss of parental authority. Certainly from the perspective of those parents whose authority declined, the experience was deeply troubling and painful. However, when we locate the erosion of authority in the broader context within which it occurred, we see that the new relationships between parents and children are better suited to enabling the young to participate in society than the traditional modes would be. Moreover, these changes have produced a more dynamic society and a vastly enlarged scope for individual expression and development. Not only has traditional authority declined but straightforward obedience makes little sense in the way it once did.

To say that parental authority is declining, however, is not to suggest that parents have less influence over the direction of their children's development. Rather, the nature of parental influence is being transformed. In the early twentieth century, childrearing manuals warned parents against becoming too friendly with their children lest their authority be diluted and they lose control of their children. As parental authority has waned, experts have discovered the virtues of close bonds between parents and children.[8] Today, parents can be very weak authority figures and still be a very powerful presence in their children's lives. Nor does a decline in authority suggest a diminution of emotional bonds between parents and children. In fact, the opposite has occurred. As parents rely less on their status as authority figures, emotional bonds with children expand. Indeed, these bonds have become the basis for intensified parental influence on children.

This change in parent-child interaction is typically experienced, and sometimes maligned, as a move toward greater permissiveness. Certainly modern parents are less strict and formal than their traditional counterparts. However, the pejorative connotations of "permissive" suggest a failure of parental will rather than an acknowledgement that parents are seeking alternative childrearing strategies. These alternative strategies are directed towards enabling children to adapt autonomously to varied circumstances rather than obediently following orders. Discipline directed toward obedience is replaced by socialization that encourages flexibility and choice.[9]

As parents grow less secure about their authority and the appropriateness of their own expertise, affection replaces authority as the culturally preferred basis of parental influence. This shift in the basis of influence implicitly acknowledges the decline of intergenerational continuity and the fact that children will be setting out on their own, entering occupations and following life-styles quite distinct from those of their parents. It is this shift in strategies that defines the differences between traditional and modern modes of childrearing and continues, down to the present, to characterize the dilemma of parents—the need to find ways of parenting that best prepare children to cope with conditions that cannot be fully anticipated or controlled.

The expansion of the role of love in parent-child relations was facilitated also by a simultaneous shift in the interdependence of parents and children. The fundamental basis for parental control has been the dependence of children on their parents for love, protection, and sustenance. All discipline plays on children's dependence upon parents, a dependence not entirely one-sided. Kinship societies were organized such that parents were reciprocally dependent upon their offspring: it was their children who would look after them when they grew too old to work; it was their children who would carry on the family name and maintain the family holdings, however modest these might be; and it was their children who would undertake the rituals and observances that would insure elders a peaceful rest.

Parents also depended upon children in more immediate ways. In most societies, including our own until very recently, children began making a contribution to the family's well-being at a very young age. Two and three year olds would help out with small chores, which would free older siblings for more demanding tasks. Weeding the garden, cleaning wool, and helping with meal preparation were small but nonetheless indispensable contributions that children made to the household economy. These contributions were concrete embodiments of the principle of reciprocity that governed parent-child relationships; they had the effect of buffering the force of parental discipline.

The threat to withdraw love, which lies beneath the surface of all parental admonition and disapprobation, was tempered by the fact that children's contributions to the family gave them a basis for self-esteem independent of parental love. Indeed, early in this century children's earnings were more important than wives' earnings in supplementing family income. To give but one example, in Chicago in 1907, 26 percent of all families had wage-earning children, while only 10 percent of families had wage-earning wives.[10]

Familial interdependence also meant that after punishment, parent and miscreant would necessarily resume their cooperative labors, in the process reaffirming the bonds that were called into implicit question as the punishment was being administered. However austere and harsh the actual discipline may have been (and by contemporary standards, much discipline in traditional societies would be regarded today as child abuse), familial interdependence was not automatically threatened by changes in mood and feeling because it was not based on volatile emotions. Filial love, commitment, and dependency tended to be mutually reinforcing, even when parents were actively insisting a child do something he or she was uninterested in doing.

Modernization challenged traditional interdependencies just as it did traditional skills and authority. Increasingly, young children became mere dependents, and childhood was practically defined by the absence of participation in any meaningful form of productivity.[11] With the development of the idea of adolescence, the age at which individuals became productive participants in society increased considerably. Similarly, the interdependencies between adults and their elderly parents changed— the elderly could no longer count on their adult children to attend adequately to their needs. By the same token, as social security and private pension plans were put in place, many of the elderly quickly came to prefer being independent of their children. The base for parent-child reciprocity shifted from material and generational interdependencies to the psychological quality of the parent child relationship. With the traditional base for parental authority reduced and traditional interdependencies truncated, emotional intensity and intimacy replaced authoritativeness not only as the primary force behind parents' power over children but also as the primary base for familial interdependence.

This expanded role for emotional intimacy creates new dilemmas for both parents and children. Parents' concerns about the adequacy of their childrearing abilities and children's strivings for identity and autonomy become enmeshed with issues of love and dependence. Parents come to measure the adequacy of their love in terms of the accomplishments or personal qualities of their children. Children come to measure their autonomy in terms of their independence from needs for parental love and approval. But before exploring this expansion of emotional intimacy we need to clarify what it means to say that socialization has replaced discipline as the primary aim of childrearing.

Romancing the Child—Childrearing in the Shadow of Tradition

All parents live in several generations at once. They carry within themselves attitudes and preferences anchored in their grandparents' generation and transmitted to them through their parents. Thus, the lines between traditional and modern childrearing are blurred and uneven. Even the most modern parents remain concerned with obedience and are thus committed to some forms of discipline. But in traditional society, a parent could simply demand that a child do something because that was the parent's will. This approach was fine for teaching obedience and is well suited to shaping an adult who can follow orders or rules within clearly structured situations. However, it is not well suited to creating persons who can respond adaptively to situations in which one needs to understand the requirements and preferences of others and knows how to act in constantly shifting circumstances. Toward this end, a disciplinary procedure in which the parent points out to the child the consequences of his or her actions for the parent's feelings is much more likely to create a person attuned to the subtleties of interpersonal interaction. It is as if, in traditional societies, the parent says to the child, "If you do X, I will hurt *you*." By contrast, a contemporary parent is much more likely to say, "If you do X, you will hurt *me*." The child learns about undesirable behavior in terms of its consequences for others. Such a disciplinary approach also helps create a child who knows in nuanced ways about parents' reactions to and feelings about a wide range of behavior and experiences, preparing the child to move into a world of new people and circumstances.

Not only do parents who have lost authority influence their children in different ways than those with traditional authority, they also ask different things of them as signs of loyalty. In place of reflexive obedience and respect, the parent whose relation to his or her children is based primarily on emotional closeness asks for sensitivity and understanding. Parents often take as a measure of the child's love the degree to which the child correctly discerns the parent's wishes, even when they have not been made explicit. Obedience results less because it is explicitly required than because conformity to parents' wishes is implicitly expected. "How could you have done that to me?" is the parental question that best reflects this sensibility. Of course, the child perceives the disappointment that this question communicates as a threat to withdraw love. This may be more coercive than outright disapproval or physical punishment.

Basing parental control of children on love also complicates children's efforts to develop their own unique personalities, to differentiate from their parents, to detach from them and to go off alone. The emotional intensity that is substituted for parental authoritativeness also intensifies the child's psychological identification with his or her parents. Identifying with parents psychologically, the child internalizes them more profoundly and consequently is, in a very deep sense, more likely to be like them.

Nor is the love between the parent and child the only contributor to this identification. Contemporary research provides evidence that as fathers and mothers more equally share both the discipline and the nurturance of children, internalization and identification increase.[12] While we value the development in children of skills, traits, and even personalities different from their parents, ironically, the increased role of love in parent-child relations makes it probable that the child will psychologically closely resemble his or her parents. Of course, the similarity need not be obvious. Indeed, the resemblance is commonly subconscious. On the surface, the child, schooled in contemporary knowledge and technology and well-versed in modern manners, values, and ideas about morality, sexuality, and relationships, may appear quite different from or even antagonistic to his or her parents. This produces a situation that is filled with confusion and paradox. Parents feel they have little control over their children even though they have a deeply pervasive influence on them. And children, encouraged to strive to be different from their parents, cannot ever be confident of their distinctiveness.

A unique personality is only one of the hallmarks of personal autonomy. Especially in the context of American culture, there is a long tradition of equating personal autonomy with independence from others. This ideal of autonomy can be traced back at least to the time of Ralph Waldo Emerson, who urged:

> Live no longer to the expectation of these deceived and deceiving people with whom we converse. Say to them, O father, O mother, O wife, O brother, O friend, I have lived with you after appearances hitherto. Henceforward I am the truth's. Be it known unto you that henceforward I obey no law less than the eternal law. I will have no covenant but proximities. I shall endeavor to nourish my parents, to support my family, to be the chaste husband of one wife,—but these relations I must fill after a new and unprecedented way. I appeal from your customs. I must be myself. I cannot break myself any longer for you. If you can love me for what I am, we shall be the happier.[13]

While these ideas have long flourished, large numbers of Americans could actually take them to heart and live their lives accordingly only when the economy and social policy made such bids for autonomy practical and reasonably safe.

It is not always easy, however, to bring psychological reality into synchrony with social possibilities. Features of the parent-child relationship that contribute to the ability to sever ties with intimates are themselves built around another complication. Preparing children to place their own development above the bonds that tie them to others requires an intense bond with parents. This bond can make leaving parents extremely difficult. When parents are deeply internalized, one's identity is so inti-

mately linked with them that no amount of geographic separation affords a feeling of true independence and autonomy. For
both parents and children then, the confounded issues of identity and autonomy evoke many of the stormiest conflicts in their
relationship. While children struggle toward an autonomous
identity, parents' efforts to develop their children's unique qualities and capacities for autonomy clash directly with their desires
for control and hopes to find some affirmation of themselves in
their children's personalities.

It is important to recognize that these dilemmas of identity
formation are not the result of inadequate parenting. Rather,
they are a direct consequence of following the contemporary
requisites of "good parenting." The features of the parent-child
relationship that allow parents to prepare their children for a
world different from their own virtually guarantee that children
will be like their parents in fundamental ways and deeply conflicted about these similarities. But it is not only personal identity that is conflicted.

When parents are unable to instill in their children appropriate standards and values; when knowing their own location
in society does not tell them how to treat their children; when
the inappropriateness of prevailing adult roles makes traditional modes of childrearing obsolete, then they must look elsewhere for childrearing advice. In the absence of relevant traditions, parents turn to professionals for inspiration and guidance
in handling the tasks and learning the techniques of childrearing. The result is childrearing methods that fuse highly charged
parental emotional involvement and instrumental rationality—
an explicit concern with producing children with particular
qualities, skills, and traits. This applies to parents across a widely
divergent range of values, ideals, and childrearing styles: those
who want their children to be conventional as well as those who
hope their children will be free-spirited; those who emphasize
achievement and success and those who value adjustment and
personal contentedness. Consequently, parental love intended
to nurture autonomy, freedom, and self-development can be experienced as inviting immaturity and personal stagnation. In
calling outside experts into the family circle, parents inadver-
tently exacerbate the very conditions in which love and intimacy

become problematic. It is in this sense that we can talk about the corruption of love.

The Corruption of Love

As parental authoritativeness declines, parents cease being their child's protector from outside authorities. Increasingly, for example, children are called upon to please parents by pleasing others—teachers, coaches, scoutmasters, and the like. Instead of shielding children from what can be a harsh and uncompromising evaluation by experts, or even protecting them from demands for performance, parents themselves come to depend upon these experts in order to know whether or not they are "doing the right thing." In this way, parents become the agents of the experts. Parents want their children to perform according to standards set by the larger society and conveyed by the media and by professional advice givers.

The message is that parental love must be earned, not taken for granted. Love becomes contingent. This can only add to the child's sense that intimacy and emotional dependency make one vulnerable, not just to the needs and feelings of the loved one but to the demands and expectations of others in general. This dynamic is captured beautifully in a passage from Sue Miller's *The Good Mother*.[14] The thoughts are Anna's, a young teenager who has gone for the first time to visit her paternal grandparents, a restrained and undemonstrative couple who contrast sharply with the rest of her family:

> I realized I was dreading leaving my grandparents' farm to go East, where I was surrounded by love, by protestations of love, but love conditional on so much: on being good, whatever that meant; on doing well; on making the family proud. The demands themselves, I realized, were often the clearest expression of the love (97).

When demands become an expression of love, feelings of love become a constant reminder of restrictions on one's freedom.

The contingency of love combined with loss of parental authoritativeness serves also to transform the value of parents' judgments of their children, as children begin to devalue judgments that are not rooted in some form of expertise. Because of the emotional ties between children and parents, praise both matters more and means less than it once did. This praise, however welcomed and gratifying, becomes suspect unless it is backed up by others' judgments as well. For example, parental delight at a child's piano recital is made more meaningful to the extent that the teacher independently corroborates the achievement. Children understand that most parents do not know how to judge and, in any case, are obliged to say encouraging things. Thus, parental praise is akin to inflated currency—more and more buys less and less. Obviously, this cycle can become self-reinforcing: declines in parental authoritativeness produce increased reliance on experts; increased reliance on experts tends to make parental love contingent; children, sensing the contingency, begin to devalue parental approval in favor of expert judgment. And then, as adults who have been shaped by this dynamic, the next generation of parents is even more likely to rely on outside experts and create an even stronger sense of contingent love.

There is another important way in which love and intimacy come to be experienced as contingent. The fact that children have largely ceased being indispensible to the household economy also bears on the nature of the change in parent-child relationships we are describing here. However much gratification parents may receive from their children, there is no denying the fact that the gratifications are almost exclusively emotional. Gone are the contributions children made to the operations of the household.[15] In place of the reciprocal dependencies of everyday existence, we have an intensified emotional interdependence in which parents need love and affirmation from their children almost as much as children need these from their parents. With parental love conditional, contingent upon the child's sensitivity and responsiveness to the parents' needs and feelings, as well as to performance in the world according to the parents' expectations, it does not matter whether the parents consciously use the threat of love withdrawal as a disciplinary tactic: the threat is an intrinsic component of the emotional intimacy between parent and child. Love is not experienced simply as something given to the dependent child, thereby enhancing his or her capacity for autonomy, but as something that creates a further dependency. Children, under these circumstances, come to associate their love for parents with their own vulnerability.

This narrowing of the basis of relationships to love and emotional intimacy permits both parents and children to enjoy greater autonomy. At the same time, strivings for autonomy become more loaded, precisely because the emotional attachments are unmediated by other forms of interdependency. Bids for autonomy may appear as rejection, as can encouragements to be more autonomous. The fact that parents make these encouragements in a context in which the predominant inducement is love (or the threat of its withdrawal), only adds to the emotional charge of the relationship. In effect, the whole process we have been describing creates paradoxes for both parents and children. The parent, valuing self-direction and nonconformity over obedience to external authority, must assume a stance that undermines his or her own authority. Ultimately the parent can demand neither obedience nor attachment. Paradoxically, the ultimate demonstration of the child's love for his or her parent is to become autonomous—loving the parent enough to leave.

Thus we arrive at yet another way in which love, intimacy, and emotional dependency—the principal if not the only bases of parent-child interaction—have been made increasingly conditional. The result of this complex and largely unintentional process has been the steady corruption of love as a basis for relationships. Needless to say, this goes well beyond the parent-child relationship, even though it derives from that initial expression and intensification. By rendering love conditional, whether implicitly or explicitly, the emotional dependency that love carries with it becomes steadily more suspect. The corruption of love produces a fear of emotional dependency at the same time that it sustains a romantic nostalgia for unconditional belonging. Intimacy, even while it is the basis for constructing an autonomous life, also becomes the foundation for feelings of dependency.

Fear of Dependency

The family dynamic we just described generates two diametric impulses: a thirst for independence and autonomy on the one hand, a desire for unconditional belonging and absorption into community, on the other. These warring impulses are opposite sides of the same coin. They are linked by their common origins in the diffusion of parental authority, the relocation of authority outside the family, and the increasingly contingent quality of love. As more and more families embody the companionate ideal, the social distance between parents and children declines, and their relationship rests almost exclusively on love. Unbuffered by multiple and reciprocal dependencies, children experience parental discipline as a threat to withdraw love. In this context, love seems contingent upon performance which, as the child grows, is increasingly judged according to standards defined outside the realm of familial interdependence. Love and deep emotional dependency become sources of vulnerability that threaten autonomous identity. The power of intimates, of those on whom one depends emotionally, is experienced as being greater and more menacing than the power of more distant or abstract authorities.[16] Some respond to this by growing reticent, by becoming leery of entering into relationships that threaten to replicate the dependency and vulnerability they experienced as children. Others seek highly idealized relationships in which they hope to discover the unconditional love they never found as children.

Romantic love offers such promise, whether it results in marriage or liaison. But in recent decades, significant numbers of people have been submerging themselves in cults or intense communitarian sects. Typically, such groups purport to provide unconditional love and solidarity modelled after romantic notions of familism. Emotional detachment and emotional immersion are both products of the growing conditionality of love. Together, they can be seen as defining polarities toward which we are all drawn with varying degrees of intensity, and often with deep ambivalence. Let us look at each response in more detail.

A rapidly growing number of American men and women are

postponing marriage and/or the bearing of children well past
what has been the conventional timing for these important family events. Moreover, though the numbers remain small, there
has been a dramatic rise in the ranks of those who deliberately
choose to remain single. The cultural meanings attached to
these preferences have also changed. Being single is no longer
reason for social isolation nor cause for pity; it is no longer seen
as deviant. These changes in preferences and cultural meaning
can be observed in a variety of settings. For example, the longstanding implicit requirement that executives of large corporations be married men seems to have passed from the scene. *Fortune* magazine, to take but one example, has periodically
profiled young, up-and-coming executives. In the fifties and
early sixties, the profiles were invariably of men, all of whom
were either already "happily married" or happily contemplating
matrimony. By the late sixties and on into the eighties, the profiles had changed dramatically. Women were now among the rising stars of the corporate world and, more salient for our purposes here, the young men and women profiled were more
often not married. Indeed, some indicate that their busy lives
and engrossing work simply leave neither time nor inclination
for marriage or, if they are married, for children. A long-term
relationship, at least a relationship other than to a firm or career, was seen as an encumbrance, a direct competitor for their
energies and drive.[17]

Of course few among us have careers and life-style choices as
alluring as the young executives featured in the pages of *Fortune*.
Though exceptional in some senses, their attitudes toward settling down are widely shared. The research arm of the life insurance industry, the American Council of Life Insurance, has
been studying the shifting attitudes of the young toward the
family, for the obvious reason that family heads are the most
logical prospects for purchasing life insurance. Their studies
have revealed a declining interest in marriage among the young
men and women they interviewed. For example, between 1970
and 1976, the percentage of surveyed youth, aged 14–24, who
indicated that they preferred to remain single ranged between
36 and 41 percent for young men and 23 to 29 percent for

young women.[18] The rising popularity of staying single is an-other indication of how the cultural value of marriage has de-clined, while the value of career success has increased.[19]

It is important to note that many of these changes are a re-sponse to the demands and expectations of corporations and professions that structure careers and define the criteria for suc-cess. Women especially became sensitive to reluctance in the cor-porate and professional worlds to support and promote people whose loyalties to their family and personal life would rival their commitment to work. Women with strong career interests began to defer marriage or childbearing, not only because of their am-bivalence about them but also as a strategy to enhance their chances for success.[20]

What is at issue is not just marriage. The fear of entering into relationships that entail commitment and carry with them the necessity of balancing one's own needs and desires with those of another increasingly controls patterns of friendship and court-ship as well as marriage. At the extreme, one sees in our culture the rapid growth of institutions predicated on what might be called relationships of limited liability. Singles bars, weekend spas intended to promote self-contained romantic interludes, and an increasingly wide array of vacation packages and con-dominium complexes all cater to men and women who want friendships and intimacy on terms that do not deflect them from the lives they have chosen to pursue. These patterns go well be-yond the "sowing wild oats" of an earlier day. They bespeak an unwillingness to become implicated in relationships that are identity defining, relationships that provide one's partner with legitimate claims on the stuff of autonomy—allocation of time, preferences and tastes, selection of acquaintances, and appear-ance in the community.

Even those who do marry have limited tolerance for the re-straints that accompany relationships. This can be seen both in our increasing propensity to divorce, the rapid rise in prefer-ence for one or, at most, two children, and a shift in parents' sense of priorities and obligations to children. It is now a cliche to observe that contemporary marriages are being dissolved for reasons that are trivial by comparison to what it would have taken to get earlier generations to end a marriage. It is not that marriages were better in the past. Rather, most people simply had fewer and lower expectations of marriage as the provider of personal happiness and self-actualization. In effect, people's tolerance for inconvenience, disappointment, and even routinization has been dramatically lowered, while expectations for personal fulfillment and growth have been considerably enlarged. More and more of us are simply unwilling to put up with relationships that become incompatible with our own needs which are constantly expanding. The result is fragility of relationships and a general wariness of intimacy.

The widespread evidence of this fragility leads to a peculiar ambivalence about the role of love in contemporary culture. Since early in the nineteenth century, love has been idealized as the primary basis for marriage. Then, love represented a person's autonomous choice, based on his or her innermost feelings, as opposed to parental preference based on social standing, economic prospects, and familial continuity. Acting on love was acting on behalf of one's independence. But as the significance of love in parent-child relations has expanded to become the basis for familial interdependence and parental control, love has been less able to serve as the vehicle for personal autonomy. The same family dynamic that amplifies the desire for intense love contributes to a creation of needs for self-actualization and autonomy that are endangered when love becomes the primary basis for establishing so-called permanent relationships. The overall result is a continued intensification of the pursuit of love along with a heightened wariness of the dependencies it creates.

The initial suppression of self-interest that accompanies falling in love is exhilarating because it is expansive, it lifts the restrictions imposed by one's own identity and creates new possibilities. But even the exhilaration becomes suspect because of the vulnerabilities and dependencies it opens up. What was first experienced as liberating can also be felt as restrictive, especially when confounded with the mundane repetitiveness of daily life and the realities of material concerns. Eventually, falling in love becomes suspect, not because of the experience itself but because of where it leads. Thus, a curious skepticism about love has emerged in the very same popular culture that does so much to promote romanticism. "Love Stinks," a long-running, top-forty rock song recorded by the J. Geils Band in the early 1980s, captures this skepticism nicely, pointing to the ways love is inevitably disappointing, intrusive, and confusing. Underneath it all, personal growth and autonomy are being promoted more than connectedness with others. Any occasion for personal growth is valued. (In this vein, even divorce has been converted to a stage in personal growth, a process by which an individual gets back in touch with his or her own deeper persona, a persona that was presumably submerged in marriage.) Marion Solomon, a psychotherapist specializing in the treatment of problems in intimate relationships, accounts for the failures of contemporary marriage in terms of the pursuit of the autonomous self:

> When the focus of life is on determining one's own needs and finding another who can fill those needs and wishes, any relationship is in danger of being flawed by narcissistic expectations. It is increasingly difficult for people to enter into loving relationships and to maintain them once they begin. Obligations to others as a primary value has become a concept either denied or distorted into a pseudo-love, a wish to embrace all mankind but no one in particular. Many have come to expect fragile relationships that break easily, although they do not usually understand the nature of that self-fulfilling prophecy. Coupled with this belief is an increasing demand for effective independent functioning without emotional reliance on others. The result is an inability to invest freely in deep feelings for others.[21]

It has been common to place responsibility for the rise of this wariness, especially towards marriage, on the reemergence of feminism. After all, it has seemed to be principally women who were discovering personal needs for growth and self-exploration, needs that seemed circumscribed, if not utterly precluded, by conventional marriage. But as Barbara Ehrenreich has argued, the earliest contemporary expressions of what she calls the "flight from commitment" are to be found among upper-middle- and middle-class men.[22] She shows that a host of psychologists and medical doctors began to be critical of the responsibilities that framed the conventional expectations for men in the 1950s. Stress, competitiveness, and the suppression of emotion were all seen as contributing to an epidemic of medical and psychological troubles. *Playboy* appeared on newsstands at this time with its own version of this critique, celebrating an ethic of self-absorption in the bargain. It described women as playmates, objects of passion and vehicles for pleasure, but not persons with whom men need full relationships. Men, *Playboy* announced, should be autonomous, free agents, not tied down with the burdens and stultifying responsibilities that come with marriage and family; sexuality should not be linked to responsibilities.

From some vantage points, men seemed to have a marvelous situation—a wife at home to do domestic service and a job and associations that were rewarding and stimulating. But, Ehrenreich argues, men felt restrained, even oppressed, by the asymmetrical dependencies the conventional family entailed. At least in their fantasy lives, complements of *Playboy*, they began to imagine a life free of the sorts of dependent relations represented by family. A decade or more later, women would begin to criticize and reject the same disempowering forms of family life that *Playboy* had begun to criticize because of the dependencies they imposed.

While Ehrenreich's analysis is a welcome corrective to the view that holds women solely responsible for the increasing frailty of the family, she clearly overstates the case. While some men may indeed find the burdens of being breadwinner intolerable and the responsibilities of being a husband claustrophobic, there is little evidence that men have less interest in marriage than women. But the value of Ehrenreich's analysis should not be measured only in how narrowly predictive her propositions are. Her book, as well as any, describes the cultural shift that has made intimacy, emotional dependence, and love problematic. That most of us still sail these troubled waters is less important than are the currents that drive more and more of us onto the shoals.

Ehrenreich portrays this shift as a retreat from the responsibilities that arise whenever two people enter into a relationship they define as "long-term." Though she is sharply critical of the conventional norms that keep women dependent upon men, and that constrain men as well, she resists rethinking intimacy and emotional dependence. Insofar as notions of commitment, maturity, and responsibility make no allowance for autonomy, the desire for autonomy must appear as a rejection of commitment. The flight from commitment appears even more irresponsible when it is the more advantaged and powerful who flee. When men walk away from a marriage, Ehrenreich points out, women and children are left vulnerable, exposed to market forces and institutional practices that have historically disadvantaged them. But the so-called flight from commitment goes far deeper than powerful men abandoning powerless women and children. Increasing numbers of men *and* women are expressing a desire to avoid being tied down, to avoid becoming entangled in relationships based on the suppression of self. When two people wish to preserve their autonomy and still have a relationship, commitment and responsibility begin to take on new meaning. The desire to keep the relationship one of limited liability does not automatically signal irresponsibility any more than divorce does. Indeed, for many people wariness of commitment is grounded in the pain of their experience of divorce.

Avoiding commitment becomes a form of self-preservation. Judith Wallerstein and Sandra Blakeslee, reporting a study of the long-term effects of divorce on middle-class families, found that "more often than not, divorce is a wrenching, long-lasting experience for at least one of the former partners. Perhaps most important, we found that for virtually all of the children it exerts powerful and wholly unanticipated effects."[23] Among the adults Wallerstein studied, there were few whose post-divorce lives came close to approximating the expansive, upbeat scenarios promised by books like *Creative Divorce* or *Beyond Codependency and Getting Better All the Time.*[24] Instead, five and even ten years after divorce, Wallerstein found a significant proportion of the adults were still feeling and showing the effects of the divorce in terms of personal problems, difficulties in relationships, and "diminished capacity to parent." Sadly, this occurs precisely when children experience an intensified need for a secure connection with parents. (It is important to note that the subjects of this study were selected initially because they were not in treatment for psychiatric problems and the children were not having difficulties in school.)

The reduction in the ability of divorced parents to respond

appropriately to their children's needs is especially significant because it adds to the wariness of relationships and commitment that arises from the vulnerabilities associated with childhood dependencies. Children in such circumstances often blame themselves for the rejection they feel from their parents. They experience themselves as unworthy of love, as unloveable. Frequently they react to the increased distance that separates them from their parents by taking on themselves the responsibility of assuaging the parents' pain. By becoming the parents' caretakers, they recover some of the closeness that has been lost during the separation of their parents. Wallerstein refers to these children as "overburdened." In addition to the immediate toll extracted by placing a child in this position, the aftereffects of divorce echo through a child over the course of its adult life. Wallerstein and Blakeslee found that some of the consequences of divorce do not manifest themselves until the child reaches an age where establishing intimate, sexualized relationships with others becomes important. In various ways the children of divorce are people for whom intimacy and vulnerability are equated. Often, both the need for closeness and wariness of closeness are simultaneously intensified. However solid their own adult relationships may appear, traces of their childhood experience of divorce haunt their adult lives. The result is a fear of abandonment that permeates their adult relationships. For many, the only way they can manage the legacy of their parents' divorce is through the avoidance or subversion of committed, intimate relationships.

Wariness of dependency and commitment extends well beyond the ranks of the divorced and the growing numbers of men and women who prefer to live singly, unencumbered by the demands of sustained intimacy with another. The rapid growth of dual-earner families is at least in part a consequence of husbands' and wives' resolve to avoid becoming disproportionately dependent upon the other. Another indication of the diffusion of this wariness is the shift in parental attitudes toward children.[25] Growing numbers of parents no longer feel automatically obliged to put their children's needs above their own. Sometimes using the language of children's rights, and sometimes using the language of personal growth, more and more parents are in effect saying that their needs are as legitimate and pressing as their children's. Moreover, since parents no longer expect to be cared for by their children in old age, they do not feel as obliged to be self-effacing or self-denying while their children are young. In one widely cited study, by researchers Yankelovich, Skelly and White, over 60 percent of the parents interviewed supported the view that "parents should be free to live their own lives even if it means spending less time with their children." Roughly the same number indicated that it was permissible for parents "to live well now and spend what they have earned even if it means leaving less to the children." [26] There can be little doubt that the corruption of love and the consequent fear of dependency has carried over into parenthood. At the extreme, children are experienced as a burden, a source of responsibility that constricts one's freedom of action, one's autonomy. Some clearly have anticipated this and decided not to have children. But others, lamentably, seem to discover this only after the fact and resent, to one degree or another, parenthood and the dependencies that parenthood entails.

In recent years many parents, even those for whom parenting has been more satisfying than frustrating, are finding that some of the responsibilities of parenthood—supporting and providing a home for adult children—have been extended well beyond expectations. Living independently away from one's parents has long been a goal for maturing children, a hallmark of full adulthood. Through the first two-thirds of this century the trend was toward people leaving home and marrying at a young age. Since 1960, however, the age at which men and women typically marry has been rising, and the rush to leave home has subsided. In fact, a new phenomenon has begun to emerge—the so-called "boomerang kids," adult children who return to live with their parents after a period of at least partial independence. The change in the timing of marriage has been most striking. The average age at first marriage has risen sharply over the past thirty years. The current median age at first marriage for women, 23.3 years, is the highest recorded in United States history. For men, the current median of 25.5 years is close to the highest on record. In earlier generations, marriage was often the only way out of the parental household; this was especially true for young women. The rising age at first marriage clearly indicates that young adults no longer see marriage as the only—or even the most preferable—vehicle for independence.

Some seek the independence of the single life, while others find striking out on their own as hard to negotiate as marriage. As a result, since 1960 there has been an overall increase in both the number of young adults, ages 18–24, living at home with their parents and in the number of young adults living on their own. In 1985, 60 percent of men and 48 percent of women, ages 18–24, lived with their parents. In 1960, 52 percent of the men and only 35 percent of the women in this age category lived at home. Especially noticeable are increases in the ranks of the un-married at precisely those ages when marriage was traditionally taken for granted. In 1960, 42 percent of the 18–24 year olds were married and living apart from parents. By 1985, fewer than one quarter of the 18–24 years olds were married.[27]

There appear to be multiple reasons for these changes. Some of them are basically economic—more education and training are required for successful entrance into the labor market; the cost of living has continued to rise, particularly the cost of hous-ing; and the relative income of young people has declined. Thus, for many the reluctance to marry goes hand-in-hand with deciding to prolong reliance on parents. Living on one's own is simply more difficult than it was in the recent past. It can also be much less comfortable—living alone can entail a drastic re-duction in standard of living. This is especially true for middle- and upper-middle-class children, many of whom are now choos-ing to stay at home because of the material comforts they can enjoy there. Why leave the sauna and the pool just to prove they can make it on their own?

But the fear of commitment also enters into the calculations of the relative advantages of moving out versus remaining at home. In the past, being independent meant being free of de-pendency on one's parents. In actuality, many people merely traded the dependency of being a child for the dependency of a spouse. For women especially, marriage meant shifting depen-dency from parents to husband. For men, marriage was seen as acquiring a dependent, a perception that helped mask the de-gree to which men became emotional and domestic dependents of their wives. Although joining one's life with another certainly carried complex commitments and dependence, at least those dependencies seemed freely chosen rather than imposed by birth. But with an increasing fear of commitment, an unavoidable recognition of the riskiness of marriage, and awareness of the often lifelong ramifications of a failed marriage, many people are finding continued dependence on parents more attractive than either the limited independence of marriage or the solitary independence of living alone.

The kids who strike out on their own but for one reason or another—financial squeeze, collapse of a career, or failed marriage—return to live with their parents are symptomatic of the increasing difficulties Americans confront in their efforts to negotiate dependencies. While there are no firm figures on the frequency with which this is occurring, the Census Bureau reported in 1988 that in the mid-eighties between 8 and 16 percent of 25–29 year olds might be living at home after a failed venture on their own.[28] When adult children remain at or return home, a considerable amount of tension and strain can be generated, even in families in which the parent-child relationship has been positive. It is not easy for a child who has lived on his or her own to return to a situation where they are or feel accountable to parents.

Nor is the situation easy or satisfying for the parents. In fact, many parents no doubt fear that they have somehow failed to equip their child for the autonomy they themselves admire. In addition to the financial drain of prolonged dependence, parents can resent the end of their new-found privacy, the time for themselves, and the opportunity to pursue activities and friendships that the obligations and concerns of parenthood had restricted.[29]

We must be careful not to write this off as mere selfishness on the part of parents. It is not simply that adults have the opportunity to pursue personal satisfaction or that they somehow lose themselves in pursuit of personal gratification. The predominant message in our culture is that one's activities ought to be pleasurable and the occasion for personal growth. There are limits to how much the satisfactions of parenting can meet these criteria. We are placing limits on the claims that dependencies make on us because we are trying to be full and decent people.

There is another reason our commitment to parenting is becoming constricted. People can undertake and endure the sacrifices of parenthood when they have reason to believe that, in some significant way, their children's lives will be better or fuller than their own. Raising children is an affirmation, an act of faith in the future. Several features of contemporary life make it hard to sustain that faith. The threat of nuclear war and total devastation are obvious factors. The increasing contamination of the earth, even excluding the prospects of war, is another. And finally, it is simply no longer realistic for most people to assume that their children's lives will be better than theirs has been, even in fairly narrow economic terms. It is difficult to pinpoint exactly how such considerations directly influence peoples' feelings about and approach to having and rearing children, but it is hard to imagine that there is no correlation.

At the same time that growing numbers of men and women have been distancing themselves from intense and presumptively lasting emotional dependencies, others have been desperately seeking such dependencies. At the margins of our culture, small but visible numbers of men and women have been seeking relationships that, on the surface, hold out the promise of unconditional love and an emotional space in which it is safe to be dependent. Why some should flee while others pursue dependency is a question we are not prepared to answer here. What is of moment for our purposes is that these diametrically opposed responses flow from the same circumstances: the shedding of the integument that surrounded parents and children and cushioned threats of rejection and reduced the constrictions of dependency.

The capacity of various religious and quasi-religious cults to recruit members, especially from among the middle and upper middle classes, seems to rest precisely on their ability to play on the themes of unconditional love and acceptance. Cults typically contrast their ways with those of the "corrupt" society in terms of solidarity and belonging, as well as purity and sacredness. They play down the individual as performer in favor of the individual as essence, essence that is meaningful particularly in the context of the group. The power of the cults resides in their capacity to make the individual untroubled by the dependency he or she comes to feel for the group. The group becomes literally like an idealized family in which the individual no longer feels vulnerable as a result of being emotionally needy. Such an idealized family stands in sharp contrast to many actual families in which, as we have seen, family members feel continually judged for their worthiness at the same time that their emotional needs make the judgments extremely charged. Distraught parents of cult members, and society generally, have difficulty believing cult members' protestations that they feel at peace, whole, and loved within the group. The disbelief stems partly from unwillingness to accept the rejection of family entailed by joining a cult. Part of the disbelief, however, is less protective than it is conceptual. Most of us cannot accept the sharply truncated selfhood that cult membership entails and when a member claims to feel self-fulfilled, we cannot understand or credit the claim. The self that they are feeling good about is one most of us do not admire because it is a self that accepts dependencies as unproblematic. It is a self that has no appetite for autonomy or independent choice.

Cults are an extreme response for those whose experience with conditional love has made them thirst for safe expressions of the need for emotional dependence. Of course, most of us avoid the extremes of either rejecting all intense emotional dependencies or submerging ourselves in dependencies. But this does not mean we escape the dilemmas that give rise to these extremes. On the contrary, these extremes represent polarities in our culture about which there is considerable ambivalence. At one time or another, we are all drawn in the direction of wanting complete autonomy; at other times we are drawn toward seeking the reassurances of emotional dependency. Most of us, most of the time, strike some sort of compromise, but the terms of this compromise have clearly shifted over time toward a greater emphasis on autonomy. As this shift has progressed, resistance (or ambivalence) has grown more noticeable.

This resistance is evident in the many current attempts to breathe new life into traditional gender prescriptions. The writing of Marabel Morgan, an outspoken defender of conventional family roles, is a case in point. Her mission is to "re-enchant" the role of wife/homemaker. Thousands of women have flocked to her seminars, and many more have bought her book, *The Total Woman*.[30] Her attempt rests in significant measure on exaggerating wifely dependence, masking the infantilization involved by eroticizing it. Thus, she recommends that wives be sure to have the children in bed early every so often so that they can greet their husbands when they return home from work in one or another outlandish, sexually provocative get-up and seduce them on the spot.

Offering a mixture of religious bromide and sexual gimickry, Morgan is extending hope to those who wish to preserve the wife's dependence in a context in which husbands may tire of the arrangement. After all, husbands have much more autonomy and, given that they spend a huge portion of their waking hours away from hearth and home, out among an array of "available" women, wives have to be ever inventive and beguiling to "keep their men." Morgan asks wives to walk a very thin line. Wives dare not make themselves so attractive as to cause their husbands to waver from the straight and narrow of providing amply for the family. The wife should be as clever and inventive as she can in welcoming her husband home at night but be resolute in getting him off to work the next morning.

Morgan is of interest because, unlike most supporters of traditional gender arrangements, she is not straight-laced. For the most part, the recent upsurge in support for tradition has been closely linked to an assault on sexual expressiveness as well. Politically conservative and religiously fundamentalist (whether Catholic, Protestant, or Jew), resistance to the steady expansion of autonomy at the expense of sustained emotional dependencies has largely focused on the putative gains of the women's movement, especially those that directly bear on sexuality—legalized abortion, sex education, widening access to birth control and pregnancy counseling, and gay rights. Sex is not only an issue on its own terms for conservatives, it also stands as emblematic of women's subordination to and dependence upon men. To deny reproductive rights to women is to reduce significantly the degree to which men and women can function independently of one another, whether as unrelated individuals, lovers, or spouses.

Love and emotional intimacy create dependencies between individuals. Dependencies conflict with aspirations for autonomy. Indeed, it may well be the case that aspirations for autonomy arise from the resentments that inevitably form within families when dependencies are used to manipulate or stymie individual wishes. Think of the idea of open marriage as the attempt to redefine autonomy within the confines of marriage. Whatever their origins, desires for autonomy have been encouraged in our society if only as the principal way to dislodge us from the webs of kin affiliation that were perceived as impediments to fuller participation in the economy, both as workers and as consumers. The internal dynamic of family life was altered by the advance of modern institutions such that even as traditional ties were loosened they came to be experienced as constricting. For increasing numbers of family members, both men and women, children and parents, the family ceased being a "haven in a heartless world." In fact, for more and more of us, the haven sought might be thought of as a heartless haven.

A Heartless Haven: Attractions of Impersonality

For all the concern over the family and for all the nostalgic evocations of family life that currently abound in our culture, the fact is that a large and growing number of Americans have been systematically, if unconsciously, reducing their expectations of family life. While marriage and children figure centrally in the intentions of most of us, fewer and fewer Americans define their lives or their expectations solely in these terms. Many express a matter-of-fact recognition that divorce is a real possibility, one for which they should be prepared.[31] And significant numbers of parents, and people who intend someday to be parents, indicate that children will have to compete with careers and other interests. In this new calculus, children no longer automatically take precedence over other commitments.[32]

In effect, subjective needs for autonomy have merged with social structural needs for high levels of mobility and private consumption to produce a context in which the delights of family life are being strenuously challenged by a wide array of competing attractions. For some, the competition comes from the workplace, though for obvious reasons this is largely restricted to those for whom highly rewarding careers, both in psychological and financial terms, are available. For others, the competition comes from avocational preferences, which entails balancing the emotional and financial demands of family life with the requirements of activities felt crucial for self-fulfillment. And for an indeterminate but almost certainly growing number of us, the pursuit of self-fulfillment has become the organizing principle of life.

While intense intimacy and love remain preoccupations, we increasingly experience these emotions and the relationships in which they occur as threatening. There may be nothing quite so emotionally satisfying as two lovers enveloped in each other, each suffused with the other such that their sense of themselves as separate beings is largely extinguished. But this bliss has by now been shattered too many times by people just like us to be taken at face value. We may still wish for "happily ever after," but it is no longer believable. Moreover, the openness and trust that such relationships imply are by no means seen as unmixed blessings or dependable certainties. Too many of us, by now, have experienced this sort of trust as children, only to have the trust violated by parents who, despite their best efforts to do well by their children, exploited that trust by guiding the development of the child's identity in a direction that met the parents' needs. Ultimately, such parents need their children to behave and even feel in certain ways so as to sustain their own fragile sense of identity. For the children of these parents, loving comes to mean adapting one's identity to someone else's needs. As a result, more and more of us question our romantic impulses and devalue our needs for dependency. The transformation of family life and the concomitant diffusion of authority have corrupted love and made us fearful of dependency at the same time that love and emotional dependency have become virtually the only bases on which family life rests. The nostalgia for family life is as widespread as it is resonant precisely because fewer and fewer of us are free to experience it in other than mythic terms.

Conclusion

As the satisfactions of family life grow more and more problematic and uncertain, the array of satisfactions offered via consumption has expanded exponentially. Though people still ritually acknowledge that "you can't buy happiness," it is clear that getting and spending have become major sources of gratification for Americans. And even though the gratifications are more often than not fleeting, the accumulation of things has become a significant measure of self-worth. In the same fashion, one of the principal ways in which we reassure ourselves of the goodness of our society is to refer to the size of our GNP: as long as we continue to consume more each year, our leaders and pundits assure us, we grow stronger and more envied the world around. The impersonality of the marketplace increasingly appears as a refuge from emotional entanglements that diminish autonomy.

Subjectively generated aspirations for autonomy are reinforced and capitalized upon, literally and figuratively, by an economy whose existence is predicated upon the atrophy of traditional familism. In order to remain profitable, the economy has to expand the sphere of needs that can be met through market-mediated exchanges. As we saw in the last chapter, the economy has done this in two ways. On the one hand, more and more of the activities that once were organized by families—food, clothing, shelter, and the like—are gradually transformed into commodities from which profits can be extracted. On the other hand, the sphere of needs itself has undergone expansion: vast new arrays of needs have been generated, needs that can only be met by spending money. Both processes are ongoing, and as they proceed, face-to-face dependencies decline and impersonal dependencies increase.

For those needs that the market has been unable or unwilling to address, the state is increasingly relied upon. As networks of kin relations wither, an elaborate network of private and public welfare measures are put in place. Pension plans, health insurance, and unemployment compensation, to name only a few of the most obvious examples, emerge in order to stabilize if not enhance the conditions needed for expanding the realm of autonomy. If children are to be able to strike out on their own, they must be assured that their parents will not be left in the lurch, just as parents must be assured that their children will not be abandoned by virtue of parental desires for autonomy. As family ties weaken, spheres of choice widen, and there is an enlarged space for the commodity form to occupy. The internal dynamic of family life, in effect, prepares us to be receptive to offers of autonomy. For much of our history, these offers have been tendered by businessmen and publicists who adhere to a particular version of autonomy—the autonomy that comes from impersonality and affective disengagement from others. In this context, families may remain vigorous while familism clearly ebbs.

There is more to this than subjective desires pliantly hitched to the purposes of profit making. Subjective needs for autonomy have meshed with consumer capitalism, but only imperfectly. As we shall see in the next three chapters, the relationship between our private world of loves and longings and the public sphere of work and consumption is less harmonious than it is dialectical. The crux of the matter resides with the ebbing of familism. But before we examine the fate of familism more closely, we need to see how the changes in social structure and social psychology have combined to reshape family life.

4

Varieties of
Modern Family Life

THE COLLAPSE OF MUTUAL AID and the subsequent dramatic expansion of consumption occurred in a context in which parental authority and love were also being transformed. These tandem changes placed an ever higher premium on autonomy, on minimizing the number of intimate emotional dependencies. Over time, as broad social and economic forces interacted with the psychological dynamics of family life, traditional family forms grew hollow. Kin networks atrophied and exerted a declining hold on our sense of obligation and commitment. Even though it remained linked to kin, the nuclear family was expected to be largely self-contained. Somewhere in this long, drawn out process, the companionate nuclear family became the preeminent family form: it became *the family*.

The emergence, in the late nineteenth century, of the idea of the "family wage" marks the point at which the modern family becomes both fully legitimate and widespread. The family wage was that rate of pay that would be sufficient to allow a husband to support his wife and children, thus enabling the wife to remain at home, keeping the house and allowing children to complete their education. Based on the companionate ideal, the

norm for family life quickly became one in which the husband
was breadwinner, the wife homemaker. Together, they were expected to maintain a home that was both materially and emotionally self-sufficient. Marriage was something of a declaration
of independence from parents, a statement of autonomy.

The pursuit of companionate autonomy requires a focus on
the present that runs against deep-seated features of family life.
Family implies a continuity between past and future. People live
among shadows cast by the traditions of their forebears. Some
of these traditions are shared with other families of the same
ethnic, racial, or religious background—the celebration of certain holidays with similar rituals or a common way of conducting
funerals or weddings. Some traditions are peculiar to a particular family—the eldest son goes to law school or one child in
each generation goes into the family business. Some traditions
are unacknowledged, revealing themselves only when we notice
certain cross-generational continuities—musical talent, business
acumen, abusiveness, or alcoholism. Parents or other relatives
tell children "that is not the way an Italian girl acts," or a child is
told, "You are just like your Aunt Emma." However the next
generation acts, whether it closely follows the family script or
tosses it aside and acts against tradition, its actions are given
meaning by traditions that define expectations.

The future also helps shape the contours of the present.
People structure their present family activities around their
strivings for tomorrow—the desire to retire early and travel or
escape from the old neighborhood at the very least influence
present priorities. At a deeper level, the desire that one's children not repeat one's own mistakes or that they fulfill one's own
unfulfilled aspirations or that they replicate one's best features
or their accomplishments permeate the dynamics of the family.

In American culture, aspirations for personal and familial autonomy affect our orientation toward both the past and the present. Often the past becomes something we strive not to repeat.
Autonomy is explicitly equated with breaking with tradition.
But when breaking with tradition is valued as a key step in
achieving autonomy, the links between generations depend almost exclusively on a personal intimacy that is difficult to sustain
given the emphasis on generational difference. Each generation

knows that it must be rejected by the next if the young are to achieve their own autonomy. But when parents cannot believe that their children in some sense represent a continuation, a link with the future, their commitment to structuring the present to assure that future is attenuated. If, in addition, parents have little hope that their children's lives will be better than theirs, then commitment to the future is weakened still more. Such is the situation confronting American families today. Neither commitment to the past nor commitment to the future makes much sense. At least they no longer make sense in the way they once did. And without these commitments it becomes necessary to rethink the companionate ideal.

Obviously, not all families strive toward the companionate ideal in exactly the same way. Attempts to achieve the companionate family ideal give rise to different family life-styles. These different arrangements represent the companionate ideal filtered through cultural and familial traditions and adapted to the concrete economic and social circumstances in which people live. Granted these variations, by mid-century, economic conditions made it possible for the vast majority of Americans to establish their families on the basis of the companionate ideal. The family comprised a husband, wife, and their children, living independently. The husband supported the family financially; the wife took primary responsibility for childrearing, housekeeping, relationships with kin, and other aspects of family social life. By the fifties, this family, long a normative ideal, became statistically "typical." It became the conventional arrangement.

In the conventional family it is assumed that a couple can come closest to the companionate ideal if the home is the central emotional focus for both husband and wife. At home together, husband and wife are free to nourish each other's psyche, free to be themselves. In effect, the home becomes the realm of freedom; work and community life, the realm of necessity. It is through work and community life that people define and seek fulfillment of their most important goals; it is within the home that they attempt to structure a life consonant with their most closely held values. A close and satisfying home-based family life is a highly valued goal of the conventional family.

Sufficient financial autonomy to be free of continuing dependence on, and obligations to, kin is crucial to establishing the home as a locale suitable for companionate living. Without the capacity for being self-supporting, a couple would be hard pressed to achieve and sustain the emotional independence or distance from family and friends that allows for intensive emotional engagement within the nuclear family. For this reason, what goes on within families cannot be understood without taking account of the ways work permeates the interior of family life.[1]

Work, whether it is beastly or sublime, leaves its imprint. To grasp its impact we need to consider differences in the kinds of work people do. At the lower end of the occupational hierarchy, work enervates: it is physically demanding, sometimes dangerous and dirty, and often stupefyingly repetitive. At the other end of the occupational ladder, work rarely enervates: it is varied, engaging, and stimulating; it is almost never dangerous and is almost always looked upon with respect if not awe.

Indeed, we call work by different names to reflect these obvious differences. At the bottom we speak of a job. At the top, we speak of a career. A job is largely only a means to a livelihood with few built-in incentives. Jobs typically leave a person exhausted and emotionally drained, used up in a literal sense. While careers can also be exhausting and emotionally draining, in comparison with jobs they tend to be addictive and nourishing. Quite apart from the dramatic differences in pay between jobs and careers, careers afford more gratification, more autonomy, and a greater sense of accomplishment and personal efficacy. Careers are predicated on a wide range of intrinsic rewards and incentives. Typically requiring extensive preparation, a career embodies an ideal of commitment, of close identification with one's work. The degree of identification with one's career is, moreover, one of the criteria used by an employer or superior to determine advancement.

These features of the world of work have given rise to two variants of the conventional family: the upper-middle-class or "professionalized" family and the working-class family. While sharing the distinctive qualities of conventional family life, each is marked by the world of work in different ways. In exploring the ways work and family life interact, we will discover sources of tension and conflict that, as the conventional family became more widespread, gave rise to new family arrangements.

The Professionalized Family

Given the central importance of economic independence for living out the companionate ideal, we might expect to find families closest to that ideal among the relatively affluent, that is, the middle and upper middle classes, the world of professionals, technicians, and managers. People in such occupations are well known for spending long hours at their work. Indeed, the institutions within which the upper middle class works have been called "greedy" institutions.[2] Such institutions demand that those who work for them invest substantial ego in their work. To be a successful doctor, executive, teacher, or minister is to organize your life around the performance of the duties expected of you.

The consequences for family life of this sort of employment should be obvious. In simplest terms, the "man of the house" is largely an absentee, sometimes even when physically present. For many men caught up in the rigors of their careers, even weekends are used for work. Indeed, the distinction between work and leisure gets blurred when business associates meet at the country club or health and fitness spa in order to cement relationships or make new contacts. In any case, career needs routinely circumscribe the time and energies the husband has to devote to his wife and family. What may have started out as a companionate relationship gradually evolves into a relationship in which husband and wife have distinctly different interests and spheres of activity, dramatically reducing the occasions for shared experience and joint ventures. In upper-middle-class families, even many of the husband's traditional roles around the house—repairs, mowing, shoveling snow, and the like— often fall to the wife. It's not that she necessarily performs these tasks, though she might. Rather, it is her responsibility to organize and supervise the maintenance of the home, as well as its day-to-day functioning. The husband might help out, but in a real sense the home becomes her arena, just as the workplace is her husband's.

The logic implicit in this arrangement was championed by prominent academic theoreticians, many of whom, not coincidentally, pursued careers predicated on family lives quite like those just described. From a theoretical perspective, the husband's dedication to work and the wife's devotion to home seemed like a functional adaptation to the demands of the modern occupational structure, a structure that shapes the choices and preferences of those within it.

Harvard sociologist Talcott Parsons, in particular, emphasized the virtues of this arrangement.[3] Parsons's ideas about the family were based on a speculative, but closely reasoned and subtle understanding of the nature of a modern, bureaucratic social order, heavily dependent upon a market for organizing the production and distribution of goods and services. He recognized that in such a society, increasing numbers of individuals are needed for highly specialized and intensely demanding work. As the sheer scale of activity expands, dwarfing the local milieu of small town and neighborhood, more and more people are obliged to become highly mobile, prepared to move a family away from kin and neighborhood in pursuit of career opportunities. Understood as an arrangement that intensifies the breadwinner's commitment to his work, the professionalized family can generate a significant degree of economic security and status, presumably enhancing the well-being of all family members. From the larger society's point of view, the professionalized family produces and sustains highly motivated and largely undistracted employees who are devoted to the world of work.

Meanwhile, still following Parsons's reasoning, the needs of family members for love and affection and for support in times of stress and discomfort are met by the undivided attentions of the wife-mother. In becoming a specialist in managing the home, overseeing both its material and emotional economies, the wife-mother becomes an expert in domestic life, a professional homemaker. Given the salary discrepancies and differences in occupational opportunity for men and women, as well as presumed differences in men's and women's aptitudes and motivations, there was little doubt but that it was men who be-

longed at work and women at home. With so rational an arrangement, Parsons expected that over time the entire society
would benefit from the production of better adjusted and more
self-confident individuals, individuals attuned to available opportunities for self-expression and advancement. Since professionalized families would be at a competitive advantage—better
able to meet the economic and emotional needs of their members than other forms of family life—he expected they would
become the dominant form of family life in America.

For some time that certainly seemed to be the case. During
the 1940s and 1950s, many people were structuring their lives
as if following a script written by Parsons himself. The post-
World War II period saw a tremendous move toward the suburbs. Everywhere, it seemed, the model of dad at work earning
money and mom at home caring for the kids was held up as the
ideal family. In many large corporations it was common practice
to interview both the job candidate and his wife before selecting
a new executive. These firms appreciated full well the importance of a man's wife as an adjunct to his career. They wanted
men whose personal lives were neatly ordered and unlikely to
compete with his job for attention. In TV and films, in the writings of child development experts, in the advice of psychologists
and counselors, and in the admonitions of ministers, all Americans, no matter what their economic resources or personal aspirations, were told this was what the family should look like,
this was the way life was supposed to be.

Given the developments of the 1960s, it is interesting to recall
that although Parsons was generally quite sanguine about this
family arrangement and its capacity to satisfy the needs of family members, he did foresee some potential sore spots. Most of
the difficulties he located sprang from ambiguities in the woman's position, particularly in the role of mother. Parsons worried
that mothers face considerable ambivalence: the child that gives
them a *raison d'être* is also the source of constriction and confine-
ment. Moreover, the mother is supposed to prepare the child
for autonomy at the same time needing the dependency of the
child to confirm her self-worth. The mother not only has to inculcate familial values (love, cooperation, affective engagement
with others), she also has to prepare the child to enter a world

predicated on diametrically opposed norms (competitiveness, self-orientation, impersonality, and objectivity). While by no means making light of these sources of disjunction, Parsons was confident that these problems could be dealt with by heightened awareness on the part of parents, particularly mothers, and increased sophistication among the counseling and therapeutic experts.

Studies of life in America's suburbs have added much concrete detail to the portrait Parsons sketched, and they have confirmed his recognition of the growing role that would be played by professionalized support services for the family.[4] The affluence and geographical mobility of the upper middle class meant that, in fact, their ties to kin were attenuated. This reduced dependence was made possible by the professionalized family's capacity to turn to the marketplace for goods and services once provided by kin.

Seeley and his associates give a detailed account of the extent to which the upper-middle-class family depends upon experts. Just as the doctor comes to depend upon a retinue of specialized assistants, so too does the wife-mother. The home becomes the focus of all sorts of technical advice: child development experts, nutritionists, interior decorators, money managers, psychologists—all these and more are called forth to assist the professionalized homemaker. These experts are, in effect, interposed between the nuclear family and kin, having emerged in significant measure as both a response and a contributor to the growing isolation of the nuclear family from the extended networks of neighbors and kin. Cut off from stable networks of association, many husbands and wives confront a set of choices they know to be important—how to arrange their home; how to entertain clients and superiors; what schools to send children to; how to deal with emotional stress and difficulties in relationships—but for which they have limited preparation or wisdom to draw from. They do know that they want to do things the "right" way, and that the way their parents or grandparents did them may be outdated or inappropriate. The result, Seeley shows, is that families become as ardent consumers of advice as they are consumers of more prosaic goods and services.[5] The contrast between the consumption of professional advice and connection to kin is perhaps most sharply realized among those aspiring to careers and upward mobility, such as families that have emigrated within the past two or three generations. Here the differences between professional advice, which is purchased, and the advice of kin, which is freely given, are often experienced as outright oppositions. For example, young adults following "scientifically" based, up-to-date manuals for childrearing or marriage often clash with parents or grandparents with very different ideas (suddenly "old-fashioned" or "unenlightened") about how to handle children or cope with marital problems. But whether or not it creates tension, it is the reliance on outside, professional resources that constitutes a new element in efforts to achieve the companionate ideal.

Given the growing availability of these resources for the family, Parsons foresaw no insurmountable problems between spouses. Ever higher standards of living, better education, enlightenment about emotional needs and sexuality—all such advances were conducive, he thought, to a deepening of gratification in marriage and a stable, integrated complementarity between husband and wife. Much of this confidence was based on the longstanding fact that the more educated and the higher the economic standing of a couple, the less likely they were to divorce. Marital instability was yet another of the afflictions of the poor and uneducated. The family that Parsons saw emerging as the dominant form possessed precisely those characteristics that would immunize it from dissolution.

For a brief while, this guardedly optimistic view seemed justified. Young men and women were going to the altar, happily expecting to throw themselves into their respective careers: work for the husband, the household for the wife. But it was not long before blemishes began appearing on the face of domestic bliss. The sharing and companionship that each spouse assumed would be theirs turned out to be hard to sustain in the face of the role segregation they embraced. Wives, alone all day (and often well into the evening and on weekends as well) felt left out, with little opportunity to be the partner or companion they had hoped to be. Many also realized that their part in the arrangement was decidedly less engaging, and ultimately unsatisfactory to minds whetted for challenge and intellectual stimulation by the advanced education that presumably was intended to make them suitable and interesting partners for professional men. For their part, many husbands discovered that the glamor and the challenges of career came at great cost. Among these costs were the restrictions on free time and the inability to be emotionally free when not working because work was so thoroughly internalized. The result was a limited capacity to pursue whatever gratifications marriage might provide. Families, for these men, became possessions entailing responsibilities that tied them even more tightly to their careers. Problems such as these became so commonplace that they appeared to be a natural part of adult development. Writer Gail Sheehy popularized the psychological research and gave us the phrase "mid-life crisis."[6] However they were labeled, these problems were beginning to have unsettling effects on the upper middle class even as Parsons was writing.

Many studies now document the malaise among upper-middle-class families. In the fifties and sixties most attention focused on women. Women's magazines regularly featured articles offering advice to readers suffering from a variety of ailments that were expressions of at least mild depression: listlessness, fatigue, lack of sexual responsiveness, the "blues," "blahs," and other catchy euphemisms for unhappiness. When Betty Friedan set out, as an editor for a prominent women's magazine, to delve deeper into the basis for this steady flow of writing, she discovered a problem that "had no name."[7] What could be wrong when most of these women had or were in the process of getting what was assumed to be everything anyone could ever want—a nice home with enough time and money to be comfortable and raise one's children unhampered by fears of economic privation or insecurity? By now, of course, it is common knowledge that the role of wife-mother was the source of the problem.

However sensible the division of roles may have appeared in theory, however appealing it may have seemed to married couples, over time many women came to feel stifled and trapped at home. That the role of wife-mother was what they had wanted and chosen only added the element of self-blame to the disappointment experienced. Whatever the pleasures of homemaking and childrearing, they do not include the satisfaction of validation in the public world. As more and more women earned college degrees, they developed skills and aptitudes that could not be satisfied exclusively at home, no matter how earnestly they tried to convince themselves that household management was a career.

Looked at as a workplace, the home suffers from being isolated, particularly the homes of the upper middle class, which are often located miles away from public facilities that might ease the separation from others. Especially when children are young and require continual supervision, suburban wives suffer from having too little contact with other adults. Looked at as a work process, homemaking is repetitive and limited in its challenges, even though it is sometimes quite hectic. Moreover, its consequences are either undramatic, in the way only the absence of dust can be undramatic, or ambiguous.

Part of any job's capacity to satisfy involves being able to recognize in its consequences something of value for which you have been responsible. Work needs an audience, some person or persons who know and appreciate the difference between bad work and work well done. In the preindustrial family, networks of kin provided just such an audience, an audience whose standards and judgments were respected, if also feared. The isolation of the modern upper-middle-class family dramatically reduces the possibility of audience. The fact that most of the audience is juvenile, and thus not a satisfactory source of approval, does not help matters. Moreover, the sharp disjunction between a wife's and husband's roles makes the husband's capacities as an audience problematic—husbands are notoriously unmindful of the work that goes into keeping a house presentable or in getting a meal to the table. ("What did you do today, dear?") In this setting fictive audiences can have inordinate and oppressive sway. And so TV commercials—"ring around the collar" only one of the more egregious of them—play mercilessly on the fears of inadequacy that bedevil many homemakers, setting extraordinary, compulsive standards that can be met, if at all, only by frenzied labors.[8]

Finally, the most important "product" of the wife's work, well-adjusted, happy children destined for accomplishment in the world, can be judged only in the distant future. At any moment

in time the indications are inevitably unstable and untrustwor-
thy. Day-to-day childrearing has little or no noticeable relationship to the long-term outcomes that matter. This produces, in
addition to the reliance on experts that we have already noted,
a tendency for wide swings in emotion. One moment there is
confidence, the next, uncertainty and self-doubt.[9] Ambiguity of
outcomes produces an intensification of concern over each twist
and turn in a child's development, adding to the mother's need
for outside advice, which in turn reduces her sense of competence. And however helpful the advice she obtains, there are
other problems with a single-minded immersion in childrearing.
The mother's intense involvement with her children works
against the children's increasing need for autonomy as they ma-
ture and creates the basis for undermining many of the satisfactions in childrearing.

With the father often absent in pursuit of career advancement
for himself and economic security for his family, children are
one of the major sources of companionship for the mother. As
untold numbers of family therapists have discovered, to the extent that children stand as emotional surrogates for the father,
there is a good chance that each move of the children toward
autonomy will be accompanied by some sort of crisis within the
family. The mother and children are in especially difficult circumstances. For the mother, holding onto the children goes
against what is supposed to be one of the major goals of her
childrearing—preparing children for an autonomous existence.
But letting go leaves her with an absence of significant daily
companionship. For the children, their own movement toward
independence can be easily undermined by guilt which leads
them to self-defeating actions which keep them tied to the role
of mother's companion, even if only as a regular source of
worry. Nor is the father likely to be of much help. Movement
away from the world of work back into the family goes against
the requisites of the career that has provided both his sense of
accomplishment and his particular *raison d'être* within the family.

Seen in this light, not only is the housewife's job extraordinar-
ily difficult, but its difficulty is not the sort that makes it challenging or stimulating, at least not for a significant number of
women. Consequently, we have witnessed widespread disillu-

sionment with the homemaking role, which has contributed, since the 1950s, to increasing numbers of wives seeking employment outside the home. At first few noticed this new development. Then, writing in the early 1960s, sociologist Daniel Bell reported that the typical pattern of wives working seemed to be changing. Up until then, wives went to work because their husbands' income was inadequate or interrupted by illness or unemployment. Statistically, the lower the husband's income, the greater was the likelihood of the wife working. Suddenly, however, the correlation was reversed—wives were more likely to work the higher their husband's earnings.[10]

The trend Bell discerned in its infancy some thirty years ago is now firmly established. Labor force participation rates of wives are greater at higher levels of husbands' income. Clearly, women whose husbands are making between $35,000 and $50,000 work for reasons that go beyond helping to make ends meet, even taking into account the greater levels of consumption and indebtedness that accompany considerably higher expectations for what constitutes an acceptable standard of living. It is reasonable to assume that under these circumstances work is providing more than just supplemental income.

Women working outside the home is obviously one of the most important changes in the family in recent decades. But before we can examine the ways this trend has altered conventional configurations of family life, we need to look also at the husband's role in the professionalized family. We have already indicated that a major source of difficulty for the professionalized family lies in the husband's breadwinning role. Technically some might say that the source of this problem resides in the structure of occupations and the expectations employers have about their employees' commitments. Whatever the source of the difficulty, it is the family that absorbs the consequences.

Careers, unlike most jobs, have stages built into them—points at which the incumbent is closely scrutinized and judged either fit to advance or not. If not, it can mean the end of employment with a given employer; sometimes it means the end of a career. In large organizations, the failure to be promoted may simply mean the end of upward mobility and the necessary adjustments to being passed over. The prospect of having to change employer or career—or of reconciling oneself to a limited future—is traumatic to someone who has spent a major portion of his or her adult life striving and competing and forgoing diversions in order to build a reputation and to advance. The problems in sustaining morale among those engaged in the pursuit of success affects families as well as workplaces.

We referred earlier to William F. Whyte's analysis of the corporate interest in the wives of managerial job candidates. The practice of interviewing the wives of potential executives was to insure that the candidate's commitment to the organization was matched by the wife's commitment to her husband's career. While scholars pondered the implications for the family of the separation of work life and home life, at the top of the occupational hierarchy work and family were seen as inseparable. The term "two-person career" was coined to better capture the degree to which a man's family was implicated in his work life.[11] Only certain kinds of family life were deemed compatible with the demands of high-level jobs. Not only did a man's family life have to yield to the requirements of work, but his family had to be something the corporation, too, could be proud of.

While not as striking as with executives, something similar occurs with families of professionals. For example, most local medical societies maintain an active wives' organization. In Martha Fowlkes's study of doctors' and professors' wives, she describes how they are, in effect, socialized into a willing acceptance of the fact that their husbands' careers will take them away from them and the children for the lion's share of each day and that their husbands will often leave work too spent to be much of a presence at home.[12] The medical wives' group offers social and service activities designed to give the wives a sense of participation in their husbands' careers as well as an ideology that justifies their particular sacrifice of companionate marriage for the greater health and well-being of others. Though most other professions are less imbued with the life and death urgency of medicine, they often present themselves as indispensable to the life of the community, thereby creating a rationale for overinvolvement in work and the consequent impoverishment of the professional's family life.

Despite all efforts to make sure that both husband and wife

collaborate to sustain the husband's commitment to work, there are many reasons for men to falter along the way. Such intense occupational demands can be constricting, relationships with others at work can become nasty, and the day-to-day routine can fail to sustain the sense of importance or idealism that makes work significant. Men, seeking respite from these conflicts and pressures, throw themselves into hobbies or sports, or participate in community associations. Alternatively, a man who has reached an occupational plateau, may feel free to channel energies once reserved for work into other pursuits in order to reduce the tensions surrounding his work. Whether to escape work or as a result of a decision to stop striving, some men may try to resuscitate the marital companionship that had been rendered lifeless by their pursuit of success. But having moved for so long in separate spheres, connected primarily around issues of the mechanics and finances of family life, it is by no means easy to revivify a routinized relationship.

We need to be very careful here. Pointing to the various complexities that make achieving personal satisfaction difficult within the professionalized family does not mean that all women, men and children living within these families are deeply unhappy or hopelessly neurotic. Clearly, there have been and still are significant numbers of people for whom this arrangement works, at least well enough for them to stay together and to give them a sense of satisfaction and accomplishment. And there are those people who turn to the conventional family after considerable time in nonconventional arrangements. Certainly, there are some women who, after pursuing a nonconventional life built around career or job, decide that the satisfactions in the world of work are not enough, no matter how successful they are.[13] Many women choose to have children, either along with or instead of an occupation. And many women find parenting a deeply rewarding part of their lives, settling comfortably into a conventional form they once avoided. The point we are making about the conventional companionate family is not that it is automatically a factory for the production of misery, but that inherent within the very feature that is supposed to be the greatest strength of that family form—the specialization of labor between husband and wife—is the basis for its vulnerability and problems. Every relevant social indicator—the divorce rate, number of working women, number of couples now choosing not to have children, frequency of extra-marital relationships, and number of troubled families—forces us to conclude that for many people, and perhaps for most women, the professionalized family is not an adequate vehicle for meeting the companionate ideal. To the extent that it can provide material autonomy and security it creates conditions that severely restrict its ability to provide sustained emotional satisfaction and intimacy.[14]

There is a certain irony here because since the middle of the nineteenth century, the upper-middle-class family has provided the norm against which other family forms have been judged and the ideals around which the media and various professional experts in morality and mental health have composed their programs for improving the lives of those to whom they minister. The dissemination of these norms and ideals was among the factors that shaped the emergence of the contemporary working-class family, the other major version of the conventional family.

The Working-Class Family

If companionate aspirations of professionalized families are stymied by occupational success, in the working-class family they are often stifled by the specter of economic insecurity. We have seen that, in the past, the traditional family made sense for most people because it was well suited to a life conditioned by economic insecurity and scarcity. However much one may have wished for independence, it was unattainable under the prevailing circumstances. People were obliged to rely upon kinfolk and, in turn, to be someone kin could rely upon. As circumstances changed and a life of relative autonomy became possible, there were significant changes in working-class people's sense of what defined an adequate family life. Most incorporated the companionate ideal into their pursuit of independence. But while many have long since left behind the values and consciousness of the traditional extended family, for a significant number, economic insecurity is a daily reality that places clear limits on the extent to which autonomy from kin can be realized. Many continue to rely upon kin for the exchange of goods and services that they cannot afford to purchase in the marketplace, for help in emergencies, and for advice and information necessary to find work, avoid legal troubles, or surmount personal problems. For some, this reliance is no doubt grudging, seen as an unwelcome necessity or one more sign of their failure. For others, the bonds of kinship are one of the sources of genuine pleasure in a life that is otherwise occupied by hard work and cruel choices. However much comfort is drawn from close ties to kin, companionate ideals of autonomy and equality are blurred by the continued vitality of noncompanionate traditions that are reinforced by economic instability.

Scarcely a study of working-class families in the past fifty years has failed to note the significant tensions and anxieties that pervade family life among our nation's workers. Dreams of companionship and pleasure in one another's company fade under the corrosive effects of deadening work and wages that never quite suffice. The feelings of inadequacy and frustration that come from the constraints most working-class families confront erode the self-confidence and esteem that a satisfying companionship requires. Though these themes are apparent in virtually all treatments of working-class life, Rainwater and his associates, in their *Workingman's Wife*,[15] were among the first to capture the pathos that so often overwhelms companionate aspiration.

Rainwater discovered women whose lives were dominated by insecurity borne either of present difficulties or the conviction that their present modest good fortune was no sure indication of what lay ahead. They had few plans for the future, not because they couldn't look ahead but because their prospects were so bleak. They were enormously fearful of indebtedness because they were certain they would be unable to meet the obligations incurred. Lest all this gloom seem gratuitous, as it seemed to those dazzled by images of affluence, let it be noted that the views of the women Rainwater interviewed were much closer to the truth than were those of the economists and promoters who commissioned the study. While aggregate statistics show steady expansion of buying power, interrupted by more or less brief downturns, the ups and downs of individual families are something else again. A recent study by James Morgan and his associates at the University of Michigan's Institute for Social Research has uncovered a startling view of the precariousness of many families' hold on economic well-being. For all but the most secure white-collar workers (the top 30 percent of all families), sharp reductions in income and living standards are by no means remote. Over the course of the ten-year study, nearly half of all families in the lower 70 percent encountered at least one year in which their total income fell to or below the poverty line.[16]

Rainwater gave an intimate account of how the material circumstances of family life affect the emotional resources of husband and wife, creating an emotional life that is in almost a literal sense the counterpart of their economic woes. The hoped for autonomy to forge their own life, free of emotional encumbrances of kin, is frustrated by material circumstances. The days and nights of unavoidable toil are simply not relieved by time off or time alone. Vacations are invariably spent catching up with home repairs and the like. Even going out to the movies, especially once there are children who need babysitting, becomes at best an occasional treat.

Lillian Rubin's recent study of working-class families updates and substantially amplifies the portrait given us by Rainwater.[17] Rubin finds working men and women seeking companionship from one another but unable to overcome the tensions and frustrations of daily life in order to find the ways in which companionship might be sustained. She shows how this difficulty is not simply one of economic privation or stress but of economic stress played out according to gender scripts that, by themselves, make it difficult for husband and wife to find a common language with which they might understand each other.

Women, attempting to show that they understand the ordeal that their husbands endure at work, seek to talk, to share innermost feelings, to express intimate engagement in one another's life. That is, after all, one of the things that women in our culture have been encouraged to do, to be expert at and comfortable doing. Their husbands, however, have not been particularly encouraged to verbalize or even acknowledge innermost feelings. Indeed, as it turns out, many of these innermost feelings are threatening, even terrifying. They involve, among other things, feelings of impotent rage at the insults of employer and the indifference and unresponsiveness of the larger society. They may also feel angry and trapped by their wife and children in whose interests they are obliged to continue to submit to danger and humiliation. They feel caught between a sense of love and duty to family and a way of meeting responsibility that robs them of self-respect and any sense of accomplishment. And so their wives find them uncommunicative, unwilling—profoundly unable, in fact—to verbalize a meaningful response to "What happened at work today, dear?" Wives feel shut out, unwelcome in the inner life of their spouse.

For their part, husbands seek companionship through a quite different mode of communication: sexual expressiveness. What they feel incapable of expressing verbally, husbands hope to express through sexual intimacy. Rubin is quick to make clear that the husband's interest in sexuality is not simple lust, a desire to satisfy only his own sexual needs. On the contrary, the men Rubin talked with expressed a desire to give their wives pleasure, to show tenderness and deep affection for her and, thereby, to acknowledge and give weight to her needs. In other words, sexual expressiveness is used as language. Unfortunately, this language is threatening to the wives in much the same way that verbal communication is threatening to husbands. For the wives, sexuality poses two kinds of risk. Most obviously, there is the risk of pregnancy which, if unwanted, would only add to her and her husband's burdens. But more important, given the wide availability of birth control measures, wives confront risks to self-esteem that sexuality has posed to women at least since the advent of the double standard. Even though married, women reported to Rubin that they still feared for their reputation: to engage in sexual experimentation and unorthodox practices (such as oral sex) was to risk loss of status—"good girls don't!" The result is reticence and what husbands perceived as unresponsiveness and rejection. For them, just as for their wives, the possibilities of companionship dwindled and the marital relationship gradually became routinized and perfunctory. Neither partner's needs get fully acknowledged, much less met.

Put in the context of economic constraint, what begins as a companionate marriage often ends in a kind of limbo between companionate autonomy and more traditional linkage with kin, linkage that is both economic and emotional. To ease financial pressures, relatives help each other out with hand-me-downs, babysitting, loans, and the like. While falling well short of the interdependence of the traditional family, the nuclear unit is less separate from kin than the companionate ideal would suggest. Husbands and wives, failing to sustain one another's emotional needs, begin to drift apart, seeking out same-sex associates with whom to pursue their own interests. Men go out "with the boys"; women chat with the "girls," go out shopping together, or gather to exchange recipes, gossip, or simply pass the time. The net effect is a variant on the companionate ideal that is probably not drastically dissimilar in its day-to-day rhythms from features of the preindustrial family: low expectations for emotional gratification, rather high levels of sex-segregated activities, low levels of engagement in community life, except around church (particularly for women), and hobbies.

To the extent that participants in arrangements such as these grow accustomed to this emotional leveling and separation of husband and wife spheres, family life can be quite stable, vulnerable only to the disruptions of alcohol, uncontrolled anger, and the temptations of extramarital sex. But to the extent that both men and women have been touched by modern expectations for emotional gratification and intimacy with one's spouse, the disappointments accompanying routinization can lead to another, less venerable, source of rupture: divorce as an effort to somehow live a better, more fulfilling life, with or without a new partner. Clearly, the men and women that Rubin studied were not reconciled to the emotional distance they felt between themselves and their spouses. Unlike partners of preceding generations, they expect more from their marriage than a dependable meeting of conventional role expectations, even though they do not have the means to sustain the richness they seek. Though it is impossible to be certain, given the inadequacies of available data, it is likely that the higher divorce rate among the working- and lower-middle classes over the past twenty years stems from heightened companionate aspiration, not from economic instability.

If economic insecurity makes it hard to sustain a companionate relationship, endemic poverty clearly makes it hard to sustain any kind of stable marital relationship, companionate or otherwise. Most analyses of the effects of poverty on family life have focused on black Americans, so we will explore this literature in order to reveal another facet of the conventional family. Though descriptions of the poor black family are still surrounded with controversy, some features are now widely agreed upon. Most significant for our purposes is the centrality of the kin network, a network largely traced through women. The mother-daughter-granddaughter link is salient and intense to a degree largely unknown among more economically secure groups. So strong is this bond that some analysts report that this bond competes with the bond between husband (or boyfriend) and wife.[18] The particular history of black Americans, coupled with the continued poverty and discrimination they face, has conspired, in effect, to make large numbers of blacks unable to sustain the minimal self-sufficiency that the companionate family requires, largely because the male has inordinate difficulty finding and keeping jobs that pay a living wage. Welfare regulations add to the woes of the black family by making it impossible to receive steady payments if the family has a male breadwinner—even though he may not be able to find a job that would actually allow him to play the role of breadwinner. The result, emergent over a long period of time, is the growth of a family that is comprised of expanded households of female kin and their children. Arrayed around these households are "satellites" made up of couples who are highly likely to dissolve, with the women returning to the kin network and detached males "in orbit" around the female network. While nuclear couples are unstable among the black poor, the family, understood as this female-oriented group, is quite stable.

The integrity and stability of this family arrangement derives from the elaborate interdependencies that are maintained by exchanges of goods and services within and between households in the kin network. Household furnishings, clothing, babysitting, and long-term child care that borders on adoption are

among the things exchanged. Each exchange vivifies the sense
of obligation and helps insure the continued participation of
each member of the network. Participants in such networks develop intense commitments to the network, commitments borne
not simply of necessity. These commitments can interfere with
courtship and other forms of potential withdrawal from the network. In many respects, this family network closely resembles
variants of the traditional family. If this is the case, why call it
modern?

There are two crucial respects in which the poor black family
is a distinctly modern phenomenon. First, though efforts at
forming companionate families are depressingly likely to fail,
there is little indication that these efforts have diminished over
time or that the ideal of the autonomous nuclear family has
weaker hold over poor blacks than others in our society.[19] It
could be argued, though, that the high and rising rates of ille-
gitimacy suggest some such weakening. But even here, it seems
clear from the literature that out-of-wedlock pregnancies typically result from the aspiration for a nuclear family, which is
tragically disconnected from achieving the conditions that
would make this aspiration more likely to become a reality.[20]
Given the means to secure autonomy for the conjugal pair—a
steady and adequate income and reasonably free choice of housing—there is no reason to believe that large numbers of poor
blacks would continue for long the pattern of female-headed
expanded families.

The second reason to regard the black expanded family as a
variant of the modern family is that it is to a considerable degree
a product of a distinctly modern institution: the welfare state.
We examined the general effects of the welfare state in Chapter
2, arguing that welfare state programs have generally enhanced
the possibilities for couples to be autonomous from kin. But in
the case of the chronically poor, welfare programs have had the
opposite effect, in part because they have been too miserly and
too shortsighted, and in part because they have unintentionally
been structured so as to penalize intact nuclear families. Welfare
programs for the very poor have never escaped or transcended
a framework that blames the victim. Benefits have rarely been
sufficient to the needs of those who are caught in a cycle of low

skills and minimal entry into stable jobs. Programs keep such people from starving (barely) but do not enable them to escape. Moreover, by directing the highest levels of support to those families in which the male head is absent (Aid to Families with Dependent Children—AFDC), husband and boyfriends are encouraged to absent themselves in order to maximize support for their dependents. Coupled with the notorious difficulties facing black males in the labor market, the result is what might be thought of as the peripheralization of males in families of the poor. In effect, modern labor markets and welfare programs combine to "modernize" families of the poor in such a way as to further marginalize men and make kin networks largely female.

This adaptation to endemic poverty and eligibility rules for welfare points the family of the poor toward the past, toward patterns of male-female interaction that are shaped by sex-role conventions derived from patriarchal traditions, and toward an integration of nuclear households within a broader system of kin. The families of the poor and the working class range from the extensive and cohesive female-centered family found in the black ghetto to the more commonly intact families of the black and white working and lower middle classes. Though the poor and working class typically start out with companionate expectations they are unable to sustain these expectations in the face of chronic economic precariousness.

The fact that family life among the poor is volatile is, of course, not new. Indeed, marital instability has long been one of the middle-class indictments of the working and lower classes. Rather than raising doubts about conventional family norms, marital instability has long been invoked as one of the reasons the poor stay poor. But when divorce began to increase among the middle and upper middle classes, as it did from the mid-1960s on, the normative supremacy of the conventional family began to crumble.

Increased instability of the conventional family came on the heels of a decade-long celebration of this model of family life. Though the model was, as we have seen, by no means new, in the 1950s it appeared that this model would become statistically predominant. Rising wages, increased availability of privately owned homes, the implementation of a mix of public and private income support programs that permitted large numbers to make realistic long-term plans and enter into long-term commitments that were predicated upon the autonomy of the nuclear family—all these changes made it possible for large numbers of young men and women to marry with the goal of attaining emotional and material self-sufficiency for themselves. More confident of their prospects than their parents could possibly have been, young couples married earlier and began having children sooner. Though there were fewer couples having five or more children, most couples had at least two and as many as four. The result was the baby boom.[21]

Beneath the surface of this spreading affirmation of the conventional companionate family, however, there were difficulties looming. Both emotional and material self-sufficiency were harder to sustain than it had at first seemed. As we have just seen, the heavy work demands on the husband, combined with a still potent legacy of patriarchal attitudes, made companionship and intimacy difficult to maintain over time. Wives were especially disadvantaged and many, particularly those who had been to college, found their lives unsatisfying. The fact that many were enjoying unparalleled comfort and equally unprecedented freedom to fashion a family life on their own terms made it all the more difficult to acknowledge the dissatisfaction.

Unable to explain the disquiet in other than individual terms, many women sought individual solutions. By the late 1960s, the nation's housewives, predominantly those from the middle class between the ages of twenty-eight and forty, were consuming enormous quantities of drugs—tranquilizers to soothe and amphetamines to energize. In 1970, the nation's pharmacists filled prescriptions for mood-altering drugs at a pace that roughly equalled one prescription for every man, woman, and child in the population. Of course, they were not being prescribed so democratically: it is estimated that two-thirds went to women.[22]

Obviously, the expectations for emotional satisfaction to be derived from conventional companionship were not easy to meet on a sustained basis. It turned out that it was also hard to make ends meet, particularly because ends were continually expanding. Home ownership brought with it a steady stream of needs which meant steadily mounting pressure on the husband's paycheck. The purchase of washers and driers, TV sets, lawn mowers, and the like helped the economy but placed enormous strain on family budgets. For the minority of men whose careers were on the fast track, income kept pace with this expansion of needs. For most, though, even for most in the middle class, it did not. As we saw in Chapter 2, indebtedness began to spiral upward and, more importantly for our concerns here, wives began to enter the labor force. As more and more families adjusted to the working wife, the wife-homemaker role began to be challenged.

Even as the nation embraced the virtues of the conventional family, a new set of assumptions about family life was taking shape. These new assumptions spoke to the need for greater equality between husbands and wives as well as for more autonomy, not just for the nuclear family as a unit but for the individual members of the nuclear family itself. As more and more wives entered the labor force, and as their wages became crucial to their families' well-being, the dual-career family began to challenge conventional arrangements.

The Dual-Career Family

There is, of course, nothing new about wives working. As long as they worked as an extension of their traditional helpmate role, to help the family get over a rough patch of financial stress or to pick up the slack of an ill, injured, or unemployed husband, the working wife posed no challenge to the prevailing ideals of family life. But, as we have seen, many of the wives who began to enter the labor force in the fifties and sixties were different. They were not driven to work by the specter of poverty. On the contrary, they appeared to be drawn to work by the prospect of affluence. By the 1970s the trend was clear: middle-class wives were pouring into the labor force, challenging traditional barriers to women across the whole array of occupations heretofore reserved for men as well as the role structure within their families.

Early on in this process of change, working wives may have continued to understand their work in conventional terms.

After all, as we have seen, there were plenty of unmet needs facing the young middle-class family. Though far from poverty, there were bills to pay, second cars to buy, and orthodontia to pay for. The significance of the change was also obscured early on because the jobs that wives were taking were, by and large, "women's work": sales clerks, secretaries, nurses, and the like. Such jobs did not strike anyone as compelling enough, on their own terms, to be seriously competitive with the attractions of domesticity. Working wives, so long as they remained in such marginalized work, could be regarded as in but not of the world of work. They were sojourners. But, as many migrants have discovered, sojourners can become permanent residents.

Even though husbands and wives may have understood their departure from the norms of the conventional family as temporary, as an expedient way of getting over an economic hump, the employment of both spouses changes many settled routines of family living. And as the period of employment stretches out, the traditional division of labor gets harder to sustain. Sex roles lose at least some of their fixity. Adjustments to the working wife give rise, again over time, to a redefinition of the companionate ideal. Equality between spouses becomes more pronounced. This, in turn, produces a heightened emphasis on autonomy, no longer just the autonomy of the nuclear family but also autonomy for each member of the nuclear family. For significant numbers of women, marrying and having children cease being the only foci of adult life; work, too, becomes a central aspect of their sense of self. Employment reduces the asymmetrical dependencies that characterize the wife's role in the conventional family. Her identity is no longer solely derivative, her sense of accomplishment no longer solely the vicarious enjoyment of her loved one's successes.

This shift was accelerated by the coming together of the several interrelated processes we have been discussing. First, economic expansion and rapid upward mobility created a mass base for steadily expanding levels of personal consumption. This, in turn, created an explosion of needs such that the income of one person almost never could suffice. Wives working appeared as an increasingly rational strategy. Second, the internal dynamics of the conventional family put a premium on autonomy. With parental authority sharply diminished and emotional dependence increasingly experienced as a source of vulnerability, more and more young men and women were desirous of arrangements that would allow them some measure of independence. The security of conventional sex roles and domesticity, especially for the rapidly expanding ranks of the middle class, seemed less a source of security than a trap. Finally, as we have just seen, the conventional family itself was not the secure haven that it had seemed. In part because of stress at the points where work and family meet, in part because the threshold of tolerance for frustration of life plans was declining, marital dissatisfaction was rising and, with it, the divorce rate. The result, already evident by the early 1960s, was an increasingly self-conscious and explicit rejection of the conventional family and the gender inequalities that were central to it. What may well have begun as a temporary expedient quickly became a new version of the companionate family.

Role symmetry between husband and wife seemed a clear and sensible response to the new circumstances: families could use two rather than one wage earner, and wives needed greater autonomy in order to be confident of their self-worth. And, given the increasingly apparent fact that marriage was not, necessarily, forever, wives needed labor force experience in order to protect themselves from the prospect of penury should things fall apart. More generally, the prevailing inequalities between men and women began to seem unjust or, at the very least, anachronistic.

In this context, it did not take long before the dual-career marriage began to be praised, not as an expedient or temporary adjustment, but as a new form of marriage. If wives could work as a legitimate expression of their own needs for independent accomplishment and publicly verified self-worth, then husband and wife would be more fully equals and genuine partners in marriage. The basis of companionate intimacy would be fuller and more durable since their interests and experiences would be far less disjunctive than was the case for so many conventional couples. By the late sixties and early seventies, myriad books and articles began appearing, praising the dual-career family as the answer to the by then abundantly evident woes of the conventional family.[23]

The rise of the dual-career family was accelerated by the rapid rise of feminism from the late 1960s onward. Though the movement of wives into the labor force began well before feminism reemerged, many of the issues that aroused feminism were the same as those that had been propelling women out of their homemaking roles. As women grew more confident of the legitimacy of their working, they grew more critical of the discrimination they encountered in the labor market. It quickly became clear that equality in the public sphere was necessary if equality between spouses was to be maintained. Changing conceptions of women's familial roles fed into and reinforced insistence that women be treated equally in schools, the courts, and by employers.

As we have noted, it was middle-class wives who were breaking this ground. As a result, attention was largely focused on discrimination in the professions and managerial, technical, and administrative occupations, as well as in the practices that discouraged women from even training to be eligible for these kinds of employment. This meant, in turn, that most attention was devoted to those families that were literally dual-*career*, as opposed to those in which the wife was employed in a routine or traditionally "woman's" job. As we have noted, there are substantial differences between careers and jobs and these differences have important consequences for family life. But it is also true that working couples, whether one or both work in job or career, face common problems borne of the ways work intersects with family: pressures that derive from the complexities of juggling conflicting work schedules, difficulties in finding time to accomplish ordinary household tasks, as well as finding the time to simply relax together. Of course, if children are present, there are the inevitable struggles with day care, coping with illness, and the like. These are issues that all working couples encounter, regardless of the kinds of work they do. In fact, the kinds of work done may make less difference than variations in the reasons both spouses work. Men and women who are committed to their work, who understand themselves as needing the stimulation and the independence that comes from working, who find the sense of accomplishment or the social life that accompanies work vital to their sense of well-being, share a great deal even when their jobs are very different.[24]

Of course, there is one respect in which careers and jobs diverge that cannot be diminished by frame of mind—careers routinely are more lucrative. While, as we all know, money cannot buy happiness, it can buy convenience. Working couples face many headaches and irritations associated with the loss of the services of a full-time homemaker (some have called working couples "two husband families"), but those who have the benefit of high incomes can often afford to hire the services of surrogate homemakers. Rosanna Hertz, in her recent study of affluent dual-career couples, found a number of couples quite dependent upon a wide range of personal services for which they paid. Indeed, some with young children have live-in help for the children.[25] Being able to afford eating out regularly, having the laundry done commercially, or having the house cleaned clearly relieves a working couple of many hassles and frayed nerves. And, conversely, not being able to do so places a working couple under constant stress.

Affluence may make it easier to cope with the hassles of daily life but what is gained on the domestic front may well be taken back at work. Careers make heavy demands on a person's time and energy and, as the incidence of ulcers, high blood pressure, and other stress-related medical problems among professional and managerial ranks indicate, they require accepting high levels of stress and pressure. As a consequence, whether discussing dual-career or dual-job families, the literature consistently reports that stress is high.[26] Apart from the mundane sources of stress, though, there are deeper problems that have often been overlooked or minimized, especially by those who have seen the dual-career family as the ideal form of family life. First, equality or symmetry in roles has been easier to announce as a goal than to achieve as a reality. This is so with both the domestic roles and the breadwinning roles. Commitment to equality is made more problematic and volatile when the couple confronts the decision whether or not to have a child. Working couples, regardless of the work they do or income they receive, wrestle with these matters. We cannot understand the contemporary family without examining how these issues shape the family life of the rapidly increasing numbers of working couples.

Equality and reciprocity are the central emphases in the dual-career couple. Sharing roles, thus blurring the distinction between the gender scripts of men and women, is the concrete way that husband and wife can demonstrate their commitment to equality. It is also the way each can be both autonomous and dependent upon one another. But role sharing is not easy to sustain. It has been easier for women to enter the labor force than to find equal opportunity there. And it appears that symmetry has been more closely approximated in the world of work than it has in the household.

Though there have been many feature stories about husbands who do the laundry and shopping or who whip up splendid soufflés, the evidence on the sharing of domestic tasks suggests surprisingly little movement toward equality in the home. No doubt all the talk about husbands who do housework has broken the grip of stereotypes on our imaginations, but it appears as though there has been much less change in behavior than attitude. To be sure, attitudes can lead behavior, and to the extent that fears of being thought a sissy or henpecked are dispelled, resistance of husbands may be softened and resolve of wives strengthened such that over time, greater equality in roles is accomplished. Unfortunately, the research to date has been far too spotty to allow us any certainty on these matters. Rosanna Hertz discovers "a markedly greater degree of equality in terms of household chores, marital decision making, and career evaluation" than had been found in an earlier study of upper-middle-class, dual-career couples.[27] However, a more recent study focusing directly on the issue of how working couples arrange domestic responsibilities suggests that there has been far less of a revolution in the home than in the labor force.[28] Whatever, it is clear that the sharing of domestic roles is still contested terrain.

Apart from the fact that there has been no systematic research on changes in role sharing over the past twenty years or so, the question is made more complex by virtue of another change—housework, including meal preparation, appears to be becoming passé. Americans are eating out regularly and at a steadily rising rate. The rapid rise of fast food franchises is clearly responsive to the fact that more and more families have two busy wage earners, neither of whom has the time, energy, or inclination to devote to meal preparation on a daily basis. Elaborate meals may well become one of the special interests of a couple, and the husband may even take the lead in these productions, but this kind of cooking needs to be understood more as a hobby than housework. The emphasis is less on domesticity than on the expression of creative impulses and the gratification of tastes that arise out of greater attention to the need for personal expression. So far as the fragmentary evidence allows, routine, weekday meals are increasingly perfunctory, often eaten on the run.

The home is not the focus for family life that it is for the conventional companionate family.[29] This lack of home centeredness has been taken to suggest an absence of family life altogether. Indeed, when taken to extremes, as when husband and wife are required to live apart in order for each to maintain their career (the so-called "commuter marriage") the concept of family can be sorely strained. Such marriages are not easily sustained over long periods of separation. But the hardiness of many dual-career families indicates that domesticity and home centeredness are by no means necessarily central features of stable and satisfying marital relationships.

In fact, the downplaying of homemaking and domesticity may help dual-career couples defuse tensions that might otherwise arise over the sharing of household tasks. Reducing the salience of these tasks makes it easier for husband and wife to cooperate, breaking down the longstanding stereotypes of gender roles. In a very real sense, though, the dual-career family moves toward equality by reducing the claims each spouse makes on the other. In our culture, careers, almost by definition, prevail over other claims. Thus, the dual-career family tends to be a streamlined family. Dual-career couples are disproportionately childless or have but one child. Ties to relatives tend to be sharply attenuated. Instead of relying on immediate family members (or relatives) for assistance, services are sought professionally. If one thinks of the modern family as one which has ceased its productive functions and has become exclusively a consumer of goods and services, then the dual-career family is quintessentially *the* modern family. It relies heavily on others whom it pays in order to have done the things that members need done for themselves. In this way, the greater equality within the dual-career family is made possible by the inequality of the larger society, which makes people, especially women, available for low-paying domestic work and child care.[30]

This larger inequality affects the dual-career family in another way: while making it easier to achieve equality at home, it is part of a structure that has routinely disadvantaged women. Though there has been much progress toward equity in the labor force, it is still the case that women are paid considerably less than men, even for comparable work, and that their chances for promotion, especially to supervisory or command positions, are lower than for their male counterparts. This fact can produce tension in couples devoted to equality. But even if this larger inequality were not a factor, joint commitment to the world of work produces tensions that bedevil the dual-career couple.

In the early stages of almost any career, life is predictable: long hours at work and absorption in the lore of the occupation and the interpersonal relationships of the office or organization. As long as each spouse is willing to accept this preoccupation, there need be no insuperable problems of synchronicity and coordination. But it is rare that two individuals have the same zeal and ability. Even if they do, it is unlikely that their particular work offers each the same opportunities for promotion and other forms of recognition or that these opportunities will become available at roughly the same time. Almost invariably, the demands on one or the other spouse increase more rapidly or the possibilities for advancement open up sooner for one than for the other.

When this occurs, the couple confronts difficult decisions, and a competitive dimension can enter their relationship. While each partner may be equally committed to his or her career, their careers may not remain equally demanding or rewarding. For many people, career success is deeply intertwined with their sense of personal worth. Taking a career seriously means accepting the importance of validation from colleagues and peers rather than spouse and family. Fast promotions for one and slow promotions for the other can skew each person's perception of his or her partner as well as of self. Obviously, differences in success in the work world can undermine the couple's ability to sustain the egalitarianism that each presumably values.

These difficulties are encountered at two levels. On one level there is the impact of differential success on two people who have built a relationship around a perception of themselves as equal. Even if these problems can be worked through, there remain the complexities of very real practical decisions that must be made in relation to career advancement. For example, we referred earlier to dual-career couples who are forced to confront the prospect of a commuter marriage because a promotion or new job requires relocation to an area where there are limited or inferior opportunities for the spouse. Often, even though only implicitly, such a moment poses a choice between career and marriage. Statistics and an array of anecdotal evidence suggest that a significant number opt for career, even if it raises the risk of divorce.[31] Kathleen Gerson's study of women who have chosen careers over marriage indicates that the stimulation of a career is very hard for many women to give up. The sense of competency as well as the sense of autonomy that a career provides are highly valued and not readily satisfied by other endeavors.

Any dual-career marriage is an acknowledgment that each partner needs much more than just the marriage for their sense of personal satisfaction and growth. The possibility of a commuter marriage forces couples into a comparison, however implicit it may be, of the relative importance of being together versus the importance of pursuing the best possible career opportunity. To accept the separation entailed by a commuter marriage means to acknowledge that, by itself, being together would not be enough. But choosing to stay together means working out an accommodation in which one spouse's career is subordinated to the other's, thereby violating the principle of equality on which the marriage is based.

Whatever the increases in equality, it is still rare to hear of a man who has forsaken his career in deference to his wife's opportunity. Typically, it is the wife who subordinates her career to that of her husband. In part this is another reflection of the continuing legacy of patriarchy. Men's career opportunities are still more numerous and men are still more likely to be first in line for promotions. And of course, men's income tends to be higher.[32] In addition, while egalitarian ideals are widespread, many still assume that a woman's commitment to her chosen career is more tenuous and work less essential to her identity than a man's. For those women committed to career, realism suggests the relative difficulty of successfully integrating career and family. A survey of Fortune 1000 executives found that while 48 percent of women executives were married (39 percent of whom had children), 95 percent of the men were married (97 percent had children), and 86 percent had wives who did not work outside the home.[33]

Nor should we overlook women's own internalized ambivalence about the importance of career. Most contemporary women grew up in families and a culture that, at best, communicated considerable ambivalence about a woman's role in the world of work. Even among highly successful women who enjoy their work, we find those who have been plagued by doubts about the legitimacy of their involvement with the world of work.[34] To this we must add the tendency of women to be the more supportive and nurturant half of a couple. Considering all these factors, it is not surprising that a wife might find herself being not so subtly eased into a position where it appears to be rational for her to let her husband's career chances take precedence over her own, precisely because his seem so much safer and predictable.

As much as husband and wife may be committed to equality in careers and in sharing household responsibilities, there is no way of equally dividing the gestation and birthing of a child. And there is no way commonly available in this country to divide up more or less equally the career dislocations that often attend childbirth. Thus, the decision to have a child, momentous under any circumstances, becomes much more entangled for the dual-career couple. Should the wife take time out from her career? How much time? At what point in her career would it be best to have a child? And of course, there is a biological clock ticking away through this deliberation, and its time scale is by no means compatible with the time scale on which careers move. From the standpoint of most careers, next year is almost always more propitious than this year—after this next promotion, or the next litigation, or the next article, or after I become a partner, or. . . . Meanwhile, the risks to infant and mother begin to mount as the time of giving birth to a first child is pushed further and further back.

In fact, increasing numbers of American couples are deciding not to have children at all. Though they are by no means all dual-career couples, it seems clear that the general increase in dual-career families has contributed more than its share to the increasing ranks of the voluntarily childless. Many simply cannot see how the demands of career can be reconciled comfortably with the demands of childrearing.[35] Since not having a family is no longer seen as a liability for men, and is much less stigmatizing for women, this trend is likely to continue. At the same time, although the pursuit of career goals may be rather all-consuming, the satisfactions careers provide remain somewhat limited for most people. While many may choose not to have children, the sense of stability and companionship provided by marriage makes marriage a likely choice even for those not compelled by tradition to be married.

But of course, the decision to remain childless is not ironclad, at least not before it becomes biologically impossible to conceive and safely bear a child. One of the more interesting changes over the past twenty years or so has been the marked increase in the number of women giving birth to their first child when they are well into their thirties. Not only has this given rise to new medical needs—it is both harder to get pregnant, the longer one puts off the first pregnancy, and harder to carry a fetus to term—it has also created a stir in executive and professional circles as women long thought to be devoted to career and uninterested in maternity, change their minds.[36] Whatever the satisfactions derived from career and getting ahead, for some women there is also the tug of motherhood, a desire to experience that aspect of self. We are not, we hasten to add, positing a "maternal instinct" here. Far from it. We are simply noting what many observers have already commented on—both upbringing and social expectations strongly incline most women to child-bearing. To resist these expectations is to resist very strong pressure, often from oneself as well as others. In early adulthood, when career demands are most fresh, exciting, and intense, and when physical energies are at their height, it is relatively easy to be disinterested in childbearing. But the anecdotal evidence available suggests that with the passage of time many career women begin to have second thoughts. These second thoughts represent not only internal conflict but also the potential for conflict between spouses, even if the husband also wants to be a parent.

The conflict is exacerbated in our society by virtue of the fact that few jobs are protected for maternity leaves. Moreover, in the context of professional and managerial careers, there remains a strong current of sentiment that holds the career in higher regard than all other claims: the desire to take time off to have a child can be taken as prima facie evidence that a woman does not really have the kind of commitment to her work that she must if she is to be taken seriously. This is especially so if, in addition to "simply" wanting to have a child, she also wants to take appreciable time off to spend with her child. If the pull toward childbearing coincides with a shift away from intense identification with career, occasioned perhaps by an accommodation to husband's accelerating career, this need not pose a dilemma and may even be greeted with relief, a legitimate way of explaining a scaling down of career expectations. But if attachment to career goals remains high, this conflict can be quite demoralizing and unsettling.

In the same way, otherwise minor differences between spouses can be magnified by this set of choices. After a significant period of time without children, couples can become quite habituated to a life that is flexible and spontaneous—whether it be in relation to work (staying late at the office to finish a project) or in relation to pleasure (deciding at the last moment to go away for the weekend). Obviously a child changes this. A husband's ambivalence in the face of this anticipated change can be threatening in the same way that his desire to have a child can be threatening to his wife if she does not want to become a mother.

However much couples may think and talk these matters through during their courtship and early marriage, the kinds of needs that are awakened or threatened by the prospect of having a child are among the most volatile.

The arrival of a child, especially a first child, sets in motion a wave of changes.[37] No matter how one reckons the changes, new needs and new ways of satisfying old needs are called into being. For many couples, family life takes on new and intensely rewarding dimensions. For most, the arrival of a baby also adds new layers of complexity and difficulty, even under the best of circumstances. The pressures on the dual-career family are simply more intense. Though there is testimony from paragons of energy and organization who claim that raising children and pursuing a career is not difficult, most mere mortals are quick to acknowledge that the presence of a child presents an almost unending series of challenges to the working couple. Child care is always a headache—insuring good and reliable care is no easy matter—but, in addition, there is the ever present possibility of the child being too sick to go to nursery or preschool programs. Simply put, it takes a number of years for a child to become habituated to adult versions of scheduling. In families where mothers are always home, schedules are flexible and responsive to idiosyncrasy. Housework can be interrupted; not so the world of work.[38]

Consequently, despite their relative affluence, dual-career families, especially those containing young children, are often families under considerable stress. The simultaneous pursuit of companionate ideals, familial autonomy, and careers requires the family to adjust its internal rhythms and schedules to the schedules, temperaments, and requisites of an array of service providers (from babysitters to repairmen) and institutions (from day-care centers to the workplace). For example, a crisis in the life of a regular babysitter, rendering that person unavailable at the usual hour, can send shock waves through the social and work lives of both husband and wife. Even something as trivial as waiting for someone to repair an appliance often requires multiple readjustments of schedules and raises the question of whose commitments are given most importance within the family. Clearly, in instances like this it is not the loss of one hour of work time that is significant but the symbolic significance of the decision about who tends to family matters.

It is not the mere complexity of dual-career family life that is most salient to understanding its internal difficulties. As much as husband and wife may attempt to compensate for the frenetic and fragmented tone of daily life by creating preserves of quality time with children or each other, maintaining equality while balancing career and companionship is not easily done. Identifying these stresses is not to deny that for many dual-career couples a livable, satisfactory balance is achieved. The dual-career family works well enough to ensure that steadily growing numbers of couples are patterning their lives around the expectation that both spouses will work.

The virtue of the dual-career family, however, cannot be reckoned in its stability: dual-career couples are at least as prone to divorce as any other kind of family.[39] Indeed, there is a higher rate of divorce among families where the wife is a professional than in the general population.[40] Even putting aside the divorce rate, there is little reason to believe that the dual-career couple, by itself, could represent the answer to the question "What is the future of the family?" For one, it is not an option available to a large enough number of people. The economy has not been able to produce enough jobs, much less careers, to go around. But more important, the dual-career family ultimately serves careers better than families. It provides a relatively secure emotional and financial base from which a couple can immerse themselves in work and relieve themselves with high levels of consumption. Given the structure of careers and the limited ancillary services available for child care and the like, the dual-career couple who decides to have children and share those responsibilities equally faces a decided career disadvantage by comparison with those couples who have chosen to not have children and those individuals who are not married.[41] For achievement-oriented people this means regular confrontations with frustration and ambivalence. Alternatively, if one spouse takes on the bulk of childrearing responsibilities, the couple loses the equality and symmetry which has been the basis for companionship in their relationship. In either case, even if the outcome is not a higher likelihood of divorce, it is certainly an increase in personal dissatisfaction and marital disharmony.

The dual-career family, for all its attractions, is by no means likely to smoothly supplant the conventional family as the normative model of *family*. In fact, our present moment, as we noted in Chapter 1, is filled with confusion about what, precisely, we mean by "family." Dual-career families do not seem to be family enough for many—the hectic pace two wage earners are obliged to keep up squeezes out many of the things people expect of family life. Moreover, once the conventional family lost its normative monopoly, other family-like arrangements grew more common. Cohabitating and gay couples, people committed to being single parents, and people committed to being just plain single have all begun to appear in discussions of the family. Before we conclude our survey of the modern family, we have to examine these variants. Since many still refuse to accept such arrangements as "families," we will designate them "unacknowledged families."

Unacknowledged Families

Today, practices that only a few years ago would have brought shame and ostracism compete with settled family life for legitimacy. While homosexual partners still contend with prejudice and all sorts of legal discrimination, the fact that they can press their claims for legitimacy, for the right to become foster parents, for example, and that they have broad support in doing so, suggests how far we have come from the day when only the conventional family was regarded as proper. Similarly, the practice of cohabitation, not long ago referred to as "shacking up" or, more decorously, "living in sin," has now become commonplace, if uneasily accepted. Our attitudes toward men and women who decide to remain single or couples who decide to be childless or a mother who decides not to marry the father of her child have all changed rapidly in recent years. Though not seen by everyone as fully legitimate, each of these arrangements is so widespread as to require matter-of-factness rather than the moral indignation that recently prevailed. Does this mean we have lost our bearings, that we no longer know—or worse, no longer care about—right from wrong? We think not.

What is striking to us about these unacknowledged families is that they each embody the same companionate ideals that have shaped both the conventional and the dual-career family. Most commentary on hetero- and homosexual cohabitation, as well as unwed mothers and singles, has focused on the ways these arrangements allegedly flaunt the conventions of monogamy and the norm that sanctions sexual relations only after marriage. Thus, unacknowledged families have generally been discussed in terms of the sexual revolution that has presumably swept over us in the course of the past three decades. Whether revolution or not, what interests us is something quite different. While they may appear deviant with respect to once prevailing norms of sexual conduct, all are shaped by the companionate aspiration that underlies the more conventional families we have been discussing. Indeed, those who have made cohabitation more than a trial marriage—merely one more stage in a courting process that leads or is expected to lead to a traditional wedding—insist that the institution of marriage itself, and the socially sanctioned roles of husband and wife, ruin companionate possibilities.

Though motives are obviously mixed, and self-consciousness is by no means commonplace, the evident problems accompanying both conventional and dual-career marriages have given rise to the allegation that marriage conventions unnecessarily constrict partners in ways that diminish their capacities to treat and be treated by one's partner as an equal. Among heterosexuals, many of those who have been affected by the feminist movement are especially sensitive to the ways in which conventional marriages so easily devolve into a system that diminishes women. Cohabitation is a way of declaring an independence from those traditional oppressive expectations while at the same time affirming a commitment to an ongoing intimate relationship that is egalitarian and companionate.[42] In other words, cohabiting couples are generally not rejecting the virtues of intimacy, sharing, or egalitarianism as these get embodied in family life. Far from it. What they maintain is that these values can best be realized outside formal marriage.

Why might this be so? Obviously, the act of getting married

itself cannot be the central issue. Rather than an aversion to ceremony, what proponents of cohabitation appear to be saying is that marriage is inextricably embedded in a set of restrictive cultural meanings that limit the possibilities for constructing the type of companionate relationship suited to the needs and personalities of each person and their interpersonal dynamics. To be married is to be treated by others according to conventional expectations about what marriage means, expectations that are imposed independent of how each wants to be treated. For example, being married subjects most people to certain expectations about involvement with their partner's family. Even with the relatively low levels of embeddedness in kin networks that characterize many modern marriages, some object to the automatic assumption that loving a person requires participation in and caring for their family. In addition, many adults, having struggled to establish their independence from their family, find marriage imposes on them a whole set of expectations for renewed involvement that they may not want. Nor is it only family relationships that are structured according to the conventions of marriage. Some who choose cohabitation rather than marriage feel they are freer to maintain independent relationships with others than they would be if married. In marriage each partner is treated like the possession of their spouse. For example, most people are less likely to ask just one person from a married couple to a social engagement than they are someone who is not married.

And then there is the question of sexuality. For the most part, marriage presumes monogamy. Even though this presumption is routinely set aside by considerable numbers of married persons of both sexes, the laws and conventions of marriage combine to make such sexual activity illegitimate. Many advocates of cohabitation, even if they are themselves monogamous, feel that not being married leaves them freer to choose how they will express their sexuality. In this way, their sexual activity continues to be an expression of their own desires rather than the fulfillment of the expectations that accompany the role of husband or wife. Of course there are also those, both married and cohabiting, who include sexual relations with others among the accepted possibilities of their relationship. For the most part, however, it appears that this freer expression of sexuality is more easily sustained outside of marriage. In each of these ways, co-habiting can be seen to be more voluntaristic than formal marriage: it says more openly what has, in fact, been steadily but guiltily occurring. The vow ". . . 'til death us do part" has obviously been altered, in practice, to mean something like ". . . 'til our needs and interests diverge and our commitment to one another wanes." By remaining uninstitutionalized, cohabitation admits the possibility that the relationship may some day cease meeting one or both partners' needs. Because the relationship is in some sense continually negotiable, unceasingly voluntary, so the argument goes, partners are encouraged to have a fuller sense of themselves and of each other. If the relationship endures, it does so because each party to the relationship wants it to, not because the inertia of social convention keeps it going.

To be sure, the longer a cohabiting relationship endures, the more it is likely to resemble a formal marriage. Over time, partners inevitably grow accustomed to and dependent upon one another such that dissolving the relationship is likely to be no less traumatic than it would had they been formally married. Of course, this is simply another way of saying that cohabitation is like marriage. However compelling the arguments for cohabitation appear, there is little evidence that cohabiting couples do in fact have an easier time sustaining companionate relationships than do their more conventional counterparts. They must contend with the full range of difficulties that beset families in general. In other words, cohabitation does not resolve the dilemmas inherent in any attempt to combine long-term commitment with recognition of each partner's needs for autonomy. What its growth does show is that conventional arrangements can no longer be assumed to be appropriate or right for everyone.

Single-parent families can pose a different sort of challenge to conventional norms by representing a rejection of long-term commitment itself. Of course, most single parents did not intend to be single when they became parents. Whether once married or not, it is likely that most have their singleness thrust upon them, either as the result of a sexual partner unwilling to assume the additional responsibility of parenting or a spouse no longer willing to sustain a marital relationship. So long as this is true, single parents do not pose a threat to the companionate ideal; they simply have failed to meet or sustain it. But of late, increasing numbers of single parents seem to prefer remaining single to the hassles of trying to keep a relationship going.

Before we even begin exploring this assertion, though, we need to make clear that what we are saying should in no way be taken as romanticizing the situation of the single parent. The majority of single parents, over four-fifths of whom are women, are obliged to endure drastically reduced standards of living, isolation, and enervating struggles with welfare, employers, and schools. Divorce has become one of the leading reasons families wind up in poverty.[43] Even a casual reading of the literature on single-parent families is sufficient to make clear that there is little that is positive in the situation.

That the challenges confronting a single parent are so enormous makes it all the more intriguing to discover that more men and women, but especially women, are apparently eschewing marriage or remarriage.[44] In statistical terms, this appears in two ways: rising numbers of never-married mothers and declining rates of remarriage. Of the two, the rising numbers of never-married mothers contributes less to the increase in single-parent families, and so we will concentrate on the declining rate of remarriage.[45] For a time, as attitudes toward divorce softened and the stigma attaching to divorce declined, the rate of remarriage for divorced men and women rose. In recent years, as many as 80 percent of men and 60 percent of women remarried after divorce. But remarriage rates have been declining of late, especially the rates for women.[46] What lies behind these statistics?

The women Arendell surveyed were ambivalent about remarriage. She writes: "Their ambivalence about remarriage seemed rooted in a new feeling of independence, a new sense of self that required protection: their hard-won gains might be lost in a new marriage" (142). It is worth quoting some of Arendell's respondents in order to get a flavor of what is at issue for these women and, finally, for us all.

I'd marry again if I found a man that was caring, self-sufficient, able to take care of himself, and willing to allow me to remain myself. I'd never be dependent like I was [in my first marriage] (142–43).

In order to become a provider for my family as a single person, I had to become an assertive person. I had to take on other roles and learn how to be assertive and take control. I don't want to give up control of my life now. But I feel like I'm a misfit because I'm not the ideal woman. I scare men to death by being able to take care of myself. . . . I find myself thinking that now that my kids are almost raised, I'll have to go back to being the submissive woman in order to relate to men. . . . But can I do that again in this life? . . . So that's part of what I've had to learn: the things that are supposed to make me successful as a woman would have made me unsuccessful as a single mother. It's not fair. There's a real need to belong. Being an individual who can achieve isn't enough for a woman (145).

What these women are saying is that they value their autonomy and fear they could never sustain it in another marriage. Another of Arendell's respondents put it this way:

I think the best thing about being divorced is being able to make some decisions by myself and be responsible for myself. I like that. The good things, for me, have been finding out that I can take care of myself, that I can make my own choices about what I want to do. It's really been a growth aspect, having room to grow (147).

Clearly, some no longer find the dependencies typical in marriage, even in dual-career marriages, inviting. Marriage carries with it a whole set of expectations that puts the individual who values his or her freedom at risk. For those who have tasted this freedom, even those who didn't want to in the first place, it is hard to return to a situation that requires more or less constant alertness to the needs of a spouse. Most single parents still do seek remarriage, but a growing number are skeptical and clearly reluctant. Their ability to raise children on their own, and to discover powers that they did not know they had, poses a challenge to the wisdom that holds marriage to be a necessary feature of adult life. Our growing appetite for autonomy and our correlative wariness of emotional dependencies has not only propelled more and more of us away from the conventional family, it has propelled a growing number of us away from marriage.

The multiple ways families can frustrate desires for companionship and aspirations for autonomy have obviously not gone unnoticed. Seeing these difficulties, some have discovered the advantages of living by themselves and found that these outweigh the advantages of living with others. Being single, for some, has become a way of life rather than a stage of life. Some come to this way of living after failed attempts at other modes—whether it be divorce after a conventional marriage or the end of a long-term, cohabiting arrangement. Others decide early on to make their life independently and to structure both their financial arrangements and their social relationships around the assumption that they will always live on their own.

Whatever the path to this style of living, it is attracting increasing numbers of people.[47] The number of people living alone has quadrupled since 1950. By 1985, 11 percent of all adults, almost 21 million people, lived alone. One-person households now account for a quarter of all households in the United States. Along with those who commit themselves to always living alone, there are now many who plan to be single and to live alone for extended periods of time. No longer do young adults jump into marriage at the earliest possible moment.

Overall, the picture that emerges is that young adults are expected to leave their parents' homes earlier and to get married later than they have for most of this century. Given the greater increase in the numbers of people living alone as opposed to getting married, it seems reasonable to assume that, were leaving home a possibility, many young adults still at home would choose to live by themselves.[48] Moreover, being single is not necessarily a brief interlude, or fling, before settling down. Particularly among young women who live independently, there are indications that the experience of living away from the parental household helps to alter the way they think about family and plan for their own lives. Studies regularly find that these women think more seriously about their own employment, expect to have fewer children, are more tolerant of the idea of mixing motherhood and employment, and have less traditional ideas about sex roles in the family than women who live with their parents.[49] While comparable effects among men are weaker, the changes in women's attitudes are bound to have an impact on the men with whom they interact.

In addition to those who live alone, there has been a substantial increase in singles in general. Between 1960 and 1980 there was a 70 percent increase in the number of single people in the United States. This includes the never married, the widowed, and the divorced. Obviously, many of the never married are simply not yet married, waiting their turn to join the ranks of the married, divorced, and widowed. And some of the divorced and widowed will remarry. Still, by 1980 there were roughly 70 million single people—roughly 40 percent of the population—above the age of fifteen in the United States.[50] Much more significant than the numbers is how singles think about themselves and how they are perceived by the rest of society. Until very recently, being single meant being pitied. At best, those who had not married, especially women, typically were described as having "failed" to marry. Marriage was taken as natural, and singleness was characterized as a form of deviance. While there are still strong residues of traditional attitudes, the hold they once had over the choices people make has decreased significantly.

In 1985 over 20 million people were living alone, 8 million men and 12 million women. This is double the 1970 figure and almost triple the number in 1960. To be sure, included among these are many who would prefer to be married or living with a partner. But by no means are most of the singles simply waiting around for the right person to complete their life. Almost 25 percent of first-time home buyers are single, and close to one quarter of all households are single-person households. While accurate statistics about the reasons for people's marital status are hard to come by, it is clear that significant numbers are either orienting themselves to life as a single or are sufficiently ambivalent about marriage to delay significantly the time at which they will make any commitment to marriage, let alone to raising a family.

However acceptable remaining single has become, it is rarely counted as a form of family life. In the strictest sense, a person living alone is not a family. But if we think of family as a self-conscious effort to structure one's private life in order to meet needs for emotional stability and connectedness as well as needs for financial security and independence, then we must include those living alone in our consideration of family life. For a long time there has been a tendency to assume that there was something wrong with people who lived alone, that they were intentionally avoiding intimacy and connectedness with others from some personal lack or failing, or that they were too selfish to structure lives of mutual dependence. But single life has never been confined to a few eccentrics and deviants, and it has emerged now as an alternative way to provide for the same needs others seek to satisfy within more traditional versions of the family. In the same way that it is now acknowledged that there are people for whom being single is an affirmation, an active choice, not merely a resignation and a giving up, there is a growing recognition that being single does not necessarily mean an empty life, devoid of meaningful relationships and interdependencies. Single life places voluntary obligations at the center of its understanding of relationships, resists exclusivity as a measure of commitment, and eschews publicly announced forms of interdependence. From this vantage point, both marriage and cohabitation are seen as threatening to personal autonomy and a companionate relationship. The tension between autonomy and interdependence that runs through contemporary family life is resolved explicitly in favor of autonomy. In a sense, staying single takes the notion of autonomy to its logical conclusion, placing a commitment to the self above any specific commitment to others.

For many singles, though, this commitment to self does not mean the avoidance of other commitments nor the rejection of intimacy and meaningful relationships. Rather, advocates of single living believe interdependencies work best when the independence of each party is unrestricted and that intimacy and emotional intensity are strongest when not diluted by the redundancy of daily routines. The following excerpt from the "Declaration of Undependence," published in the newsletter of Interaction, a large singles organization in Dayton, Ohio, captures this attitude, albeit in idealized language:

I resolve to think for myself in all situations rather than allow an "expert" to decide the course of my life. While I will remain open to wise counsel, I will make the final decision in personal matters and make myself heard when there are shared decisions to be made.

I resolve to remain aware of my identity and my wholeness at all times, particularly when in a coupled relationship. I will exercise my need for personal space without impinging on others.

I resolve to be a loving friend and to nurture worthwhile friendships, realizing my self-sufficiency is not equivalent to isolation. I will cultivate relationships with those of all ages, occupations and marital statuses as long as they meet my needs.

I resolve to become acquainted with the other gender burdened with a minimum of bias, recognizing they are neither alien nor enemy. I will focus on our similarities and develop real relationships with them, establishing authentic intimacy rather than superficial sexuality.

I resolve to plan for my own life for myself insofar as is possible; career goals, family future, my personal intentions to develop and grow.

I resolve to maximize the possibilities for growth and freedom within my singleness. I will keep my eye fixed on its positive aspects.[51]

Living alone places individual responsibility and self-development at the center of one's life, presumably avoiding the conflicts and restraints imposed by formal dependencies and interdependencies. Whether ascetically self-denying in the pursuit of higher ideals or narcissistically self-indulgent in pursuit of pleasure, it is the person's own interpretations of what is important and relevant to the self that become the desiderata of all action. But, as we have seen, in all forms of family life there is a discrepancy between the promises of the ideal and the limitations of reality, discrepancies that originate within the contradictions of the ideals themselves.

In the world of singles, the flip side of autonomy is loneliness. Even those who are basically satisfied spending lots of time by

themselves report needs for companionship, desires for an audience, and longings for intimacy. Being removed from the
obligatory commitments that come with family life, they also
lack the guaranteed presence of others when desired. For many,
independence from family obligations means increased dependence on the marketplace. We noted earlier how the dual-career
couple becomes enmeshed as consumers in relationships and
dependencies necessary to maintain their autonomy and make
companionate living a possibility. Dependence on kin and
neighbors is replaced by dependence on the marketplace. Perhaps even more than with dual-career couples, consumerism is
important for sustaining the autonomy of the single person.
Many singles, despite the rhetorical "pledge" cited above not to
allow experts to compromise their independence, rely heavily
on these experts for help in making choices and depend on the
marketplace for structuring social occasions. Dating services,
singles' bars, singles' nights in supermarkets, health and physical fitness centers flourish because of single people's needs. For
singles more than for others, the marketplace is a setting for
social encounters. Louise Bernikow, in *Lonely in America*, reports
on the informal information network in the singles culture that
identifies not just night spots but particular supermarkets and
department stores as good places for meeting people.

More significantly, consumerism provides singles not just a
means to meet certain needs but the very logic of their relationships with others. Novelty and choice, long the mainstays of consumer activity, become central criteria in personal relationships
as well. The single person is committed to relationships in a way
similar to the way a consumer is committed to commodities—
you seek them out and keep them so long as they provide the
satisfaction for which they were acquired, and when they no
longer work, or when you are dissatisfied with them, they are
replaced by new ones. Always the central focus is the individual
self. And herein lies one of the major limitations of single life—
the narrow base for personal satisfaction. Many of the satisfactions that come from a focus on the self are of limited duration.
Even among the most successful, those earning excellent salaries
in work they find challenging and satisfying, with active social
and sexual lives with interesting partners, there are reports of

something missing. For most people even the best careers provide only limited satisfactions. Work that was once the center of a personal universe can suddenly seem insignificant. Similarly, the satisfactions of the dating scene and limited liability relationships can wear thin. Some singles no doubt find themselves longing for more permanent attachments to others.

Unacknowledged families wrestle with the same sorts of dilemmas that more conventional families confront. It is not easy to combine companionate intimacy with needs for autonomy. As we grow more attentive to personal needs and more committed to the importance of psychological satisfaction, the bonds of kinship and familism are necessarily experienced as constricting. And they become more volatile. The result has been a proliferation of life-styles and, overall, a dramatic reduction in the sense of normative cohesion and consensus about what is apropos.

Conclusion

We have been describing ways of arranging one's private life that represent sharp departures from what we ordinarily think of as "family." The rise in popularity of cohabitation, the declining rate of remarriage in the face of persistently high divorce rates, and, last, the rising proportions of singles can all be taken as signs of confusion about, or the collapse of, the norms that have informed our sense of family life. This chaos arises less because family is being rejected than because there is no particular version of family life that seems generally appropriate or satisfying. Marriage was once taken for granted as normal, a bond that virtually everyone was expected to forge and then maintain "for better or worse." Clearly, this is no longer the case.

Most people experience several different versions of family life in the course of a normal lifetime, and for many the different versions are perhaps better thought of as phases of a life rather than fixed forms. A "typical" person growing up today might well live for the first ten years of his or her life in a conventional family and then, following the parents' divorce, live with a single parent until going away to college or leaving to work. This could easily be followed by living alone for five years, cohabiting with someone for a year or two, returning to single life for a year, marrying and having a child after four years of marriage, divorcing when the child is six, returning to the parental home with the child for a year, and then living as a single parent until the child leaves home. Each of these different arrangements represents efforts to combine intimacy with personal autonomy. In this sense, although very different in important respects, each of these arrangements is informed by the companionate ideal.

But more is involved. The ideal itself is not constant. What for one generation seemed egalitarian can seem, for another, highly repressive. Until quite recently marriage was a declaration of autonomy. Autonomy was understood to mean, more or less, freedom from direct parental supervision. Marriage took the young man and young woman out of their respective parental orbits, allowing them to embark upon their own life. The promise of autonomy is no doubt one of the important contributing factors to the steady decline in the average age at first marriage that started in the nineteenth century and continued steadily until the 1960s. The desire to escape the watchful eye of parents led many young men and women into hasty and ill-considered marriages and so, as age at first marriage declined, the divorce rate rose. Until very recently, there was no social space between the parental home and marriage for young people, especially women. The army served this capacity for young men in time of war, and college was such a space but was available only to a tiny minority, again until the decades after World War II.

As college became more widely available and as a large peacetime standing army became routine, autonomy from parents quickly became possible without rushing into marriage. It took only a little over a decade, by the mid-1960s, for the trend toward earlier marriages to slow and then be reversed. It is clear that a modified understanding of what it means to be autonomous is emerging along with new ways of organizing private life in order to reach for this newly defined goal.[52] Marriage is no longer an unambiguous vehicle for the realization of autonomy. Indeed, for many, marriage constitutes an impediment to autonomy and to maintaining companionate relations with others.

Thus, the families we have been describing ought not be seen as frozen "family types." Instead, they constitute a moving sys-

tem that simultaneously describes past practices and new departures arrayed around attempts to fit private life to personal
needs and socially sanctioned possibilities. In this sense, families
can be thought of as existing along a continuum that overlaps,
at one end, with preindustrial family forms and continues toward an ever fuller expression of the unique elements of the
companionate ideal. The family life of the nation's underclass
obviously shares some features with preindustrial families: activities tend to be sex-segregated and relations with kin tend to
be both close and extensive. Though a visitor from the eighteenth century would no doubt be appalled at how little control
parents have over their children and how much autonomy wives
have, many features of family life would bear resemblance to the
visitor's own family. By contrast, though roles remain organized
around gender, the upper-middle-class family is far more egalitarian: the wife has considerable autonomy and scope for shaping her own milieu—as long as she retains the central identification of wife-mother. Though interests may diverge over time,
she and her husband entertain together and her role is often
seen as an important adjunct to her husband's career. But equality remains an issue in the professionalized family. It is a
stunted, equivocal equality. By contrast, the dual-career family
takes equality one step further, a significant step indeed. By
couching equality in terms of occupational engagement, however, much of the couple's family life becomes truncated, forced
to find expression in the interstices between two busy schedules.
In order to attain the equality that companionate aspiration
makes compelling, the dual-career couple forgoes much of the
content of companionship.

   Over time, the companionate ideal has become more explicit,
more central to the organization and continuation of family life.
Each family is more autonomous from kin and each, in succes-
sion, is more solicitous of the needs of individual family members. In each, the prospect of greater intimacy both promises to
fulfill and threatens to undermine the equality essential to companionate living. The modern family, seen in this light, is less a
type of family than it is a trajectory, a movement toward a small,
independent family unit that places heavy emphasis on equality
and autonomy. This trajectory entails high levels of disruption

and produces considerable anxiety about identity and self-worth.

These anxieties are perhaps most clearly illustrated among singles, where autonomy takes precedence over companionship and equality is achieved through emotional distance. While the recent growth of the single population is an especially significant phenomenon, we should not exaggerate its meaning as a sign of things to come. Single life has acquired an unprecedented legitimacy, but it is not in any way likely to become the answer to the crisis in the family. What is interesting is the degree to which, along with cohabitation, single life has begun to provide the ideals against which varieties of family life are measured. Personal autonomy, self-sufficiency, and individual development are the criteria used in the media and by experts in assessing the quality of all family relationships. Whether we are examining the relationship between husband and wife, cohabiting lovers, or parents and children, the emphasis is on the individuality of each partner. From a variety of perspectives the traditional features of family life—the intermeshing of identities, the blurring of boundaries, and the perpetuation of dependencies—are seen as problematic. Family life forms that enhance prospects for individual autonomy are promoted by experts, preferred by employers, and reinforced by the organization of career opportunities, markets, and social services. While interdependencies are acknowledged as inevitable, the emphasis is on controlled reciprocities that produce the kind of companionate intimacy that facilitates individual autonomy. It is the general movement in the direction of this ideal that leads us to refer collectively to the forms of contemporary family life as *the minimal family*.

Yet it is this very minimalism that leads each new elaboration of the modern family to give rise to consternation, lending an aura of sanctity to forms of family life that contain, or seem to contain, elements of the more traditional family. Thus, for example, in the face of the rapid increase in dual-career families, we see a rising nostalgia for the professionalized family, even though many working wives of today are, in effect, refugees from professionalized families.

This simultaneous pressing forward and nostalgia for what

has been left behind may be one of those features of our behavior that makes our hindsight so superior to our foresight. But this duality, ambivalence even, is also a function of the pursuit of autonomy itself. Autonomy is a contradictory goal. On the one hand, the desire for autonomy is a desire to be taken seriously by others, to be regarded as an individual worthy of others' esteem and affection. One needs to be a member of a group, large or small, in order to satisfy this aspect of autonomy. On the other hand, the desire for autonomy is also a desire to be left alone, to be allowed to follow one's own impulses free of the constraining and circumscribing influences of others. Autonomy, in this aspect, is autarkic, anti-social. As the pursuit of autonomy intensifies, families get smaller and commitments get more volatile, precisely because family commitments are constricting, even if they can also be among the most deeply satisfying of human relationships. The result, over time, is an enlarged scope of individual initiative and action and a correlatively reduced scope for family life. But ironically, greater autonomy, understood as individual freedom, produces longings for the sorts of solidaristic associations that the family has historically provided, precisely because the decline of such associations greatly intensifies anxieties about identity. The result is a general tendency to romanticize the family even as more and more of us abandon its more traditional and solidaristic features.

However, as increased autonomy evokes needs for connectedness with others, it results in more than nostalgia. With the family less and less able to satisfy these needs, people begin to turn elsewhere, both to anchor their sense of personal identity and for the supports that will enable them to pursue their individual goals. This has produced a bewildering variety of life-styles and family patterns. For some, it is the variety that is troublesome. For others, what is troublesome is less the variety than the volatility of life-styles and family patterns. Nothing seems settled. We seem no longer to have a clear normative sense of what the family is or ought to be. Under these circumstances, it is not surprising that the family has become an important component of the political tumult that has characterized the last three decades. It is to this subject that we now turn.

5

The Limits of
Autonomy and the
Fate of Familism

BY THE EARLY 1960s the logic of consumer capitalism was in full
sway. The changes in both public and private life described in
the preceding chapters converged in the late forties. During the
fifties they became mutually reinforcing. Institutional imperatives and subjective desires were apparently complementary.
Rapidly growing numbers of men and women were forming
families predicated upon high levels of autonomy for the couple
as well as for each individual. In turn, this autonomy was premised upon expectations of expanding opportunities for work
and rising living standards. It was in private consumption—in
the shopping centers, department stores, and realtors' offices—
that the objective requirements of capital and the subjective desires for individual autonomy appeared in exquisite harmony.
It seemed society was getting precisely the kinds of people it
needed—people who were ambitious, willing to take risks, and
psychologically strong enough to chart new paths. They were
also sensitive and emotionally open, able to cooperate in the
workplace and be loving in the home.

Celebrations of this achievement were evident, marred only
by a few critics who persisted in pointing out the shallowness of

the new consumerism. The rapid expansion of employment in bureaucracies and the equally rapid development of suburbs was producing a generation of Americans profoundly anxious about their status and self-worth. As a result, the critics said, people were uncertain of their needs and cut off from any sense of purpose beyond loyalty to the hierarchy at work and the standards set by advertising.[1] Most of the social criticism of the day, however, focused on the need to extend the reach of affluence to groups and strata heretofore excluded from consumer society. For the working class, the only impediment to full inclusion was their presumably irrational fear and timidity. This impediment could be removed by "education." For others, most notably blacks, exclusion was seen as a complex and vexing problem, the persistence of which took some of the edge off the otherwise unabashed optimism that prevailed.

There were also adjustments needed in the nation's families. Many people required assistance in their efforts to constitute autonomous family life. It was "natural" for men to be breadwinners and women to be homemakers, but the dramatic separation of these roles amid rapid suburbanization and the equally rapid expansion of the salaried middle class was not without its difficulties. Many couples were unprepared for affluence and the demands that social mobility made on family life. Childrearing was a particular source of concern. Parents were being asked to socialize their children for participation in a world they themselves only dimly understood. Preparing children to be autonomous tends to make them precocious, even unruly, yet there was reason to fear that imposing rules would inhibit or stultify a child's movement toward autonomy. Parents, the experts seemed to agree, needed to walk a fine line between encouraging independence and insisting upon respect for authority. Still, there was a virtual consensus that the fine line existed and could be walked.

It is hard, today, to capture fully the sense of optimism, even of perfectibility, that permeated the discourse of the 1950s and early 1960s. The economy was thought to be cured of its disastrous nosedives; the threat of class war and revolution had been ended. The economy no longer cried out for transformation, and it appeared that a smoothly working political order had become the arena for resolving conflicting interests. It seemed as if people's private lives echoed the harmonies of the political order and the economy. Personal consumption was steadily expanding, educational levels were steadily rising, and there appeared to be a broad-based willingness to support modest state programs designed to extend the reach of affluence to the poor and the victims of discrimination.

Of course the euphoria was short-lived. The unraveling began from several directions. The tolerance and openness that flourished in the immediate wake of McCarthyism was sorely tested by blacks insisting that they be included with dignity—now. While a majority of whites appeared ready to spurn old racist shibboleths, the economy and the cultural patterns on which economic relations rested (including real estate patterns as well as assumptions governing employment decisions) effectively made most blacks unwelcome. Conservative resistance to government programs intended to equalize access to affluence began to be augmented by whites who no longer felt responsible for the fate of blacks.[2] Growing numbers of whites thought that since segregationist laws were struck down, all institutional barriers to equality had been removed. Now it was up to blacks to show that they had the stuff to succeed. "Hand outs" would only perpetuate their lowly status. But even with unprecedented rates of economic growth, there were not enough jobs being created for those who sought work, and this exacerbated the relations between blacks and whites. Moreover, many whites found that their needs greatly exceeded their incomes. The fixed costs of mortgages, the repayments on auto and other consumer credit purchases, the costs of privately acquiring goods and services that once were public or available through kin, as well as the steady elaboration of "necessities," put increasing pressure on family finances. Wives began to drift into the workforce in order to ease the pressure on the family budget, thereby increasing competition for jobs. The steady squeeze on family budgets, even among those who by any standard would be judged comfortable, generated increasing resistance to higher taxes, especially when it seemed that so much of the tax dollar went to the poor and to blacks. In other words, the base of support for the expansion of the welfare state began to grow restive.[3]

The civil rights movement helped fuel another, contradictory sort of unraveling: a cultural and political revolt of youth that in turn gave impetus to the rebirth of feminism as well as other social movements critical of consumer capitalism. Young whites who were attracted to the civil rights cause were remarkably alike in one crucial respect: they were largely the children of middle-class parents whose family lives emphasized the centrality of autonomy.[4] These young men and women were among the first, in any significant number, to have been raised in family settings in which authority, love, dependence, and autonomy collided in the ways we described in detail in Chapter 3. The liberal values transmitted by parents, values that emphasized egalitarianism and an obligation to act justly and fairly toward others, were undermined in the daily life of family members outside the home. When white students saw blacks barred from restaurants and degraded in myriad other ways, it was hard to reconcile with their own freedom and security. Many young people experienced this disparity as emblematic of adult hypocrisy. Striving for unity between personal morality and public action, many found the civil rights movement exhilarating.

It was attractive for another reason: here was a chance to discredit adult authority. Young people made a principle of their disdain for the experience and authority of the adult generations that nominally governed them. In large numbers they joined civil rights groups, anti-war organizations, campus-based political action groups, and life-style communities. Some conservative observers saw the youth rebellion of the sixties as an oedipal revolt, a refusal to grow up.[5] In a way they were right, but not in the narrow and dismissive sense of mere psychological perturbation. It was the compromised adulthood of their parents they were rejecting, not adulthood per se. The fact is that a significant portion of the generation born in the late 1930s and 1940s came to young adulthood under the auspices of parents and other adults who were unsure of their authority, not because they were weak or vacillating but because history had conspired to destroy central features of their cultural confidence.

The depression demoralized more than the unemployed: it undercut faith in the system generally. Some of the disillusioned were drawn to radicalism and militant trade unionism; others were drawn to ideals of activist federalism embodied in the New Deal. But disillusionment stalked these convictions too. The old left, bedeviled by its links to the Soviet Union, spent its considerable moral authority in sectarian squabbles and was internally too weak to withstand the ferocity of post-war anti-communism. New Deal liberals, too, got swept up in the binge of purges, unable to separate their dislike of communism from the reactionary impulses to purify. The result was the birth of a cold-war liberalism epitomized by John F. Kennedy's muscular interventionism abroad and half-hearted support for reforms at home.

The bankruptcy of the old left, celebrated by many who were once its youthful boosters as "the end of ideology,"[6] combined with a paralyzed liberalism to produce a vacuum into which the post-depression/post-war generation moved. The emptiness of the larger political culture mirrored, on a large scale, the homes in which many of the nation's middle- and upper-middle-class young were being socialized. If oedipal dynamics were involved at all, it was in a struggle that resonated far beyond the specificities of father-son or mother-daughter relationships precisely because both familial and social authority had collapsed, the former permanently, the latter only momentarily. The self-satisfaction of the fifties and early sixties was replaced by the realization that society was not, after all, getting quite the kinds of people it needed. The relationship between the larger social structure and the family, which observers had been happily assuming to be a functional relationship of harmonious interacting parts, turned out to be a dialectically conflicting relationship in which apparent harmonies exploded into discord.

The family circumstances common to many Americans were producing a generation of young people who were ideally suited to some aspects of the society and at the same time were quite out of step with others. Many young people clearly desired autonomy and were committed to self-development, both as an end in itself and as a means to the larger goal of helping to bring forth a more just social order. Though sympathetic at a superficial level to anti-commercialism and simplicity of material needs, the sixties generation was thoroughly accustomed to high levels of personal consumption. To be sure, their consumption was moderated by low levels of income associated with being students and new entrants into the labor force. Young people spurned the tastes of older generations, masking their consumption patterns beneath an anti-materialistic veneer. Nevertheless, the youth market was a high-growth market.

Quite apart from propensities to consume, the generation that came to young adulthood in the sixties and early seventies was the bearer of the desire for autonomy, which had been steadily nurtured for many generations but only became realizable for substantial numbers in the sixties. Society could assimilate the desire for autonomy as long as it was channeled into consumption, but found autonomy much more difficult to accept in virtually all other realms. The freer life-styles that became widespread challenged nearly every article of traditional belief. The pillars of the community—family, church, and school—came under a barrage of attack. These attacks had a common element in that each focused on the ways prevailing institutions stifled individuality and creativity, thereby reproducing the hierarchy and repressiveness of the system. The family reproduced gender differences that many men and women began to regard as oppressive. Schools, it was asserted, reinforced class and racial differences by making hierarchy seem the logical, consistent, and fair outcome of individual ability and striving. And many insisted that churches had largely abandoned their spiritual role, serving instead to join in the celebration of Americanism at home and abroad.

As disaffection spread and criticism intensified, defenders of tradition began to assert themselves more and more vigorously. Appalled by the counterculture's open contempt for traditional values and authority, culturally conservative forces rallied around opposition to federally funded day care, the Equal Rights Amendment (ERA), and abortion. By the early 1970s they had become a serious political force. At the heart of their program was an attempt to make the family once again the central organizing focus for people's private lives. They believed a reinvigorated family would teach respect for authority and would restore the distinction between right and wrong. With strong families, people need not look to government or employer for assistance and succor.

Bolstering the Family

Though Americans flocked to the nation's emporia eagerly once the old restraints of thrift and self-denial were lifted, there has always been a nagging, if sometimes only barely discernable, doubt about consumption as the main determinant of the good life. Of course left-wing critics regularly deplore the crass materialism, "commodity fetishism" as Marx put it, that identifies personal fulfillment with new cars, hair fashions, and home stereos. But there has been another source of concern about these matters that, in the United States, has far deeper roots and more widespread resonance than the idealism of the left. Found principally in the themes of otherworldly religion, celebrations of self-denial have struck recurrent chords in American life. The downplaying of earthly treasures (and their associated pleasures) in comparison to the joys of eternal heavenly bliss has regularly appealed to significant numbers of Americans, especially, but by no means exclusively, the poor and the marginal.′ One of the principal pillars of this religious view is a strong commitment to the family. Family is understood not simply as individuals bound to one another on the basis of love. Rather, it is seen much more traditionally, as a web of individuals whose love for one another may wax and wane but whose mutual obligations must nonetheless be acknowledged and met.

Throughout the 1950s and 1960s, as ever increasing numbers were drawn into the delights of expanding consumption and as the web of kin affiliations and obligations were further reduced, a small but growing network of fundamentalists clung to a conception of family life that stressed respect, order, and a clear subordination of individual desires to the needs of the family. Most were politically as well as culturally conservative, and to the extent that they caught public attention at all, it was as a result of their hyper-patriotic responses to the growing dissent over the Vietnam War. But for the most part, religious teachings of the fundamentalists were directed at the concerns of private, not public life. The cultural ferment of the late sixties and the

seventies changed both the character and the focus of conservative religiosity.

Drugs, sex, and rock 'n' roll—the self-parody that the counterculture used as a credo—was a galvanizing red flag for the
devout. Mortified by the breakdown in public order and by the
increasingly audacious flouting of conventional morality, the religious right began to mobilize in defense of their imperiled values. There emerged a group of leaders, sophisticated in the use
of television, who preached the basics of fundamentalism—a literal interpretation of the Bible, the subordination of wife to
husband and children to parents, respect for authority, and opposition to atheism and its pernicious agents, whether communists or secularists. More important, they urged their followers
to do more than pray for a better, more righteous world: they
encouraged political activism to staunch the tide of sinfulness.
The politicization of the religious right was accelerated through
the 1970s by the ascendence of the women's movement, the legalization of abortion, and the emergence of gay rights as an
issue of moment.[8] Each of these developments directly challenged the integrity of the family as traditionalists understood
it. The Equal Rights Amendment, for example, was seen as directly attacking the conviction that a woman's proper place was
in the home. Circumstances might, from time to time, dictate
that she work outside the home, but this was to be understood
as a part of her obligation to be a helpmate to her husband, not
as an expression of her need for autonomy nor as an expression
of her fundamental equality in society.

When the Supreme Court made abortion constitutionally protected in 1973 (the year after Congress approved the constitutional amendment for the ERA and sent it to the states for the
required ratification), the religious right had an even more potent issue to organize around. Not only did legalized abortion
conjure the taking of "innocent life," it also implicitly authorized
a view of sexuality that was anathema to most fundamentalists.
By reducing the link between sexual activity and procreation to
a voluntary and potentially self-conscious decision, the most obvious basis for the biblically sanctioned sexual division of labor
was transformed into an option, not an invariant rule. Moreover, along with birth control (the spread of which was also

greeted with dismay, though with less outright and explicit resistance), legally sanctioned abortion fully legitimated the notion of sex as a pleasure unto itself, which many fundamentalists found objectionable even between married partners.[9]

"Right to Life," as opponents of abortion dubbed their movement, became a widespread, grassroots movement almost overnight. Though given considerable support by the Roman Catholic Church, it was by no means dependent solely upon its doctrine or resources. Fundamentalist Protestants (as well as some conservative and orthodox Jews) have played central roles in many successful electoral and lobbying campaigns aimed at unseating legislators deemed unsympathetic to the presumed "rights of the unborn." Animating this otherwise heterogeneous movement has been a commitment to the "traditional family." Of course the traditional family the religious right has in mind is not, literally, the preindustrial family, commonly referred to as the "extended family." What they have in mind when tradition is evoked is a family that remains the sole repository of familism—of mutual aid, loving obligation, and devoted self-sacrifice, especially by mothers; a network of more or less closely linked households, each of which is structured around a clear sexual division of labor, wife the homemaker and husband the breadwinner, and which mediates between individual family members and the larger public order.[10]

It is this last point that links the religious right to a broader conservative agenda concerned less about private morality than about the steady expansion of the welfare state. What began in distress over declining morality, embodied first in concern over diluted parental authority and juvenile delinquency, later was expressed in reactions to the tumult of the sixties, and finally and most vigorously, in efforts to repel frontal attacks on the family led by feminists, gays, and their allies. This coalesced and cohered into a sustained and well-organized political force when the government itself became the target of the religious right. Prohibitions on school prayer, federal programs promulgating contraceptives for teenagers, legalization of abortion, and similar governmental intrusions into private life came to be seen as the source of the alleged breakdown of order. Courts, emulating eviscerated parental authority, turned criminals back out on the streets. Welfare administrators showed more solicitude, it was argued, for drug addicts than for the victims of addicts' crimes. Under federal mandates and guidelines, schools were inculcating skepticism, moral relativism, and a "secular humanism" that directly challenges belief in a divine being.

The focus on government as the source of society's troubles resonated with the longstanding laissez-faire principles of secular conservatism. Though the evolving partnership between government and business described in Chapter 2 was conceived and brought into being by leading businessmen and public figures, they have never been of one mind. A large section of America's elite has always been at best grudging in the face of the growing interaction between the federal government and the economy. They resented the legitimacy this partnership lent to labor unions, and there was considerable opposition within the upper class to the steady elaboration of welfare measures, whether government sponsored or negotiated labor-management settlements. Conservatives continued to believe that virtue inhered in thrift and hard work and that the welfare system largely rewarded just the opposite.

These views were not the stuff of which electoral victories were to be made, however, at least not at the national level. The combination of still-fresh memories of the depression and the evident successes of the post-war economy led by the partnership between government, business, and labor meant that conservatives were cut off from a mass base through the 1950s and much of the 1960s. Only the appeal of anti-communism allowed conservatives to avoid complete isolation from the electorate. Goldwater's capture of the Republican Party's presidential nomination in 1964 showed that conservatism had considerable financial clout and dedicated cadres drawn from the ranks of the upper and upper middle classes. But the Right could not parlay these strengths into popularity with any but a narrow slice of the electorate, at least not with the program that it offered.

But by the late 1960s, concerns over so-called "social issues," the code name for assertive blacks, rising crime, and young people scornful of prevailing social norms, began to broaden conservative appeal. Coupled with the disarray within the ranks of liberals occasioned by the war in Vietnam and a waffling on civil rights, Richard Nixon won election to the White House. Though he ran on a promise to end the war, his votes came from people who were less troubled by the war than by domestic disorders, people who hoped he would return the nation to the "good old days." Nixon was not sufficiently conservative for some, however. In fact, though his rhetoric was conservative and his impulses were essentially Babbittesque, Nixon was too pragmatic to suit the ideologues of the Right.[11] Nixon was contemptuous of labor and the poor, but he was too committed to his own electoral successes to let personal biases jeopardize the kinds of compromises and coalitions needed to govern the country effectively. As a result, and with no small degree of irony, Johnson's Great Society programs, as well as those welfare programs originating in the New Deal, grew faster during Nixon's first term in office than they had in Johnson's. But with the help of his pugnacious vice president, Spiro Agnew, Nixon helped the new conservativism gain coherence. The social-issues conservatives came together with the laissez-faire conservatives in the Nixon years, and Nixon helped chaperon the resulting courtship.

Although Nixon funded Johnson's programs, he also made it clear that new programmatic advances were going to be very rare. Funds bought votes, but new programs could jeopardize his base. And so, in 1971, Nixon surprised many who had been distracted by the good fortunes of the social welfare sector under his administration by vetoing a bill authorizing federally supported day care. In a strongly worded statement, Nixon echoed the concerns of the religious right. Day care, he insisted, had "family-weakening implications." Rather than weaken the family, the federal government should pursue policies that would "cement the family in its rightful position as the keystone of our civilization." Presumably, federally supported day care would represent official acknowledgement that a woman's place need not be in the home, that children need not be reared solely in their own homes by their own parents, and that the state has an interest in making these changes accessible to all those who want or need them.

It was one thing to rhetorically celebrate parental authority by insisting that all protestors really needed was a trip to the woodshed, to extol motherhood by making it harder for mothers to find surrogates so they might work to help support their children, and to call for policies that would buttress the traditional conception of gender and family relations. It was quite another to actually do anything to achieve these ends. Nixon pandered to conservatives alarmed by what they perceived to be disintegrating traditions, legitimated their conception of how government ought to behave toward families, and delivered very little. In fact, there was little Nixon could have done to reverse the changes that so disturbed traditionalists—indeed, change accelerated during the Nixon years. Employment of women (and especially of wives and mothers) surged as more and more women sought autonomy as well as income to bolster precarious household budgets. Divorce steadily rose and legal barriers to divorce were lowered.[12] As already noted, the ERA initiative passed Congress at the start of Nixon's second term, and the Court, with two Nixon appointees, including Chief Justice Burger, declared a woman's access to abortion constitutionally protected. Everywhere, the feminist agenda seemed ascendent—in the media, the schools, in mainline churches, and in politics. Nixon spoke to, but ultimately not for, the forces of cultural reaction. His denouement—amidst scandal, deceit, and publicly aired blasphemy—made clear to conservatives that they needed one of their own to carry the torch of preservation.

While central casting groomed Ronald Reagan for the task, socioreligious conservatives and fiscal conservatives continued the courtship begun under Nixon's aegis. Together they billed and cooed about the evils of big government. Government was the problem—it interfered with the private sector and in doing so upset the natural harmonies and self-correcting capacities of economic and social life. Government was forcing the businessman to defy the laws of the marketplace. The result was inefficiency, lowered productivity, and erosion of the work ethic. At the same time, government was encouraging people to turn their backs on religion and family life by promoting birth control, abortion, and divorce while protecting homosexuals, pornographers, and those who were determined to belittle the role of religion.

A powerful movement was in the making, as heavily financed

as any in our nation's history. Throughout the 1970s, think tanks were lavishly funded by wealthy conservatives. The result has been a remarkable celebration of the virtues of free enterprise and a broad attack on government "interference" in the economy. A return to basics will reverse what has been, we are told, a steady slide toward socialism and immorality at home and decline of U.S. influence abroad. Virtually every aspect of the institutionalized partnership between industry and government was seen as contributing to our decline: regulation was strangling innovation and lowering profitability; social programs were rewarding the least energetic and imaginative; and the taxes to support these programs were demoralizing the productive and energetic among us. The conclusion invariably reached was straightforward: reduce the role of government and the people will respond with a burst of innovation and energy to propel us back into the uncontested leadership role we had at the end of World War II.

Evangelical religion took the message to the nation in a less academic vernacular: people had allowed themselves to become too wrapped up in pleasures of the moment, thus losing sight of the larger purposes that should guide life. As a result, peoples' capacities to shape and give meaning to their lives had diminished. When faced with adversity, people lacked the inner resources to fend for themselves. They looked not to God for strength but to government for a handout. The result was a nation at risk of losing its source of strength: a self-reliant, God-fearing people capable of shouldering responsibility and making sacrifices when they were required.

The programmatic link between these two strands of conservatism turned on two themes. One was the old standby, anti-communism and national defense. But the other was a new meeting ground—the family. Cultural conservatives had put the family at the center of concerns from the beginning. But now policy-oriented, political, and economic conservatives (who ordinarily left family and morality to their wives and preachers) realized that the family theme was crucial to their efforts to dismantle public and private welfare policies and benefits. They saw welfare choking initiative and saddling business with the costs of health, unemployment, and retirement insurance. Welfare, it was argued, relieved men of the responsibility to provide for their families. Moreover, this subtle erosion of male initiative contributed to the desire of women for more power, setting up a cycle of reaction and response that was eating away at the motivational substructure—that is, the work ethic—at the same time that it was tearing apart the family. And as the family weakens the need for welfare grows. Bolstering the nation's families, then, would directly translate into reduced demands on government. If families could be strengthened, if the old sense of familial mutual aid could be resurrected, balance could be restored between public and private life and between the public sector and the private sector. The steady increase in what people felt entitled to expect from government could be halted. Once halted, the process could be reversed and welfare programs could be phased out or at least drastically reduced.[13]

Interestingly, this confluence of concern over rising welfare dependency and family instability was first signaled not by a conservative but by a liberal—Daniel Patrick Moynihan. As an Assistant Secretary of Labor in the Johnson administration, he authored an extremely controversial (and misunderstood) report on the black family.[14] In what quickly came to be known as the Moynihan Report, he noted with alarm the rapid rise of black female-headed households and the equally dismaying increase in births among unmarried black women, particularly teenagers. These trends, Moynihan warned, were producing an expanding stratum of blacks who would have no choice but become chronically dependent upon welfare. Marginalized, unemployed men, pregnant teenagers, and poorly educated, unemployable single mothers would transmit a "tangled web of pathology" to successive generations, creating a permanent, demoralized underclass.

Critics were quick to see the victim-blaming possibilities in Moynihan's report, though it is clear that this was not his intent. His policy recommendations centered on giving black men the training, skills, and incentives to work so that they could become responsible heads of household. Needless to say, Moynihan's recommendations went unheeded, in effect lost in the vortex of eroding white support for welfare programs that appeared to go only to blacks and rising black consciousness that rejected all negative characterizations, even if well intended, of the black community. In such a context, it was a short step to argue, as Gilder did, that welfare is the problem because it undermines masculine dignity and, hence, initiative.[15]

Enchanting the Family

Nixon spoke of the need to strengthen the nation's families, but his administration came forward with no proposals to this end. It did not take long, however, before conservatives began to make clear what they had in mind. In 1979, after filing several preliminary pieces of legislation that had died in committee, Senator Paul Laxalt, close friend of soon-to-be-president Ronald Reagan, introduced the omnibus Family Protection Act before the U.S. Senate. The bill began:

> The purpose of this act is to preserve the integrity of the American family, to foster and protect the viability of American family life by emphasizing family responsibilities in education, tax assistance, religion, and other areas related to the family, and to promote the virtues of the family.

Among the provisions of Laxalt's bill were

1. a prohibition of federal funding for instructional programs that seek to "inculcate values or modes of behavior which contradict the demonstrated values of the community;"
2. a prohibition of federal funding to any program that supports educational materials or studies that would tend to denigrate, diminish or deny the role differences between the sexes as it has been historically understood in the United States;
3. restriction of funding to any group, foundation, commission, corporation or association or other entity that presents homosexuality, male or female, as an acceptable alternative lifestyle;
4. a prohibition of federally funded programs that provide contraception or abortion counseling or services to unmarried minors without notifying their parents; and
5. forbidding lawyers funded by the Legal Services Corporation (a federally funded agency) from litigating any cases involving abortion, divorce, or homosexual rights.

Aside from trying to write into law the conventional husband-the-breadwinner and wife-the-homemaker nuclear family, an effort that no doubt doomed the bill, Laxalt and his conservative colleagues meant this legislation as an accompaniment to their persistent efforts to roll back welfare benefits and coverage and their equally vigorous efforts to weaken unions in collective bargaining. In order for either of these efforts to succeed, families had to be *made* to function in the ways they once did. And this meant that families would have to be forced into a single mold: husbands working, wives at home caring for children, and kinfolk assisting one another. If family-based networks of mutual aid could be resurrected, there would be less need for welfare, fringe benefits, day care, and the whole panoply of programs that, taken together, make the relatively isolated and fragile nuclear family in all its contemporary variants possible.

Of course the Family Protection Act never passed, though some states took up some of its provisions, most notably the attempt to require teenagers to get parental permission before being granted an abortion. But even though it failed as legislation, Laxalt and his fellow conservatives were clearly establishing a social agenda that broadly shaped the debate over domestic policy throughout the Reagan-Bush era. Unwittingly, Reagan's predecessor in office, Jimmy Carter, lent a bipartisan credibility to at least the family component of the emergent conservative agenda.

Carter's views on the family were quite unambiguous from the start and were also grounded in evangelical assumptions about the proper relationships between men and women and parents and children. Though Carter was far more charitable than his more zealous and politically conservative evangelical brethren, he made it plain that "good old-fashioned family life" was what he respected. There might be lust in his heart from time to time, but fidelity was the guidepost for this president. He also wistfully urged his staff to work less so that they might have more time to spend with their wives and children, thus helping to preserve those precious relationships.[16] But here, in microcosm, was the larger dilemma that the conservative agenda faced: the requirements of family stability and of an enveloping familism clearly collide with the requirements of the job. Moreover, the so-called pro-family advocates had no account of how wives could stay at home raising children when their husbands' incomes were insufficient to meet the steadily expanding needs upon which the economy depends. Carter, like Nixon before him, could only offer up ritual nostalgic evocations of family life because he was unwilling to initiate a restructuring of the society that would oblige all other institutions to accommodate to family life. Carter's tolerant pro-family stance was empty piety, harmless but for the fact that it helped to strengthen the forces on the right who were determined to put teeth into their pieties, not by making political and economic institutions more congenial to settled family life but rather by making a certain kind of family mandatory.

With the election in 1980 of Ronald Reagan, the fusion of old and new right was confirmed, and an electoral base for a crusade to return America to its beleaguered traditions was in the making. Praise for the family was raised to new levels. It was as if the new president had invited us all to Disney's "enchanted kingdom," walked us down Main Street, and invited us to rediscover the joys of being at home in a "typical family." As the Moral Majority railed against homosexuality, premarital sex, equality for women, and divorce, the Reagan administration began its assault on the welfare state. At the same time, in order to combat the soaring inflation that Carter had been unable to control given the political constraints he worked under, Reagan plunged the nation into its worst economic nosedive since the 1930s. Unemployment benefits were cut, even as unemployment soared to 12 percent and more. Food stamps, hot school lunches, job training, low-income housing subsidies, aid to the disabled, these and more were cut. And how did the nation's families respond?

One response was almost immediately apparent: household composition changed. The steady growth of single-person households came to an abrupt end, principally because many young adults ceased being able to support themselves in the face of rapidly rising rents and even more rapidly rising unemployment rates. Many who had set up housekeeping on their own were obliged to return to their parents' home; others found friends or associates with whom they could share living quarters, or they simply put off leaving home. In any event, the Census Bureau reported that the average size of the nation's households declined more slowly in the early 1980s, principally because the rate of increase in single-person households slowed down significantly. There were fewer single-generation households, more households in which adult children resided with parents, and a slight increase in the number of households housing non-nuclear family members. In other words families, as they have done for millennia, began to reabsorb those members who could not sustain independence and autonomy in the face of straitened circumstances.

No doubt many—conceivably even most—families accepted this gracefully, buoyed by assurances that the interruption of normal expectations would be but temporary. But lest we stand too quickly to applaud the resilience and warmth of the family, we need to note other statistics as well:

> *Item.* The incidence of intrafamilial violence rose through the 1980s. In fact, studies made of the rates of child abuse and wife beating show a direct positive correlation to rising unemployment rates and other economic stresses on family life. Increases in unemployment are also directly correlated to elevated suicide and homicide rates, as well as increased admissions to mental hospitals and to state prisons.[17] Though we know of no thorough empirical studies of the effects of adult children returning to their parent's home, or of the consequences of elderly parents (or other relatives) being accommodated in a household, the anecdotal evidence that has appeared in newspapers and magazines over the past several years gives a very sobering side to "familial resilience."[18] Adult children bridle at the sudden resumption of dependence. Parents who have become accustomed (and many report being astonished at how quickly they did so) to having more privacy and freedom in the absence of their children, also report tension and resentment at the result of the return.[19]
>
> *Item.* The incidence of teenaged runaways has also continued to rise. This is due, at least in part, to greater tensions in households as they attempt to respond to the constrictions on autonomy that have come as a result of the combination of economic and social policies of the Reagan administration. Experts estimate that in New York City alone there are thousands of teen-

agers living in the abandoned buildings, "crashing" with acquaintances, and making a living by prostitution, drug dealing,
robbery, and the like.[20]

Item. The incidence of homelessness continues to rise. In spite of
the likelihood that many displaced persons and young families
find a temporary home with a parent or relative, more and
more of the recently unemployed, displaced elderly, and young
families with children—those who work with the homeless call
the "new homeless"—are living in their cars, seeking housing in
shelters, or making do, somehow, on the streets. Clearly, the ab-
sorptive capacities of many families is not great.[21]

Item. The divorce rate continues its long-term trend upward,
though the rate of increase has slowed during the 1980s. This
leveling of the rate of increase does not indicate increased per-
manence in marriage, however. Instead, the rate seems to be
responding to the fact that more and more men and women are
delaying marriage, just as increased numbers are cohabiting.
The proportions of never-married men and women in their late
twenties and early thirties has roughly doubled between 1970
and the present while the number of unmarried couples has
virtually tripled in this same period.[22]

Item. Along with a declining marriage rate and a high divorce rate,
the nation's birthrate continues its downward trend. Polls show
that while large numbers continue to plan to have children, the
desire for large families (four or more children) continues to
drop sharply. And as Americans have fewer babies, more babies
are being born out of wedlock. By 1988, 40 percent of all first
births to women aged 15 to 29 were conceived out of wedlock,
a 30 percent increase since the early 1970s.[23]

Item. Throughout the 1980s, American housewives have continued their exodus from the home in search of employment. The
percent of married women in the labor force increased from
50.1 to 56.5 between 1980 and 1988 (the last year for which data
are available). Even more striking has been the increase among
mothers with at least one child still under six years of age. Between 1980 and 1985, labor force participation of these women
increased from 45.1 percent to 53.4 percent. Indeed, 1987 was
the first year in which over half of all *new* mothers remained in
the labor force after the birth of their baby.[24]

Obviously, these developments do not mean that the conservatives' policies are unworkable. However, they do suggest that

shifting more responsibility for the care of the nation's young, old, and "unfortunate" away from the state and toward the family will not automatically restore the family to its presumed golden age. Such a shift will lead to a reduction of autonomy and will force the society to accept a good deal of misery and suffering. For the religious right, misery and suffering can be taken as signs of our sinfulness, tests that God puts before us to strengthen our faith in Him. In that event, misery is small price to pay for the promise of eternal bliss that awaits the believer. For the secular conservative, misery and suffering are but schools for pluck, determination, and the desire to improve. In short, the evidence that many families buckle under the pressures of adversity does not necessarily move conservatives to conclude that government ought to do something.

But there is another source of difficulty facing the conservative agenda that is not so easily avoided by the mystifications of divine judgment or the free market. As we have shown in Chapter 2, autonomy has been a central premise of consumer capitalism. Though capitalism did not invent autonomy, it came to depend heavily upon the aspiration for it, not only as advertising motif but, far more importantly, as the source of what appears to the individual as self-generated need, need that can best and most naturally be met through consumption. Without the desire for a home and a car of one's own, and all that this has come to entail, our economy would simply be in shambles. In fact, it would scarcely qualify as a modern economy at all. Anything that threatens to constrict or diminish the desire for autonomy threatens to undercut the emotional basis upon which much of our consumption rests.

As Gilder and others have argued, close-knit families have been important in the process of capital accumulation, though not for the reasons Gilder assigns. However, these same close-knit families are quite ill-suited to ever expanding levels of personal consumption. Close-knit families depend for their solidarity upon comparatively low levels of individuation and a willingness to forego individual gratifications in order that others within the family circle can be accommodated. In the aggregate, this translates into a lowered readiness to seek satisfaction of needs in the marketplace. Moreover, the conservative's desire to reaffirm the traditional prescriptions that keep the wife at home raising children and maintaining the household collides with the fact that a single income has long since ceased being adequate to meet the consumption needs of even a modest family budget. It is only when a husband's income tops $75,000 a year that we find a dramatic decline in the proportions of wives working. But no more than 1 percent of all husbands earn $75,000 or more. Without the income of wives, the vast majority of American households would have to sharply reduce their consumption. Reductions of almost any sort, much less of the magnitude that wives leaving the labor force would occasion, would send enormous shock waves through the economy and give rise to almost immediate calls for the government to take countermeasures. The plain fact is that the family ethos that conservatives cherish is inimical to the health of the economy that they are so committed to preserving. In this contest there seems little doubt but what the economy's requirements will prevail. For all the rhetoric of upholding family values, conservatives in power will be obliged to pursue economic policies whose effects will be devastating to families attempting to embody traditional familism. Alternatively, if by some miracle more and more families are able to model themselves on the family of conservative imagination, it is almost certainly going to be the case that consumer demand will decline.

It is no accident, nor is it mere oversight, that conservatives today have largely dropped admonitions to thrift from their list of prescriptions for what ails us. Quite aside from the profligacy of the Reagan administration and its utterly cavalier disregard of deficits, under conservative auspices the Federal Reserve has encouraged sharp increases in consumer credit, without which recovery from the 1982–83 recession would have been deeply problematic. Once again, we see that old nostrums and nostalgia, however much they may have inspired affection for a president, do not serve as reliable guides to the real policy options and consequences that await us. Conservatives are correct to see a connection between the functioning of the economy, the family, and the state, but they have the connections all wrong. Their policies will do little else but lead us back to the experiences that gave rise to demands for state supports for family life decades ago. Try as they might, it is unlikely that Americans in appreciable numbers will fall for the enchantment of the family that the Right is attempting. The desire for autonomy has been nurtured too long, and in too many ways, for it to be more than sporadically and temporarily squelched.

Conclusion

As compelling as the motifs of traditional familism may still be, the family forms that Americans now prefer are quite thoroughly predicated upon programs and policies that are anathema to the New Right. Though the Right has had electoral success playing upon our nostalgic attachment to the idea of the self-contained family, they have not been able to erode broad popular support for programs that sustain our diverse bids for autonomy. The clearest expression of this is the unassailability of Social Security, long a favorite target of the Right. Since his days as a spokesman for General Electric, Reagan has been on record favoring the abolition of Social Security. As president, however, Reagan was unable to halt even cost-of-living increases, much less end the program. This is so not simply because the elderly now form a significant electoral bloc but, more importantly, because Americans of all ages support the system in overwhelming numbers.[25]

Virtually every other welfare measure also continues to enjoy majority support, in spite of the steady barrage of anti-welfare publicity from the White House. Unemployment compensation, food stamps, school lunch subsidies, low-income housing subsidies, prenatal nutrition and care—all these and more were supported by majorities that ranged from a narrow 51 percent to decisive margins in excess of 80 percent, as reported by public opinion polls taken during the Reagan years. Even support for a constitutional prohibition on abortion has repeatedly fallen short of majority support among the nation's voters.[26] However much of a rightward shift there may have been in the last decade, the shift has not substantially eroded popular support for those policies and programs that have made it possible for more and more Americans to pursue life plans significantly unconstrained by the needs of kinfolk.[27]

The development of what, in the last chapter, we called the "minimal family" has been rapid. Conceivably, it has been the rapidity of this change as much as the change itself that has fueled resistance. Certainly, the abstract ideas behind the minimal family are not new. What is new is that the minimal family has become an explicit normative model. Arising first in the upper middle class—the post-war, college educated men and women whose living standards rose rapidly from 1950 onward—the minimal family was initially shaped by the heavy workplace demands that husbands encountered as the condition of their upward trek through corporate hierarchies and professional ladders of advancement. Upper-middle-class husbands played a peripheral role in their families. This, in turn, set in motion the forces that began to propel women out of the home, if not initially to seek autonomy, certainly discovering its attractions once at work. In turn, this led to more emphasis on developing children's capacities for autonomous action.

The norm of autonomy is no longer confined to the upper middle class. Indeed, it has come to broadly shape public as well as private life. Behind the demand for equality that has been raised now by virtually every imaginable group that departs from the abstracted norm of the "average American" is the implicit assumption that equality means granting the presumption of capacity for autonomous action in one's own behalf. Whether a stigmatized racial minority, the physically disabled, or the mentally retarded—all are entitled to autonomy. The barriers, be they physical or cultural, that have kept individuals dependent in the past have been steadily assailed over the last two decades.

The unfurling of the classic liberal principle of individualism—its extension to women, children, the old, and the disabled—has been both a product of and the condition for the further spread of the minimal family. Each incremental reduction in the degree to which the family enfolds and protects its members has enhanced the scope for individual action at the same time that it has occasioned a greater reliance on non-familial networks of support. This support is based on one's claims as citizen or employee or member of an objectively constituted group (e.g., veterans); it is not based on kinship. The steady accumulation of these claims has produced a web of impersonal dependencies that, in the aggregate, form the social structural basis for the autonomy we savor. Though it has gone largely unacknowledged in these terms, each concrete public program or policy that is an element of this structure has its own considerable constituency made up of people who recognize that their prospects for dignity as autonomous actors in society are bound up with the fate of such programs. But as long as these impersonal dependencies go unacknowledged in these terms, it is also possible for people to sustain the illusory notion that they are free agents whose only responsibility is to their own experience and growth. The result is that while each specific program or policy is popularly supported, a generalized conception of welfare is not.

With the expansion of the welfare state after World War II, the attractions of autonomy became widely shared even as recognition of the structural bases for this increased autonomy remained obscure. Since expression of autonomy was largely mediated by consumption—the "deal" struck with an otherwise conservative business class—increased emphasis was placed on income and immediately available lines of credit as the vehicles for autonomy. With growing aspirations for autonomy, pressures on family budgets are relentless, helping to create resentment of taxes and welfare, even as more and more Americans increase their reliance on the very programs the welfare state embodies.

Although the failures of liberals after 1964 were linked to sacrificing domestic reform in order to finance the Vietnam War, in fact liberals had begun to flinch as the implications of their rhetorical commitments to equality and social justice were seized upon by strata not yet blessed with much autonomy. As momentous as the gains of the civil rights movement were, they only whetted black people's appetites for substantive as well as procedural equality. Those whose patient forbearance had helped bear aloft the aspirations of a large white male middle class— women, the young, gays, the handicapped—also began to press their claims for equal access to autonomy. Even to begin to accommodate, much less encourage, this onslaught against the vestiges of repressive self-denial obviously requires far more than rhetorical commitment to equality. As important, to begin to meet appetites whetted by the marketplace and the prospects of autonomy requires the systematic and self-conscious use of the state as social planner. In other words, the playing out of the liberal celebration of the self requires democratization of politics, the economy, and the culture.[28] This was—and remains—more democracy than any plausible coalition of extant forces now has the political muscle to put in place.

The result has been, in a sense, the worst of two worlds. On the one hand, we encounter a culture that celebrates the individual and rewards achievement through highly privatized and alienating consumption.[29] On the other hand, we have created a welfare state that demoralizes those who must depend wholly upon it, precisely because the autonomy it underwrites for most is denied them. In effect, the reluctance to face squarely the relationship between autonomy and dependence has distorted both and, in the bargain, has increased pressures on the family. For the upper middle and middle classes, these pressures have accelerated movement toward minimalist forms of family. At the same time, the lower classes are obliged to find succor in kin networks that reduce even further an individual's chances for autonomy. The result is volatility and instability from top to bottom.

As we have already seen, this volatility has provided fertile soil for right-wing appeals for a nostalgic, "enchanted" family. It has also been fertile soil for a proliferation of expressions of "enchanted" selfhood. The whole array of awareness, therapy, and self-enhancement movements that have waxed and waned over the course of the past two decades are the counterpoint of the right's celebration of family virtue. But neither version of enchantment can possibly suffice: each denies essential and inescapable features of social life. Conservatives want the family buttressed so that the accumulation process might proceed unfettered by entitlements pressed upon the state or upon employers. They fail to see how the accumulation process has depended upon the demise of the very forms of family life they venerate. They have no answer to the question "Who will buy?" once the accumulation cycle has run its course. Liberals want more scope for individual autonomy but have been unable or unwilling to generate sufficient political will to acknowledge that this can come about only if we accept responsibility for new, more generalized forms of dependency. And so we struggle with an increasingly irrelevant tradition whose defenders are inspired either by a blind or cynical faith and a poorly charted future whose midwives are, generously, timid and reticent.

6

✦

The Familial
Public

WE HAVE COME A LONG WAY from our discussion of the Massachusetts controversy over a homosexual couple's desire to be foster parents. We have tried to place this controversy in the broadest possible context, taking into consideration not just contemporary attitudes about what is appropriate for family life but also the connections between the family and other social and political controversies. Our analysis has led us to examine two especially important and complex historical transformations. One involves the ways in which we meet material needs and dependencies. Impersonal private markets and public agencies now provide many of the goods and services that once were the province of families and small, more or less cohesive communities of people who were quite familiar with one another. The other shift involves the diminution of parental authority, a change that has been accompanied by a dramatic increase in the significance of the emotional bond between parents and children.

Taken together, these changes have produced a tremendous elaboration of the possibilities for individualism and autonomy. They have also given rise to a concomitant wariness of dependencies and emotional entanglements. Combined with the varied cultural traditions and economic opportunities that have characterized our society over time, these changes have resulted in a variety of family forms ranging from the elaborately inter-dependent networks of largely female-headed households of poor blacks to the highly independent, affluent households of dual-career couples. All told, these changes are leading to a new family norm—the minimal family. The conventional family, consisting of a working father and a home-based mother, is no longer the ideal toward which most people aspire. Instead, most of us seek arrangements that emphasize the autonomy of indi-vidual family members as well as the nuclear family's indepen-dence from extended kin. This has meant that our families have grown steadily smaller and that the claims made in the name of family solidarity are reduced, often to a bare minimum.

This emphasis on personal independence has been accompa-nied by a considerable degree of family instability, which has raised a host of questions about social welfare. With families un-able or unwilling to be fully responsible for matters such as child care, care for the elderly, and emotional support of family mem-bers, where does the responsibility rest? Americans are divided about the proper locus of familism. Moreover, since many see the family as a pivotal social institution, controversy over related issues such as sexuality, child discipline, men's and women's roles, abortion, and divorce have become intertwined with broader disagreements over public policy. Because both con-servatives and liberals place special importance on the family, each fears that the realization of the other's vision of the ideal form of family life would undermine individualism, subvert po-litical freedom and, ultimately, cause social decline. That is why even more is at stake than disparate notions about the ideal form of family life. There is no agreement about the kinds of people we ought to be, and more importantly, this absence of consensus occurs within a climate of resurgent intolerance for diversity. Family forms that vary from those we value are re-sponded to as if their mere existence constituted a frontal as-sault on our most deeply held values.

The roots of our present impasse run deep. Even in colonial times, when the family was unambiguously at the center of the community and its governance, Americans were divided about what kind of people to be, what kind of individuality to sanction. As we have already seen, there is a basic tension between the thrift and self-denial that form the psychic basis of the incentive structures of modern industrialism and the possibilities for unparalleled self-gratification and indulgence this same industrialism makes possible. From the beginnings of European settlement there has been a conflict between self-restraint and self-expression. Though every epoch has had its own version of this conflict, its basic form has changed little since the guardians of self-control, led by Miles Standish of Plymouth Colony, arrested and deported Thomas Morton, a fur trader. Morton's fondness for whiskey and feasting and his embrace of native Americans' attitudes toward work offended the sensibilities of Standish and his cohorts.[1] When the forces of order tore down the maypole around which Morton and his associates had cavorted with the Indians, they were, in effect, striking a blow for the god of accumulation. Little did they know that, ultimately, this god would test the faithful by making escalating consumption and self-indulgence a necessity of the social system.

The conflict between self-restraint and self-expression sustains two quite distinct and antagonistic conceptions of individualism in our culture. On the one hand there is the individualism that Standish was defending when he arrested Morton, what we might call "repressive individualism." On the other hand there is the individualism Morton personified: "expressive individualism."[2] Not only are both variants of individualism deeply rooted in American cultural traditions, but each is nourished by contradictory impulses of the economy and defended by opposing political groupings.[3] Repressive individualism is especially resonant with the accumulation phase of capitalism. It is sustained today by conservatives who see in the prospect of a steady expansion of profits both national preeminence and domestic prosperity and harmony. Expressive individualism, by contrast, has been nourished by those worried that capital accumulation will come to naught if markets do not steadily grow. If markets are to expand, people have to be encouraged to amplify their appetites for experience, novelty, and personal growth.

At times this has played itself out as a conflict between savings and consumption. Of course, each is necessary, and there has to be some balance between the two. But balance is hard to sustain because the conflict is not just about proper mathematical proportions of savings and consumption. A preference for either savings or consumption symbolizes dramatically different value choices about style of living, about work and play, about self-denial and self-expression. In attempting to balance savings and consumption, each individual and individual family struggles as well with the deeper meaning of these choices, with the kinds of selves saving and consuming allow them to be.[4] Standard of living is not the point: the high-living bon vivant has more in common, in these terms, with an unemployed youth interested only in immediate thrills than with a grey flanneled account executive who is more nearly his social equal.

There is more to the conflict between the two individualisms than differences in orientation toward savings and consumption. Repressive individualism stresses restraint imposed by the injunction that we each take responsibility for our own moral life and standing in the community. Each person stands alone in striving to attain grace and respect. This view of the individual sees the person as the bearer of virtue, virtue that is acted out in the faithful meeting of responsibilities and obligations. From this orientation, social order emerges from each individual acting in ways that sustain and affirm the community's norms and values. Sumptuary delights are anathema because they threaten withdrawal into self-absorption. Ostentation is bad not only because it signals unbecoming pride in self but because it can lead others to envy and greed. In this conception of individualism, family, church, and community are indispensable institutions through which one's individuality is expressed and from which the self draws strength and purpose.

Though this form of individualism roots the person in groups, it is decidedly anti-collectivist. For example, it is believed that the community ought not to interfere in people's lives in any way that reduces the incentives to meet their responsibilities. One of the purest examples of this attitude can be drawn from a controversy between Congress and the Office of Education in the mid-eighties. Several Reagan appointees had announced their intentions to end federal guidelines and support for efforts to reduce the barriers handicapped persons encounter as they endeavor to lead full and active lives. Stipulations that public buildings be made accessible to persons in wheelchairs were to be withdrawn. Similarly, regulations mandating the mainstreaming of handicapped children in the nation's schools were to be ended. When asked by an irate and incredulous senator (Lowell Weicker, R., Conn.) for the rationale for this rollback the answer was straightforward: the federal government ought not interfere in people's lives. Each of us has been dealt a hand of cards, so to speak, to do with what we might. To tamper with God's will by trying to minimize the consequences of His will was unfair—not to the rest of us so much as to the handicapped themselves who, if life were made too easy, would not have the incentive to become as strong, self-reliant, and pious as they might.[5]

Adversity, for the repressive individualist, is the occasion for steeling the self, for testing mettle, for showing character. "Collectivists," from this vantage point, wish to deny the sanctity of the individual by making people dependent upon groups rather than making groups dependent upon individuals. And so, just as Andrew Carnegie could commend poverty to one and all (it was, he insisted, the finest school for initiative and character), being in a wheelchair can be seized upon as an opportunity to deepen one's faith and strengthen one's character. Public charity, even when well-intentioned, is a disservice; it makes matters worse.[6]

Charles Murray, a critic of most of the welfare programs of the last thirty years, has brought Carnegie's thesis up to date. In his recent book *Losing Ground*, he purports to show how virtually all of the Great Society elaborations of the New Deal have succeeded only in miring the poor more deeply in poverty. Things will improve, he argues, only when we stop interfering with the processes by which individuals sort themselves out. In doing so, people will come to regard themselves and their responsibilities with pride and a determination to succeed.[7] Of course Murray's analysis has been devastatingly criticized. He has misread or systematically ignored data that, if properly taken into account, show just the opposite of what he contends. The programs he criticizes for making matters worse have, in fact, improved the lot of the poor while reducing their numbers.[8] Moreover, the most comprehensive and systematic analyses do not show that receiving welfare produces family instability (expressed either in divorce or in terms of out-of-wedlock births).[9] The overwhelming majority of welfare recipients relies on welfare for a brief time, to get through short-term adversity. But as we have seen, when adversity stretches out, as it does endemically for many blacks, welfare dependency can become demoralizing, especially when welfare combines with racism and persistently foreclosed options.[10] Cutting welfare supports does not demonstrably reduce despair; nor does it notably invigorate erstwhile recipients. In fact, research has repeatedly shown that programs that assist people in completing their education, in acquiring vocational skills, and in linking them to meaningful jobs have had positive effects.[11]

At base, repressive individualists are not interested in such results. Their interest lies in preserving tradition and hierarchy, respect for authority, and the conviction that familism is appropriate only in families. Improving life and reducing despair by welfare measures is opposed because doing so upsets hierarchy, promotes equality, and moves responsibility for one's well-being from the individual and his or her family to the broader society. Repressive individualists see individualized responsibility as the cornerstone of free enterprise and a free society. The family, in this view, is the only institution that can develop the necessary sense of individual responsibility. They fear that by generalizing responsibility beyond the family, ambition and entrepreneurial zeal will be diminished, as will the appetite for liberty. Reagan advisor Gary L. Bauer writes:

> Families save; and even more importantly they teach children the values upon which savings are built—delaying gratification now for some future goal. In fact, "the family is the seedbed of economic skills, money habits, attitudes toward work, and the arts of financial independence."[12]

Bauer continues:

> [O]nly in a society that allows individual freedom can family members exercise the initiative and responsibility that makes for strong family life.

The breakdown of the American family in recent years merely confirms the interdependence of strong families and secure liberties. Irresponsibility, self-seeking, and contempt of authority erode not only the family but respect for law and civility as well. *Children who do not learn to live out commitments to others in a family do not learn to live within a larger society either. If we wish to see a renewal of liberty, we must work for a renaissance of the family* (14, emphasis in original).

There is no mistaking his message: self-control, deferred gratification, and the honoring of family responsibilities produce prosperity and sustain liberty. Familism must be restricted to families; they are the basis of American success. In none of these deeply problematic assertions is there any recognition of the paradoxical relation between self-restraint and economic growth. While accumulation and economic growth historically have depended upon initial self-restraint, they cannot be sustained without stimulating our appetites to consume. And once the desire to consume has been tickled, the psychic and familial bases of self-restraint begin to erode. The very successes claimed for repressive individualism give rise to expressivity.

Expressive individualism has its own paradoxical qualities. Expressive individualism is distinct from its repressive cousin in that it encourages individuals to have a robust sense of entitlement and a dramatically reduced inclination to defer gratification of needs. "You *deserve* a break *today*" (emphasis added), a McDonald's advertising slogan, captures a recurring theme in contemporary marketing that derives its persuasiveness precisely from the conjunction of feeling deserving and needing immediate confirmation of that fact.

In a sense, expressive individualism is the Protestant ethic stripped of any trace of asceticism and otherworldliness. Rewards are to be savored here and now. In this context, work ceases to be an end in itself. Instead, it becomes a means to an end—if not *the* good life, at least *a* good life. If work cannot deliver this it is not worth doing. Expressive individualism is not directly at odds with the work ethic, but it does have the consequence of devaluing much work in our society, especially work that is low paying, unconnected to ladders of advancement, or otherwise unaccommodated to the needs of an expressive self.[13]

Thus, expressive individualism encourages a sense of entitlement while relaxing the connection between hard work and reward. If repressive individualism can be understood as glorifying the rigors of hard work, expressive individualism embodies the spirit of self-indulgence.

Though expressive individualism has been permeated with the themes and motifs of consumerism and plays itself out on a field that has been contrived by merchandisers, the "good life" is not defined simply as getting and spending. Expressivity also reaches into the fabric of relationships. The expressive self is one eager for challenge, for change, for new experience. Played out in the middle class, expressivity translates into competitiveness, desire for achievement, and need for recognition: in short, upward mobility. Played out in the lower class, it becomes "action seeking": the constant, restless quest for stimulation and excitement.[14] Needless to say, action seekers are anything but upwardly mobile. But like those who are, they are highly self-oriented. For both action seekers and the upwardly mobile, relationships are often seen as instrumental rather than as ends in themselves. So long as a relationship is personally satisfying, so long as it fits in with one's own needs and plans, it will be maintained. When it ceases to be rewarding it is ended. One's principal obligations are to one's self. Wider networks of obligation—kinship, friendship, collegiality—may be acknowledged, and failure to meet obligations may be a source of regret and guilt, but even these can be rationalized away.[15] The key is that expressivity, regardless of the context in which it is acted out, accentuates individual needs and diminishes the strength and durability of ties and obligations to others.

Of course intense, single-minded commitment to upward mobility is no more typical of the middle and upper middle classes than hell-raising and action seeking are among the poor and destitute. There are ways of seeking stimulation and challenge that lie between the extremes of upward striving and hard living. Indeed, the steady expansion of leisure time has been legitimated, at least in part, by seeing leisure as the occasion for meeting a wide range of needs for expressivity and self-development. In fact, concern has grown that too many people have begun to invest more ego in their pastimes, their avocations, than in their vocations.[16] In any event, what is clear is that for significant numbers of Americans, from all social strata, the need for self-exploration and self-development is deeply felt. People are increasingly unlikely to acquiesce in arrangements that threaten to impede the satisfaction of this need.

Expressive individualism has been fed by the blandishments of merchandisers and advertisers, augmented by changes in patterns of family interaction, and legitimated by broad acceptance. Over time it has become the dominant, though obviously not uncontested, form of individualism in our society. Expressive individualism produces, in the extreme, the perfect alternative to the idealized family of the repressive individualist's imagination: the idealized self. Whether in Emerson's essays and lectures, Whitman's verse, or in current celebrations of psychological independence and personal growth, the message is the same: BE TRUE TO YOURSELF.

Expressive individualism subordinates relationships (and the dependencies and obligations that are the stuff of relationships) to the unfolding needs of the self. In the extreme, it is antagonistic to familism, particularly as it is manifested in conventional versions of family life. Expressive individualism is more closely suited to the minimal family with its limited obligations and enlarged scope for self-actualization. While efforts to make private life a domain of self-fulfillment have been accompanied by the ambivalence and anguish associated with divorce and reluctance to marry and/or have children, moves in this direction have nevertheless been broad based. Indeed, many old evils get reframed as positive contributions to maturity and personal growth—divorce becomes a "developmental stage," infidelity is transformed into "open marriage," children left unattended are being encouraged to be "autonomous." Even the U.S. Army uses the theme of expressivity to recruit young men and women: "Be all that you can be."

Expressivity reached its zenith in the late 1960s and early 1970s. In the blush of excited experimentation and exhortations to "do your own thing," few paid attention to the casualties, the people who could not sustain life on the edge of experimentation and change. Alongside the celebrations of freedom, altered states of consciousness, and the return to nature, there were disturbing stories of emptiness, exploitation, and shattered lives. The love-in atmosphere of the earliest days of the Haight Ashbury in San Francisco all too quickly gave way to predation as some took advantage of the naivete and vulnerability of the flower children. To compound matters, while some cooperative ventures flourished, the individualism of the so-called counterculture made it hard to sustain communal institutions that could offer protection against the predatory dangers inherent in laissez-faire expressiveness.[17]

There were other experiences that raised misgivings about expressive individualism. Many women found that it was easier to escape the trap of domesticity than it was to forge a new life predicated on greater autonomy. Autonomy did not eliminate the need for depending upon others, yet prevailing conceptions of autonomy made it difficult to acknowledge dependency needs. Affordable day care became a widely felt need, in spite of the fact that many mothers still believed that there was something wrong with them if they couldn't manage on their own.[18] The search for greater independence led, in other words, to the discovery of needs for support. In the women's movement, what began as consciousness raising was gradually transformed into support groups that functioned to sustain relational connections for women increasingly committed to autonomy.

The realization that autonomy and independence were difficult, if not impossible, to sustain on one's own led to something of a backlash. Indeed, some prominent feminists, most notably Betty Friedan, began to explicitly and sharply criticize those within the movement who insisted that women needed complete autonomy vis-a-vis men. The goal, Friedan insisted, was not to end women's familial commitments but rather to make those commitments more compatible with a woman's full engagement in career and public life.[19]

What the women's movement has been struggling with is nothing less than the central paradox of individualism itself: individuals cannot secure their desires solely by their own actions. Some, like Jean Baker Miller, recognize that

> autonomy carries the implication, and for some women therefore
> the threat, that one should be able to pay the price of giving up

affiliation in order to become a separate and self-directed individual. Women are quite validly seeking something more complete than autonomy as it is defined for men, a fuller not lesser ability to encompass relationships with others, simultaneous with the fullest development of oneself.[20]

Miller recognizes that autonomy, the central preoccupation of expressive individualism, is illusory. Individuals can be freed from one or another set of constraints, but not from mutual obligations in general. As importantly, she insists that mutual obligations need not be thought of only as constraints that restrict self-development.

While Miller may exaggerate the ease with which one can encompass relationships with others as well as pursue the fullest development of one's self, her vision of the autonomous person at least includes acknowledging connections to others. Autonomy, from this perspective, consists of choosing which mutual obligations will shape one's life or, alternatively, choosing the kinds of supports one wishes to rely upon. But expressive individualism makes obligations and restraint problematic. Unalloyed, it promulgates an idealized version of the self, the notion that individuals can discover solely within themselves the powers and resources necessary for fulfillment and actualization. As promoted by myriad gurus and self-proclaimed therapeutic or awareness experts, the self can be made to seem virtually enchanted, its celebration the path to both individual fulfillment and social reconstruction.[21] While it is easy to poke fun at the combination of hucksterism, credulity, and Panglossianism that surrounds such promotions of the self, the pathos cannot be ignored. Advice books that proclaim the advantages of "looking out for number one" or manuals that suggest "how to be your own best friend" are testimony to the competitiveness and loneliness inherent in expressive individualism.

At the extreme, expressive individualism dissolves the emotional basis upon which crucial aspects of social life rest, precisely because it disparages all forms of constraint. Consequently, expressive individualism has been accommodated to the rationality that was once confined to the marketplace. If self-development is the organizing principle of a life, then relationships to others become instrumental, subject to calculation and a "bottom line": Am I enhanced more by this relationship than by other possibilities? Seen in terms of marital relationships, this translates into what sociologist Bernard Farber has called "permanent availability."[22] Spouses, Farber argues, are coming to see themselves as permanently available for courtship. Stability in relationships connotes stagnation rather than maturity.

The result is a blurring of the distinction between public and private spheres, but on terms diametrically opposite to those that once prevailed. Increasingly, the private sphere is experienced as an extension of the public. All life, not just working life, becomes a series of transactions and negotiations between parties, each of whom brings to the relationship a bundle of interests to be jealously guarded lest he or she be taken advantage of.[23] Notions of affection, responsibility, and common fate get squeezed out: they are not relevant to instrumental concerns.

In the absence of any sustained attention to the issues of connectedness, exponents of expressive individualism can offer little defense to charges of self-indulgence, narcissism, and irresponsibility. Though elements of the left have joined in on the attack, conservatives have dominated the critique of expressive individualism.[24] For conservatives, expressive individualism must be opposed because it threatens the conventional family, thereby upsetting the delicate balance that sustains free enterprise and democracy. But so long as the alternative to expressive individualism's enchanted selfhood remains an equally enchanted family, our capacity to turn genuine and well-founded concern into coherent social action will be blocked. The terms of this discourse must be changed.

Whose Interests?

The late British economist Fred Hirsch, in his book *Social Limits to Growth*, argues that capitalism's success has entailed the steady erosion of the "moral legacy" on which capitalism has rested.[25] The manifold benefits that derived from freeing individuals and markets from the constraints of feudal restriction were compelling so long as the logic of the marketplace was leavened by the traditions of familism, traditions that gave substance to the impulses of sympathy and mutual aid. But over time this reservoir of good will has been depleted. As we have seen, networks of mutual aid get overwhelmed, and in the process people are rendered less and less capable of offering sustained, day-to-day resistance to the forces of the marketplace. Consequently, the market and the mentality it promulgates gradually permeate all realms of social life.

In effect, economic growth is achieved by rendering more and more of the repertoire of human activity into commodity forms, thereby creating more opportunities for profit. But this process goes forward at the expense of traditional forms of self-reliance and self-sufficiency. When the home ceases to be a place of production, when venerable skills are obliterated by the techniques of mass production, then people become almost entirely dependent upon markets over which they have no control. In this unfolding context, Hirsch argues, the layers of precapitalist sentiment are successively stripped away. The market encourages self-interest, driving out other bases of purposeful activity. Though Hirsch does not go beyond this, he might well have gone on to say that the family becomes the principal bearer of precapitalist morality. As Lasch has put it, the family becomes a "haven in a heartless world."

But the haven was more wishful thinking than reality, even in the nineteenth century. The idea of the family as a haven merely privatized and personalized the manifold social problems that accompanied the rise of the market and the industrial mode of production. It was a haven that was surrounded and beleaguered from the start. To exist, much less prosper, in society required that the family let the "enemy" into the very haven it was supposed to construct. Because parental skills were undermined, parent-child relations were transformed, making it necessary to relinquish more and more of the upbringing of children to the schools and to other adults more knowledgeable in the emergent ways of the world. Parents, rather than being buffers between the larger world and their children, became accomplices of teachers and childrearing experts. Over time the family ceased being a counterpoise to the market mentality. Instead, it became one of its promoters.

For many social critics, Christopher Lasch being the most widely known, this process has been an unmitigated disaster.[26] In ways reminiscent of Marcuse, Lasch depicts our society as one whose elites endeavor to create an irresistible system in which corrupt shallow ends masquerade as the will of the people. Under the guise of therapeutic concern we are manipulated into passivity. Even efforts at criticism or rebellion, in Lasch's view, have been turned against themselves, thereby contributing to the decadent stability of the overall system.

While aspects of Lasch's critique are telling, he is so focused on decline and co-optation that he loses sensitivity to areas of contradiction. Though hopeful that enough people will refuse to be hoodwinked and bought off, thus keeping alive the possibility of radical restructuring, the bases for such resistance and radical initiative are portrayed as fast disappearing. In particular, the family, once the buffer between the market and the self, is ceasing to be a source of resistance. Largely the result of the intrusions of professionals, parental authority has been decimated, thus depriving children of the psychological context within which they can test themselves and elaborate self-conceptions that are able to withstand the blandishments of the capitalist order. Lasch sees no points of resistance arising from within the expressive ethos of a consumption-oriented capitalism. Autonomy is, at best, only thinly disguised irresponsibility.

Hirsch sees a different possibility. By no means sanguine, he nonetheless holds out the possibility that as the social limits to growth are reached, people will begin to move in a more constructive (or reconstructive) direction, a direction he calls "reluctant collectivism." For Hirsch, precapitalist sentiment was essentially collectivist in the sense that it raised community—and familial—interests above the interests of the individual. The Enlightenment and the incorporation of notions of individual distinctiveness into the bourgeois ethos of enterprise dissolved that spirit of collectivism. As individualism flourished, self-interest was lionized and a mad rush for the good things in life was set in motion. But, Hirsch argues, it turns out that the good things in life are for the most part intrinsically scarce. Moreover, their capacity for satisfying us lies precisely in their exclusivity. Without the old restraints, there is no legitimate exclusionary principle to fall back on. The result is that more and more people strive to attain homes, education, stylish automobiles—to name only a few of the many trappings of success—and as they succeed, the satisfactions derived from success decline because they are surrounded by others who are equally "successful." Instead of a valued education, one encounters a labor market glutted with graduates. Instead of convenience, a car yields traffic jams; homes in tranquil, green countryside become sprawling suburban tracts with many of the problems and virtually none of the amenities of the city. While commercial interests may temporarily prosper on the basis of such steadily receding incentives, in the longer run such an order can only produce heightened disappointments, frustrations, and anger—as well as perceptibly declining living standards. If everyone tries, individually, to gain what they can, no one is likely to end up with what they individually need most.

It is this paradox—a restating of the ancient problem of the commons—that Hirsch thinks will ultimately force modern industrial capitalist societies to move in the direction of recapturing collectivism: some way of modulating individual appetites such that everyone is likely to get more of what they need. But it is hard to return to a condition of restraint once the prospect of the free pursuit of self-interest has been savored. After all, the community's best interests may not correspond directly to any one individual's best interests. Hirsch argues that we will come to a grudging recognition of the common interest because the consequences of not doing so are steadily becoming more evident and intolerable. As the traditional reservoir of good will and selflessness evaporates, the effects of an increasingly privatized pursuit of the good life undermine and distort the ends sought.[27]

Moreover, Hirsch argues, over time interest groups form, each one of which endeavors to maximize its interests at the expense of all others. The result is an economy and a polity that no longer function in the ways they were meant to. One gets neither free markets nor planning in the economy; and in the polity, voting loses its central role in the frenzy of lobbying, influence peddling, and special interest politics. Legitimacy ebbs and the system tends toward endemic crisis.[28]

Hirsch argues that cumulative personal dissatisfactions and deepening social crises will move people toward an acceptance of the need for some sort of central guidance, some combination of private and public initiatives that can embody the moral legitimacy on which an assertion of the common good can rest. The recent resurgence of the Right suggests that the move toward "reluctant collectivism" is currently more reluctant than collective. Hirsch is correct to see deliberate, democratic planning as necessary for the preservation of a liberal society, a society committed to enlarging the scope of individual rights, including the right to a minimally decent standard of living. But he underestimates the strength of sentimental attachments to the legacy that roots collectivism in families, not in public policy. The symbolism of precapitalist traditions remains potent and has demonstrably weakened the resolve of liberals (and many further to the left) and strengthened the determination of conservatives. Something in addition to structural necessity is needed to get us to acknowledge that the private pleasures we seek require concerted public action. Only a new vision of the connections between private and public life can provide a base on which to rest the structures of planning and public succor that high levels of personal autonomy require.

This new understanding may, as Bellah and his associates have argued, draw significantly on traditional morality and our ancient attachments to kin and village. But if this is to be something other than a renewed celebration of the enchanted family, it will have to involve a decisive break with the distinction between public and private, between kinsman and stranger, that permeates our tradition.[29] At the same time, this renewal will have to avoid the temptations of the enchanted self that are also woven closely into the fabric of our heritage. What will be needed, in other words, is a new consensus that reverses the steady siege that has been laid against familism by the advance of marketplace rationality. If we are to be able to be expressive, self-actualizing people, if we are to have families that encourage autonomy, then we shall have to insist that the institutions of work, commerce, and governance embody the values and traditions we associate with the family.

Our history has been a history of rationalizing familism, of rendering human activity into forms pegged to the convenience and needs of employers, managers, and merchants. We have reached the point where it is necessary to challenge the norms that have guided this history. What is needed is a "familization of the public."

Familizing the Public

We have been trapped in a dilemma largely of our own making. We have created only two choices: pretending either that the family is the only legitimate repository of humane impulse or that the autonomous self can be emotionally (and morally) self-sufficient. Neither alternative can be sustained because neither speaks to irrepressible features of psychological and social life. The enchanted self gives way too quickly to the predatory calculus of looking out for Number One. The enchanted family requires the subordination of the wife-mother which is as unacceptable psychologically, given the changes of the past century, as it is economically, given the majority of families now thoroughly conditioned to the wages of both husband and wife. Although these two enchantments are contradictory—and it is their apparent opposition that has made them seem as though they were genuine alternatives—they share an important convergence. Each is premised upon a sharp distinction between public and private realms: familism is located in the private realm of the family, and the public realm (the arenas of commerce, industry, and policy making) is characterized by impersonality, efficiency, and instrumental rationality.

Cast in slightly different terms, we are offered the choice of two arrangements. One arrangement features an employed husband supported *at home* by a wife. This, of course, is the normative model of the conventional family that has been with us at least since the industrial revolution. Though many, even most, families departed from this norm at least from time to time, it remained the normative standard until very recently. As we have seen, in the last two decades another arrangement, the dual-career family, has emerged to challenge the dominance of the conventional family. This arrangement extends the breadwinner role to the wife, thus exposing both husband and wife to the logic and demands of the world of work.

When the early theorists of liberal capitalism, most notably Mandeville and Adam Smith, celebrated *homo economus*, they were celebrating individuals released from myriad sentimental obligations that derived from a family-based social order. From their point of view, these obligations were only so many impediments to rational calculation, efficiency and, most crucially, economic growth. Freed to pursue self-interest, individuals would be possessed by boundless energy, ingenuity, and creativity. The market—with its "invisible hand"—magically transforms all this self-interested activity into the collective good by winnowing out the foolish, the dangerous, and the outmoded, thus maximizing the likelihood of rising productivity, expanding varieties of goods and services, and higher standards of living. What these theorists did not acknowledge, though, was that economic man was predicated upon *noneconomic woman*: a wife who forgoes the rigors of the marketplace in order to attend to the moral and emotional needs of men and children. Wives and mothers became the moral force, the bearers of familism, while men became the economic, even the mercenary, force.[30]

This arrangement is by no means stable. Even when women were not particularly interested in pressing claims to equality, the economic forces set in motion by industrialism and the spread of commercial culture undermined this arrangement and, with it, women's "place." By the mid-twentieth century, economic pressures on the family, as we saw in Chapter 2, combined with the psychosocial dynamics discussed in Chapter 3 to produce a dramatic shift in men's and women's ideas about gender, commitment, and family. Wives and mothers began leaving the home in droves in order to enhance family standards of living and to expand the sphere within which they could develop their own autonomy. Economic man was being joined by economic woman. When both husband and wife embrace an economic perspective, it becomes unclear who preserves the familial perspective.

The tensions and asymmetries inherent in the conventional family have produced efforts to achieve greater equality between spouses. Many of these tensions arise from the unequal distribution of opportunities for personal development. Wives were denied the possibility for expressive individualism. Wives, in effect, were the principal bearers of repressive individualism; they were the ones expected to set aside personal needs for the sake of the greater good. They were expected to be the keepers of familism, thereby linking familism and repressive individualism and yoking women's capacities for emotional expressiveness and interpersonal sensitivity to those features of family life that emphasize self-restraint and self-denial. Women, in the conventional family, instruct family members in the importance of responsiveness to one another's needs. Of course, taking responsibility for the needs of others conflicts with possibilities for fulfilling the ideals of expressive individualism. By placing responsibility for meeting the emotional needs of family members on the wife-mother, the husband-father can distance himself from these commitments. Ironically then, while men are typically less expressive personally than women, it is men who have had the opportunity to pursue expressive individualism. In context, this makes expressive individualism appear to be a rejection of familism and a flight from commitment.

Efforts to diminish inequality have concentrated largely on expanding opportunities for women to participate in the public sphere, the arena of expressive individualism that is antithetical to the modes of personal expressiveness with which women are most adept. This has meant that recent changes have dramatically accelerated the spread of what are essentially marketplace values at the expense of familial values. Women's entry into the public domain, seeking income as well as greater scope for self-expression, has been contingent for the most part upon acceptance of the ethics and logic of the marketplace. Cooperation, self-sacrifice, and nurturance give way to careerism, getting and spending.

The picture is by no means totally gloomy. To be sure, as we become more autonomous, less constrained by the obligations to kin, we become more dependent upon consumption and more easily tempted by the manipulated symbols of merchandisers. But contrary to such critics as Lasch, this has by no means assured the unmixed triumph of the bourgeois ethos. The decline of familism has also brought with it attitudes and expectations that have been the basis of repeated challenge to the dominance of marketplace rationality.

As we become more autonomous we also become more insistent about our entitlements—our right to dignity, fair treatment, and the freedom to pursue (and change) life plans. Passive and manipulable in some respects, we have grown more contentious and self-assured in others. Both children and adults are harder to discipline in the home, workplace, and in public life. We have grown more litigious, less likely to accept an outcome as inevitable and more likely to seek redress of grievance, even when the grievance is against someone considerably more powerful than oneself. Disruption of a life plan is less likely to be shrugged off as a trick of fate and more likely to send us looking for redress. The spread of medical malpractice suits exemplifies this process nicely. When the delivery of medical care was embedded in structures of sentiment that were fundamentally familial—the *family* doctor—the idea of suing for malpractice was unthinkable. But when the doctor-patient relationship becomes more impersonal, more rational and efficient, the willingness of the patient to trust the doctor and submit meekly to his or her authority is dramatically reduced. Mistakes are no longer suffered stoically.[31]

In each instance, this readiness to press claims, whether by litigation, publicity, or civic action, may be criticized because it appears to be guided by selfish motives. But this growing litigiousness can be read very differently. To insist that employers accommodate to their employees' private lives, or that municipalities protect their residents from toxic substances, or that state and federal governments protect citizens from the ravages of the business cycle, is to insist that the protections and solicitude that once characterized only our familial relationships be extended to our relations in the public sphere—as workers, consumers, and citizens. In short, the ensemble of guarantees and protections that form the structure of public policy in all advanced societies, and the complementary protections won from employers by collective bargaining contracts or by legislation (protections against arbitrary dismissal, unsafe working conditions, as well as pensions, health coverage, and the like), represent the generalization of reciprocal obligations that were traditionally organized by families.

So long as the family retains its meaning as the *rightful* source of succor, other sources of support and solace remain suspect, if not illegitimate. Even as more and more of us come to take for granted the benefits of humane social policy, significant numbers still regard government programs as "handouts," degrading to the recipient and oppressive to the taxpayer.[32] But unemployment compensation is not intrinsically more degrading than moving wife and kids to a relative's home in the wake of job loss. Likewise, there is nothing demeaning about receiving federal assistance in order to defray the costs of caring for a retarded child or an aged father or mother. In fact, social security is a vast improvement over reliance on children or relatives for support in old age. In the aggregate, the younger generation can care for the elderly far better than each of us, as the children of particular elderly parents, can. While many older folks may resent not being cared for by offspring and many children may feel guilty for not caring for parents, it is clear that young and old alike find the impersonal means of meeting filial duty crucial to their sense of well-being.

It is this shift in the locus of responsibility for well-being, one's own as well as that of others, from the family to the broader community that we think of as "familization of the public." It is a process by which the manifold dependencies we enter into in the course of our lives cease being the sole responsibility of our families. Instead, these unavoidable dependencies are being shifted to the whole array of societal institutions that together comprise what we think of as the realm of our public lives. But more is involved than a simple shift of functions from the family to the larger society. The rising tide of entitlements—expectations that society owes its members dignified retirement, workplace safety, access to medical treatment, education, assistance when unemployed or disabled, safe products—involves a growing insistence that the society's institutional orders be more responsive to the personal, even idiosyncratic needs of clients, employees, recipients, and consumers.

Family networks simply cannot protect us. Even if they could, the protection they offer entails dramatic reductions in personal autonomy, in our capacity to develop expressive individuality. We would be, as our ancestors were, weighed down by an elaborate web of obligations the sum of which would foreclose many of the choices we now take for granted. We would live out our lives within far narrower perimeters. In part because families could not protect and in part because familial protection carried too great a burden of constricting obligation, we have sought other more impersonal modes of negotiating our dependency needs. The expansion of these impersonal expressions of dependency—reliance on the state and/or employers—has meant that the dominant experience of the past several generations has been one of declining obligations. With fewer people dependent upon us, we feel freer to pursue our own agendas and interests, unmindful of the fact that we remain as fully dependent upon others as ever. But we often do not know those on whom we depend. Even if we do know them, our relationship to them is defined as a market relationship—a narrow instrumental relationship. As a result, we do not feel deeply implicated in their lives nor do we expect them to feel implicated in ours.

The sense of independence that results from this impersonality is paradoxical. In fact, as Lasch notes, we are far more dependent than our forebears. They, after all, could grow their own food, repair their own tools, and build their own houses. By contrast, our personal autonomy derives from a staggeringly elaborate division of labor that renders many of us incompetent in all but narrow specialties. And all of us are at the mercy of other specialists and professionals who mediate between us, advising us about which specialists to consult for this or that particular need.

In this sense our autonomy is illusory, less a condition of self-sufficiency than of a larger irresponsibility. But the self-sufficiency against which modern helplessness is measured is also illusory. Few were resourceful and intrepid enough to be literally *self*-sufficient. They relied upon family, friends, and neighbors. Seen in this light, the issue is not self-sufficiency versus helplessness, nor autonomy versus obligation, but rather how we experience and act upon the ineluctable dependencies that are part and parcel of the human condition. Familial obligation was, in traditional societies, the way dependency was framed. Kinship provided the metaphor for most interaction, even when it was non-kin who were interacting. Familism was the prevailing ethos and it required each individual to see his or her own needs and interests inextricably bound to the needs and interests of others, such that a broader, common good was at least glimpsed, if not fully articulated.

Repressive individualism kept familism more or less intact, though over time the domain of familism was narrowed to family life alone, with residual energies left available for neighborliness and localized community spiritedness. Expressive individualism cuts deeply into the family's ability to sustain familism. As expressivity spreads, encouraged by economic forces as well as by the psychic dynamics of the family itself, families cease to modulate individual appetite and project a sense of broader common good. Attempts to project such a sense of broader common good are limited by laissez-faire doctrines, the faith that the free market is the only legitimate model of public life. Unfortunately, the market is an impoverished source of conceptions of the common good. The market all too regularly gives us what we think we want accompanied by consequences that diminish or destroy the benefits sought. The result, following Hirsch's reasoning, is we get neither the private comforts nor the public order that we desire.

The plain fact is that familism can no longer be sustained by our families. However, without familism we are without a means to connect our private longings deliberately to larger social purposes. Our autonomy is, in effect, a cul-de-sac. What we experience as a crisis of the family is less a family problem than it is a breakdown in the means by which individuals feel connected to their milieu. Though some people have begun to explore new ways of acknowledging connections, ways that preserve their autonomy, these explorations are largely carried out in isolation from each other. There is little in our experience that leads us to see our personal needs in more general terms, as legitimate social needs—and, thus, of broad political significance. But that time is coming.

The balance between public and private life has decisively shifted, even though we still labor under old conventions.

Trapped between a nostalgic attachment to family and a celebration of detached selfhood, we have been hesitant to demand that the public institutions on which we depend and within which we find shape and significance for our lives be more responsive to our needs. As our families gradually lose the capacity to sustain familism with sufficient intensity to countervail against the weight of self-interest generated in the public sphere, there has been a consistent, albeit intermittent, pressure to modify the premises that shape the public sphere. These struggles have resulted in the establishment of the rudiments of a welfare system, amplified by health and welfare benefits derived from collective bargaining, as well as the modification of work rules that regulate hours, conditions, and access to employment and promotion. In large measure, these benefits have sprung from the collapse of mutual aid organized along familial lines.

The aggregate of policies that help people sustain their private lives are what we take to be "public familism." It does not matter whether these policies are enacted by legislation, negotiated through collective bargaining, or instituted by "enlightened" bureaucratic organizations in their efforts to attract and retain talented and energetic employees. In effect, what has been going on fitfully for several generations has been the renegotiation of dependencies such that our private lives grow steadily less burdened by the needs of kinfolk. In place of reliance on family members, more and more of us have come to rely on programs we collectively pay for through taxes or are entitled to as a condition of employment.

The elaboration of public familism has allowed growing numbers of Americans to pursue life plans with considerable freedom of movement and room for idiosyncrasy. Though this expansion of personal freedom and choice has been the source of popular support for public familism, legislatures and employers have gone along for reasons of their own. In Chapter 2 we explored how freeing people from family obligations also made them more easily coaxed into being avid consumers and more responsive to rapidly changing labor force requirements. In effect, two distinct consequences can be associated with most of the social reforms of the twentieth century: directly or indirectly they have made it possible for nuclear families to be more free-standing, more self-enclosed; and they have, especially in recent decades, made it easier for individuals, inside or outside nuclear families, to enjoy greater autonomy.

We have already seen how the variety of standard welfare programs and fringe benefits have formed the foundation upon which Americans have been building their families. Of course, this process of "building families" continually throws up new exigencies and gives rise to new aspirations. The result has been recurrent pressures for expanding the scope of public familism. The present period is no exception. In fact, for reasons that should by now be fully apparent, we are entering a period in which the rapid change of the past three decades is throwing up a broad series of initiatives whose net effect, once acted upon, will be to expand significantly the breadth and depth of public familism. When the dust has settled several decades from now, public institutions will be more responsive to the varieties of private lives Americans will be living. A brief inventory of these initiatives will make clear the change we envision.

Largely as a result of the very rapid rise in the numbers of wives and mothers in the labor force, the pressure for changes in work rules and work-based benefits has increased markedly in recent years. The introduction of reforms like flex-time is clearly designed to make work life more accommodating to the diverse rhythms of people's private lives. By 1980, slightly over 10 percent of the nation's non-farm labor force worked on flex-time schedules. An additional 2 to 3 percent of the labor force compresses their full-time job into three or four days per week. Coupled with job sharing for spouses, "time banks," and the provision for personal days in addition to conventional sick leave, such modifications in work scheduling reflect the beginning of recognition that families can no longer automatically be expected to adapt to fixed and inflexible schedules. [33]

As more and more of the nation's women define themselves as workers, there has been a steady insistence that employers make it easier for women to take maternity leave. Studies have shown that maternity leave policy in the United States lags significantly behind that of most other industrialized societies.[34] Given this and the likelihood that the vast majority of the nation's women will want to resume working after the birth of their child(ren), it is understandable why parental leave policies have become a source of growing agitation. Several states have already passed legislation requiring employers to offer unpaid parental leave. Minnesota was first to require that leaves be offered to both mother and father. Oregon put into effect similar legislation in 1988. A survey by the *New York Times* in 1987 found that twenty-eight states were considering legislation in this field, much of it modeled after federal legislation introduced that same year by Rep. Schroeder (D., Col.) and Sen. Dodd (D., Conn.). This legislation requires employers to offer both male and female employees up to eighteen weeks of unpaid leave upon the birth or adoption of a child.[35] Though Schroeder's bill has yet to achieve legislative passage, it has steadily gathered backers since its initial filing. And, perhaps sensing the inevitable, conservatives have begun to offer weaker legislation of their own in this area. All of these initiatives pale by comparison with the *paid* leaves granted in many European countries, but it is nonetheless clear that employers are going to feel increased pressure to adjust their policies to the needs of their employees.

This is signaled in a related way by the mounting calls for day care. As a political demand, day care reached its zenith in the Nixon administration. Since that defeat at the federal level, proponents have focused more on community-based or workplace-based day care arrangements. But as with maternity/paternity leaves, day care is now reemerging as a national issue. Though researchers continue to debate the comparative virtues of primary child care at home or in day care, more and more children are being cared for outside the home. They are also entering day care at earlier ages and spending more hours per day away from home than ever before. In response to this trend, some corporations have begun to provide day-care centers for the children of their employees. Data reported by Galinsky indicates that the number of firms providing direct day care increased from 105 in 1978 to over 1200 companies in 1985.[36] In 1989, the Conference Board reported that roughly 3,300 companies were offering employees a range of benefits directed at easing child-care headaches.[37]

This is, of course, a drop in the bucket when one considers that there are well over 500,000 corporations in the United

States, but the growth rate is nevertheless significant. While Congress continues to debate the matter, states and municipalities have begun to try to enlarge the availability of day care. Connecticut, for example, now offers employers a 50 percent tax credit for costs incurred in establishing day-care facilities. As the pressures for well-regulated, comprehensive, and affordable day care grow, even conservatives have begun to waver. In the 1988 presidential campaign, George Bush unveiled a plan of tax credits to help give poor mothers access to day care. Senator Orrin Hatch, long identified with the New Right's attempt to discourage mothers from working outside the home, has become a co-sponsor of the Schroeder-Dodd bill. In fact, as the 1989 session of Congress began to shape its agenda, it seemed that political wrangling over which party would be able to take credit for day-care legislation was more important than ideological positions. Hatch and Dodd worked together to guide it through the Senate. In the wake of Senate passage, Hatch was excoriated by many fellow conservatives but his support for the bill was firm. He responded to his critics from the right that it would do no one any good to deny what is now an accomplished fact: like it or not, the nation's mothers are working. Of course, the day-care bill still has many hurdles to jump, including a threatened presidential veto. But whatever the fate of that particular piece of legislation, a significant shift in the way we think about day care and childrearing is now evident. This new reality is making itself felt in both boardrooms and congressional hearing rooms.

Day care represents only the beginning of the process of revising our ideas about parceling out what were once exclusively family responsibilities. A recent Conference Board report, for example, raises the prospect of broadening corporate responsibility from day care to include provisions for the care of employees' aged parents. Citing the steadily mounting number of studies showing how stress in private life impacts upon job performance, the report argues that companies should help to ease the burdens that arise when families try to take care of everything themselves and thereby benefit from higher morale, lower rates of absenteeism, and greater employee loyalty.[38]

Indeed, employers and public authorities are also under increasing pressure to expand the reach of benefits and protections to include members of what we have called unacknowledged families. With the numbers of gay and lesbian couples and heterosexual cohabitants steadily rising, benefits such as family health coverage are now beginning to be extended to these couples. In 1989, San Francisco voters narrowly defeated a "Domestic Partners Bill," which allowed a civil procedure for certifying such partnerships, thereby entitling the partners of municipal employees to the same benefits that now only accrue to legally defined family members. The defeat in San Francisco means it will be some time before such laws become widespread.[39] Nevertheless, as with the much-publicized palimony cases of a decade ago, it is clear that as the norms governing private life change, so too will our laws and our public practices.

The way work is organized and the norms governing behavior in the workplace are even undergoing revision. Traditional hierarchy and minute job specialization, standard features of industrial organization, have become targets of reform. Many employers are experimenting with ways of reorganizing work processes in an effort to locate more initiative and responsibility in work groups rather than with supervisory personnel. Various job enrichment schemes also attempt to introduce more cooperation and egalitarianism into work processes that have long been modeled more on a military chain of command than on the give-and-take ideal of private life.[40] We have also become more alert to violations of personal integrity in the workplace. A prime example of this change is the growing sensitivity to sexual harassment. Procedures for punishing sexual harassment are now commonplace. Behavior long regarded as "private" and beyond regulation can now become publicly scrutinized. As the implications of these new norms sink in, it is reasonable to imagine a changed atmosphere in the workplace.

Of course it would be naive to claim that social relations in the workplace are well on their way to becoming loving and family-like. But it is clear that standards of public conduct are changing. The widespread reliance on sensitivity training and the teaching of conflict management skills are further indications that emergent standards are informed by notions of dignity and regard for others that have a closer affinity to the informal relations of family than the long prevailing formal and hierarchical norms of the workplace.

While the most dramatic changes involve the articulation of workplace and family life, there has also been a significant change occurring in the foundation of our commercial ethos. *Caveat emptor*, the norm governing the relationship between seller and buyer that affirms the sharp split between public and private realms, has been under mounting attack for some time now. We noted in passing earlier, in connection with the spread of entitlements, that the rise of product liability suits represents yet another way in which public life is beginning to be held accountable to standards traditionally reserved for the private sphere. The worlds of work and commerce are slowly being made more responsive and responsible. The right to be left alone, the classic liberal guarantee of liberty, is being supplemented by the right to humane treatment at work and in the marketplace.

Another cluster of initiatives revolves around the need to assist the growing numbers of mothers and fathers who, largely as a result of divorce, find themselves in need of a wide range of supports in order to maintain their own independence. In the mid-seventies, Congress passed several pieces of legislation designed to assist "displaced homemakers," divorced or widowed women who had been principally housewives and mothers, to acquire the training and work experience necessary to become gainfully employed and financially self-supporting. Some states have added their own support through job training and university scholarship and loan programs for displaced homemakers. Though programs vary considerably, most include provisions that assist a return to college, help to defray child-care costs associated with education or job training, and provide career and personal counseling associated with such an abrupt shift in life-style.

In a similar vein, more and more public schools are now offering special programs for student mothers in an effort not only to help young mothers finish high school but also to give them training in the skills of parenting.[41] And, reminiscent of the kindergarten movement earlier in this century, some educators have begun to talk about extending the mission of the public schools to include day-care and preschool programs. Though this will no doubt guarantee continued attacks on the schools from those who feel that such programs represent an unwarranted intrusion into family life, in one way or another schools will continue to broaden their instruction as well as expand the age range of their student population.

The schools have also been asked to respond to varieties of disability that were once the responsibility of parents. Federal and state law now broadly mandates schools to provide a very wide range of psychological and pedagogical services to children who even a few decades ago would never have entered a conventional school. Recognizing that parents can no longer be expected to be the sole nurturers, caretakers, and educators of their retarded or physically impaired offspring, the public sphere has begun to offer substantial supports. As a corollary, the public sphere has also begun to be more responsive to the needs of the disabled. Whether in the form of special parking spaces; wheelchair accessible ramps, elevators, and lavatories; or recreational facilities designed for people with widely varying abilities, public spaces are becoming steadily more accommodating and inclusive. People once condemned to the privacy of households can now pursue a far more active public life, a life far less dependent upon the narrow circle of family members that was once the only alternative to grim institutionalization.

To complete this brief illustrative overview of the range of ways familial modes have begun to inform public life, let us turn to the ways the tenor of public institutions have been changing to reflect styles closer to those of a family than an organization. One area in which change has been occurring has been in the ways we treat the ill and dying. Though change in this realm is spotty, the spread of institutions like the hospice signals a tendency to familize what have been quite impersonal, even austere, settings in hospitals. With or without family members in close attendance, hospices afford terminally ill persons the flexibility, self-control, and warmth that hospital wards rarely provide. Indeed, hospitals themselves have begun to loosen up in some areas, most notably in obstetrics. The newest model is the "birthing center," a far cry from the cold and hierarchical settings of the labor and delivery rooms of a generation ago. Now, fathers are welcomed to attend the birth of their child, and even grandparents and friends are allowed in some hospitals.

The treatment of the mentally ill has been transformed, too, by attempts to make treatment centers more family-like and community based. The move toward deinstitutionalization for residents in large state mental hospitals that was begun in the 1960s was largely animated by a family model of care. Patients were discharged from the large, very nearly penal, hospitals into small residential halfway houses where small groups of former patients and a small staff could model their activities on the ways a family might live. The hope was that the greater flexibility of such an arrangement would lead to more autonomy for former patients and that as their self-confidence grew, their self-esteem would rise and they would be able to live richer and more meaningful lives.[42]

We must inject a note of caution into this brief account of the multiple ways in which the public sphere is being transformed. The developments we have just surveyed are more a hodgepodge than they are a concerted program or agenda. The notion of public familism is neither a coherent nor a conscious political program. Indeed, virtually everything we have identified as contributing to public familism has developed as a more or less ad hoc response to particular needs or difficulties. So far, each initiative taken separately has had modest effect at best. This is probably the only way such a thing as public familism could emerge. Were it fully articulated, it would likely be the political equivalent of a lead balloon. It would strike most people as either far too idealistic, even utopian, or too sharp a break from how we are accustomed to think of our family and our public lives. At the very least, were it presented as a full-fledged agenda, it would loom as horrendously costly. In any case its political prospects would be grim. But as a piecemeal, unsystematic, and nonideological series of pragmatic responses to specific problems, public familism has been spreading gradually.

This is not to say that there have been no attempts to achieve broad and sustained political mobilization on behalf of reforms that make private life more viable and satisfying. Most notably, Patricia Schroeder's brief run in the Democratic presidential primaries in 1988 on a platform based on the kinds of initiatives

and reforms we have been discussing suggests that public familism might soon become a much more explicit political force.[43]
At present, however, the pressure to transform public life has
been more evident in the workplace than in the political arena.
This is partly the result of our deep ambivalence about reliance
on government and programs that smack of welfare, attitudes
that depend heavily on nostalgia for traditional forms of family
life. Additionally, social supports organized through employers
can be selective and their impact kept narrow. Benefits can be
directed at particular groups or used as enticements or rewards
for desired behavior. For example, the fringe benefit of maternity leave currently extends only to those employees covered by
disability insurance, at most 40 percent of the labor force. In
fact, many of the recent examples of steps toward familizing the
public have been corporate programs aimed at young managerial, technical and professional employees—so-called yuppies.
Sensitive to discrimination and harassment, the young upwardly
mobiles have been on the cutting edge of the challenge to conventional hierarchical structures of work in the last two decades.[44] In an effort to attract or keep highly trained and able
employees, many organizations have been obliged to institute
maternity and paternity leaves, day-care provisions, and other
provisions that make work more consonant with private life.
Proponents of these initiatives claim that the results—higher
morale, greater energy devoted to work, and higher levels of
loyalty, which mean lower turnover rates—make these programs economically rational for the organization.

   To be sure, many of these challenges have been deflected or
co-opted, in the process enhancing managerial control and increasing productivity without concomitant increases in either
wages, benefits, or satisfactions.[45] But we are not claiming stunning triumphs here, only the slow, tentative emergence of a new
conception of how public life and private life ought to intersect.
That organizations manage, in the short run, to defend traditional prerogatives should not be surprising. The question is: To
what extent will they continue to do so?

   Of course, there is no way to give a definitive answer to this
question. But changes well under way and not easily reversed

are likely to make defense of traditional organizational prerogatives ever more difficult, if only because dual-earner families will continue to grow in numbers and this will inevitably mean that more of us will form and be raised in minimal families. In turn, more couples will experience the need for an expanded array of services in order to make their private lives liveable. Not only will there be a growing insistence that employers provide day care (or offer allowances for those who need day care), the ranks of those who feel this need will grow more diverse. Reforms begun in response to the emergent needs of highly valued executives are likely to become a general expectation as families structured by the needs of two wage earners become more common. If corporations balk at the expense or the organizational burden entailed in providing such services, it is likely that a well-established pattern of reform will be repeated: business leaders will grudgingly come to acknowledge the necessity for change and will throw their support behind state provision of the services.[46]

Whether change comes from prescient elites or from popular agitation (or a combination of both, as is more likely), what seems clear is that change will come. In significant respects, the change is already upon us. What remains is to acknowledge this change and recognize its implications. Families simply cannot function as they once did. Neither our subjective desires nor our institutional means of realizing these desires could long tolerate the subordination of self that nostalgic versions of the family require. Families that stress solidarity more than autonomy have given way to those that emphasize autonomy.

To fail to acknowledge this change, to pretend that people's private lives are unchanged, is to risk not only the further erosion of family life but also the spread of malaise into the public sphere. Further declines in productivity, lower worker morale, and increased mean-spiritedness are the likely results if individuals are forced to scramble to defend what little comfort and security they have. Continued foot-dragging is also going to be very costly in the long run, even though many may balk at the price tag of an expanding public familism. The nations with whom we will be in sharper and sharper competition in the dec-

ades ahead are all nations with substantially more developed
forms of public familism than we have thus far seen fit to promote. One immediately thinks of Japan in this context.

The heavy involvement of the Japanese corporation in the
private lives of its employees is one expression of a familized
public. In the case of Japan, the provision of housing, education, medical care, and related services by the corporation derives from the accommodations that businesses had to make
with labor shortages and the strong family tradition in Japan.[47]
Given its origins in tradition, public familism in Japan is deeply
paternalistic. However well the Japanese manage, it is unlikely
that our movement toward familization of the public will be as
paternalistic, and ultimately autocratic, as their arrangements
seem to be. Paternalism, even when patriarchy was still very
much taken for granted, has never worked for long in our culture. More importantly, the aggregate of demands that constitute what we are calling familization of the public are demands
that go far beyond the desire to be passively taken care of. Just
as the American family has long been suffused with egalitarianism and a participatory ethos, so too is it evident that our expectations for a more familial public reflect these qualities, not
the qualities of hierarchy and deference that still permeate Japan's social and family life.

This is not to deny that there are profound risks. The impulse
to save us from ourselves can all too easily become oppressive, a
latter-day version of benevolent despotism, all the more pernicious because it appears self-willed rather than straight-
forwardly imposed by an autocrat. The double-edged nature of
public familism is captured nicely in a recent workplace innovation that is another example of the shift that we are discussing—Employee Assistance Programs (EAPs).[48] As more and
more studies show that private woes have considerable impact
on work performance, employers have begun to explore ways of
offering assistance to employees, such as alcohol and drug programs and counseling programs for employees experiencing
marital difficulties or troubles with a child. These services are
offered as part of the overall benefits package and give workers
access to an expanding array of services, often available at the

workplace on company time. By making professional services directly available to employees, the employer is acknowledging the need to take their private lives into account. In doing so, however, the employer can become intrusive and manipulative.

The difficulty is especially acute when therapy or counseling is linked to continued employment. In some firms, if an employee is deemed in need of counseling and refuses it, that refusal is cause for termination. So long as an employer's primary interest is to increase efficiency and productivity, expressions of concern and solicitude are inevitably contaminated. Public familism can become just another veil for social control. By seeming to be concerned, those in power simply manipulate us into compliance. George Orwell's Big Brother lurks persistently behind the facade of benevolence in the modern world.

Lasch's fear is precisely that we will become ever more pliant and passive given the prospect of being cared for by our employers and/or by the state. Philip Reiff, in his *The Triumph of the Therapeutic*, raises similar concerns.[49] These critics worry that if all we are interested in is personal growth and sustaining a sense of personal satisfaction, no one will be willing or able to take risks for fear of rocking the boat. Moreover, as firm moral guidelines and certainty give way to relativism and expediency, no one will be able to stand up for what they believe. "Feeling good" will take precedence over doing the "right thing."

These fears have recently been forcefully restated with specific reference to the changes in family life we have been describing. David Popenoe, a sociologist who studies Sweden and has written extensively on the ways private and public spheres interact, argues that the changes that have brought about what we have called the minimal family (and what he calls the "postnuclear family") are changes for the worse.[50] Preoccupation with self-development and gratification have devastated our capacity to provide children with an emotionally secure environment in which to grow and have made us all less able to form lasting bonds of deep intimacy. In Sweden, where a version of public familism is most fully embellished and institutionalized, Popenoe reports that voluntarism and community involvement are at a low ebb. With the state and employers so involved in people's lives, and with most husbands and wives working, people have little interest in and often little time for thinking about or helping others.

Aside from representing a departure from longstanding pieties and thus creating a diffuse sense of loss, it is not at all clear that Swedes are losing anything but a tradition that is no longer sustainable or relevant. It certainly cannot be claimed that they have become passive or indifferent to their freedom or to their rights to free expression and self-determination. They have not ceased being citizens. This is not to say that Sweden is perfect or to claim that public familism will necessarily be superior in all regards to the traditions it is replacing. Nor are we claiming that public familism is without risk. There *is* a risk of becoming passive and self-absorbed. There is also a risk that among the growing numbers of single individuals there will be many for whom autonomy is really plain old loneliness.

These risks are real. As importantly, the principal means of reducing the risks of suffocating paternalism require levels of involvement in public life that are hard to sustain over long periods of time. The odiousness of any given paternalistic intrusion may be too slight or too easily shrugged off to be worth the investment of time, money, and energy required to thwart its implementation. Moving solicitude from the private to the public sphere means that the normal give-and-take in family life over what needs are legitimate and whose needs prevail must get translated into public discourse. We may become passive, content to let others define issues and determine priorities, just as in our families we are often unable to resist the strong-willed or manipulative family member who always gets his or her way. But it was almost always possible to leave home, to get out from under an oppressive father or mother. It is not possible to escape the public sphere, except by psychic withdrawal and self-absorption.

Popenoe argues that this appears to have happened in Sweden. Churches, neighborhoods, and voluntary organizations have all declined as vital forces in the average Swede's life. However, it is by no means clear that this sort of withdrawal will occur here. Even with the rapid growth of public familism, Americans' fabled "belongingness" has remained vigorous. To take but one example, the proliferation of support groups shows that we remain able to assert ourselves and invent ways to collectively shape our interests. Of course, there is no guarantee that we will continue to be both assertive and inventive. We are headed into uncharted waters.

The fact that we are on a new course is itself a source of concern. But for all the uncertainties and risks, it can no longer fairly be said that we would be better off, or freer, if only we could be left to our own devices. Coping with a drug dependency or a failing marriage is not easier if employers and the state steadfastly refuse to acknowledge these private travails. Nor can it be claimed that our citizenship would be more robust if we were more reliant on our families and friends and less dependent upon the public sphere. The real issue is not whether there is a role for government or employers in our private lives but what public policies seek to attain and how accessible they are to the will of the people affected. In other words, we must put a premium on citizenship, on making involvement a central feature of adulthood. Whether at work or through leisure pursuits, whether around special needs or interests or through neighborhoods or churches, we will continually need to invent ways for increasingly autonomous individuals to be linked to others. Since there is no serious prospect of return to a presumed golden age, our efforts should be focused on developing ways to make our public life more responsive and all of us more self-consciously engaged in collectively shaping and representing our needs.

Families are supposed to be respectful of individual needs and idiosyncrasies, even while maintaining a sense of cohesion and cooperation. It is not farfetched to expect this same solicitude from the organizations we work for and are presumably served by. Though neither farfetched nor unreasonable, there is still the problem of money. Moving familism from the private domain of the household into the public sphere means replacing essentially volunteer activities with programs that require paid labor for their delivery. As we have already noted in passing, were public familism put forward as a unitary full-fledged social agenda, it would strike many as too costly. There is no way to be precise about the costs, but it certainly would require substantial outlays by employers and/or taxpayers. Can we afford it? We think the answer is yes, but only in the context of drastic changes in current priorities. It is hard to see how we can continue expanding public familism if the share of taxes paid by the nation's businesses continues to decline. Similarly, it is hard to see how change can come without reversing the tax policies of the Reagan-Bush and Bush-Quayle administrations. Clearly, public familism will not advance if the tax burden continues to be shifted away from the wealthy. By the same token, the budget priorities of the last several decades will have to be sharply altered: the Pentagon will need to settle for far less than it has been accustomed to in recent years, and the government will have to be far less generous in its willingness to subsidize corporate incompetence and corruption.[51]

Moreover, it is wrong to see public familism as only "expense." Expenditures that go to making us saner and less harassed must be seen as *investments*. Virtually all of the industrialized nations of the world now spend more than we do on human services broadly conceived. The fact that we do far less than most has scarcely enhanced our productivity or competitiveness. If anything just the reverse is true: our lagging investments in "human capital" and our reluctance to relax the rigidities of organizational life are quickly making us a second-rate economy. And insisting that each of us meet our personal needs privately insures that we will continue to run up staggering private debt.

Money, seen in these terms, is at most a minor impediment to the continued advance of public familism. Of far greater moment are the quite substantial cultural changes that will be required. It is one thing to restructure one's own family and work life in response to what appear to be opportunities for a better life. This kind of ad hoc pragmatism permits people to remain attached to one set of values even while practicing something very different. An example of this is the women Kathleen Gerson interviewed who were strongly committed to working and had no intention of becoming mothers. Gerson found that they held very conventional views about motherhood. They rejected motherhood for themselves but were not particularly interested in seeing it redefined.[52]

In sum, there are several reasons why moves toward expanding public familism will continue to be halting, half-hearted, and piecemeal in the near future. People do not abandon long-cherished assumptions eagerly. Resistance to a radical restructuring of the social contract will be able to draw upon nostalgic attachments as well as hostility to taxes for some time to come. But the current wave of conservatism will run its course. For all the rhetoric celebrating the virtues of "the family," Americans continue to move toward minimal family forms. As they do, they come to depend ever more heavily on the public provision of services that are the foundation of autonomy. Those services, and the politics that democratize and humanize them, can be thwarted momentarily because many people are still ambivalent about the autonomy our culture offers. For all our ambivalence, however, for all our attachments to both the enchanted family and the enchanted self, we grow more demanding of our public institutions. Though we still lack the language of a public familism, the sensibility is becoming evident.

Unfortunately, many of the demands for human services are now framed in the language of individual entitlements—a language that takes for granted traditional notions of autonomy and individualism and obscures interdependence and mutuality. Even when voicing desires for programs whose enactment would have implications for all people, advocates for such programs are dismissively categorized as representing special interests. For example, environmentalists are seen as taking a position peculiar to the narrow sensibilities of partisans in competition with other special interests. Advocates for the handicapped or the mentally ill, or for welfare or universal health insurance, are labeled the same way, as if the programs they espouse will only benefit the lives of a few unfortunate persons. So long as we cling to the tradition of family-based familism, there is no way to acknowledge that a society that makes room for the handicapped and provides decent health care and develops an adequate program for criminals would be a better society for everyone. Likewise, child care is seen as a need of parents, especially working parents, rather than a requirement of the larger society and a recognition of generational interdependence.

If public familism is to become even a part of an explicit political agenda in this country we will have to rethink our notions of autonomy and dependence as well as the relationship between them. Autonomy has been mostly wedded to what we have been calling the enchanted self—a person who brings the competitive ethic and a performance orientation to all relationships. This type of person always calculates the personal advantage to be gained from each encounter or relationship and feels free only when unencumbered by the weight of ties to others. For such persons, autonomy means self-reliance and self-sufficiency in all domains—work and play. In the extreme version of this persona, others are important only insofar as they can further the individual's goals for advancement, for success, for pleasure, or for a sense of importance.

Power is the most salient dimension of all interactions for people who believe that the only way one can trust others is when they themselves are in control. Relationships of true equality are threatening because the other's capacity for autonomous action leaves such people vulnerable to the independent desires of the other. This is automatically threatening because such persons can only assume that others are as self-serving and dangerous as they themselves are. Every effort must be made to deny or minimize interdependencies and to transform those interdependencies that cannot be eliminated or constrained into controlled dependencies. In effect, this entails the denial of dependency or, as Philip Slater put it twenty years ago, "the pursuit of loneliness."[53]

Ironically, such a version of autonomy perverts the possible forms that mutuality can take and makes equality itself appear to be a threat to mutuality. Systems that value autonomy must then be hierarchical, and persons desiring equality in such systems have no choice as individuals but to aspire to the top positions in the hierarchy. Interestingly, the rapid rise in the number of women seeking permanent positions in the labor force has probably produced an increase in the number of people who live out conventional notions of autonomy. The increase in the numbers of women in positions that require that they see themselves in terms of the conventional conception of autonomy sets the stage for conflict between the desire for autonomy and women's typical sex-role socialization. Most women are brought up instilled with an orientation toward mutuality and self-sacrifice which is obviously incompatible with conventional notions of autonomy.

The resulting tension has begun to give rise to efforts to recast conventional conceptions of autonomy. In the recent work of Jean Baker Miller, Carol Gilligan, Sara Ruddick, and others, one encounters versions of autonomy that are centered on the recognition of intersubjectivity and interdependence.[54] Within this emergent framework, interdependencies provide both the support and the recognition that are essential for a strong notion of independent selfhood. Such a self is actualized only through the full acknowledgement of his or her interconnnectedness with others.

Though it never quite gets put this way, what critics of conventional notions of autonomy are saying is almost directly analogous to the critique Fred Hirsch has leveled at those who insist that the free market is the most rational means of distributing goods. Agonistic autonomy is the psychic equivalent of laissez-faire: neither is capable of delivering sustainable satisfaction or meaning. In fact, both result in fetishistic consumption, the one of commodities, the other of identity. The move toward public familism thus can be seen not only as the elaboration of a new relationship between our public and private lives; it also entails the creation of a new context within which we come to self-understanding. We will have greater choice and fewer immediate, face-to-face dependencies. We will also have a fuller sense of the manifold ways our personal choices carry consequences for others.

In other words, if public familism is to mean anything, it will have to embody the egalitarianism and democracy that has come to characterize the aspirations for family life of significant numbers of Americans. In this way, private desires and public purpose may become less antagonistic than they have been through much of our history.

Conclusion

The history of family life for the past three centuries has been a history of families accommodating themselves to the requirements of our industrial system. To be sure, this has never been a one-way street: the requirements of family life, however they were defined at any moment in time, have often set limits on what the industrial system could expect. But over the long run, the industrial system seems to have gotten the kind of family it has needed. This fact has led many observers to conclude that the relationship between the conventional family and the institutions that comprise the industrial system is essentially harmonious: each is complementary to the others, together forming a well integrated, mutually reinforcing system.

What some see as harmony, others experience as tension-filled and fraught with contradiction. Balance, to the extent that a society can ever be said to be in balance, appears to be the result of contradictions temporarily canceling each other out or of the exercise of more or less raw power on behalf of one set of institutional needs over the competing claims of other institutions. Relations between institutions, from this perspective, are less functional than they are dialectical. Institutions never quite get the kinds of support they would like, just as societies never quite get the kinds of people that prevailing social norms and values dictate. The result is that social life is marked by conflict and uncertainty at least as often as it is by harmony and predictability.

Seen in this light, the ways in which the family has changed over the course of the last century have been accommodating in some respects and conflicting in others. It is unquestionably the case, as Lasch has insisted, that the family has largely ceased being a haven, a respite from commercialism and what, following Max Weber, we know as instrumental rationality.[55] The decline of familism has produced a general decline in the degree to which individuals feel insulated from the blandishments of the larger society. At the same time, this decline in familism has meant a correlative increase in autonomy. As we have seen, autonomy has been encouraged in many ways. In the family, autonomy has been nurtured by changes in parental authority, which have, in turn, fundamentally altered the character of parent-child interaction. Autonomy has also been stimulated by the two agents of the marketplace, the employer and the merchandiser. As we have seen, people thirsty for autonomy are, paradoxically, relatively easy prey for the advertiser. In this sense, the decline of familism can be read as a script for the rise of mass society, just as Lasch suggests. Increasingly, individuals confront the social sources of authority without buffer. But this has not meant, as critics of mass society have feared, that we are without either the social or psychic resources to analyze, criticize, or resist. What it has meant is that we have become more insistent about our rights to live life as we see fit. For some, this has meant an attempt to restore traditional ways. For others, this has meant pressing claims on the government and employers to make organizational imperatives and balance sheets more responsive to their private lives.

A choice now confronts our society: do we insist that only families be the bearers of familism or do we insist that familism be embodied in public policy? The consequences of this choice could scarcely be more momentous. To pretend that families in general can be havens—preserves of cooperativeness, sharing, and love arrayed against an impersonal public realm in which competition, self-interest, and rational calculation prevail—is to condemn family life to permanent instability. This instability has two sources. First, someone has to guard the barricades of the family against the ravages of the public realm. Whoever the guardian is—and it is almost certain to be a woman—that person will necessarily have to subordinate self-interest to the task of keeping the home fires burning. Such selflessness, in a society otherwise committed to the celebration of self-interest, must produce ambivalence, anger, and guilt along with whatever benefits supposedly derive from such an arrangement. Needless to say, such circumstances do not, for long, promote stability.

Second, there are the "objective" circumstances the family encounters. They too give rise to instability. As we have seen, both the threats and promises that now characterize society make it virtually impossible to rely exclusively upon one breadwinner, just as it is impossible to rely exclusively on kin networks for mutual aid. Attempts to do so lead inexorably to poverty, either directly or by virtue of marital dissolution. The business cycle, the advance of technology, and the steady expansion of the commodity form have cumulatively robbed the family of its sources of stability: parental authoritativeness, self-sufficiency of the family unit, and reciprocal bonds of dependency. The results have been all too apparent.

The public realm is simply overpowering: either its character will be transformed such that the nature of its impact on personal life is changed, or personal life will become merely a reflex of the impersonal dictates of public convenience. Familism will continue to decline, as will our capacity to see beyond immediate gratification and to see meaning and purpose in others beyond their usefulness to our own private ends. A sense of crisis will become endemic. And as this unfolds, the solace offered by the enchantment of the family, on the one hand, or the escape offered by the enchantment of the self on the other, will become more evident and irresistible, even though they will remain profoundly illusory solutions.

This crisis, which appears as a crisis of the family, is better understood as a crisis of the public realm. The contemporary resurgence of conservatism affirms this view, though conservatives respond to this crisis perversely—they attack one sector of the public realm, government, as if reducing its power will restore power to families. But such is not the case. Indeed, the opposite is more nearly true. If the public realm can be made to reflect the values of familism, families may well find themselves more able to meet the emotional needs of their members. This being so, it is also likely that more of our families will produce individuals who will not be content to be passive recipients of a benevolent bureaucracy, whether public or private. If we can acknowledge our manifold dependencies, if we can see those dependencies as the links between our private lives and the larger social patterns our private lives constitute, we might then be able to forge a society in which autonomous individuals are capable of consciously shaping their own families and, in doing so, constitute a world in which "caring, sharing, and loving" are broadly incorporated into both our public and private lives.

Notes

Chapter I

1. *Boston Globe*, 25 May 1987, 1. Subsequently, Babetts and Jean sued DSS and won the first round of what is likely to be a long, drawn out court battle. In finding for the two gay men, Chief Justice Thomas R. Morse of the Massachusetts Superior Court wrote: "Any exclusion of homosexuals from consideration as foster parents, all things being equal, is blatantly irrational. . . .It is the children whose interests are paramount, and prospective foster parents should be selected on the basis of their ability to provide temporary care and support for children, not on the basis of an arbitrary factor such as marital status." This statement is taken from William F. Schulz, "Fostering Prejudice," *The Progressive*, January 1987, 15.

2. "Court Widens Family Definition to Gay Couples Living Together," *New York Times*, 7 July 1989, A 1.

3. In a closely related area, airlines are now beginning to allow their frequent flier ticket holders to share them, in the words of Mark Buckstein, T.W.A.'s general counsel, "with any companion of their choosing." Until recently, the airlines stipulated that their free tickets could be transferred only among family members. *New York Times*, 16 July 1989, A 19.

4. Even now, when especially close ties develop with nonfamily mem-

bers, it is not uncommon to assign family titles or use familial referents to acknowledge the closeness. Thus, we describe a very close friend as being like a brother or a sister. And we will extend emotional or financial support to such fictive kin, in much the same way we would to blood relatives. Similarly, children are often taught to refer to significant friends of their parents as aunt or uncle, simultaneously acknowledging both the respect due elders and the intimacy that goes along with family.

5. John Demos, *Past, Present, and Personal: Family Life and the Life Course in American History* (New York: Oxford University Press, 1986), 28.

6. See Mary Jo Bane, *Here To Stay* (New York: Basic Books, 1976). A similarly upbeat interpretation of the contemporary family is offered by T. Caplow and his associates, based on their return to "Middletown," the site of the pioneering social science study of the Lynds. See *Middletown Families: Fifty Years of Change and Continuity* (Minneapolis: University of Minnesota Press, 1982). Also see Sar Levitan and Richard Belous, *What's Happening to the American Family?* (Baltimore: Johns Hopkins University Press, 1981).

7. Among many others, Andrew Cherlin's analysis of long-term trends in the statistical patterns of marriage rates, fertility, and divorce provides a counterweight to Bane's cautious but nonetheless optimistic reading of the state of the family. See his *Marriage, Divorce, and Remarriage* (Cambridge: Harvard University Press, 1981).

8. See Carl Degler, *At Odds* (New York: Oxford University Press, 1980), 20. Roger Thompson's study of sexual mores in colonial America, *Sex in Middlesex: Popular Mores in a Massachusetts County, 1649–1699* (Amherst: University of Massachusetts Press, 1986), demonstrates, among other things, that the struggle between parents and children over courtship and marriage was common early on. It is plain that the much heralded sexual revolution of the 1960s has venerable roots.

In the most comprehensive study of contemporary premarital conceptions we know, limited in its usefulness only by being restricted to 15–19 year olds, 11.6 percent of teenaged girls reported having become pregnant out of wedlock. For details, see Melvin Zelnik and John F. Kanter, "First Pregnancies to Women Aged 15–19: 1976 and 1971," *Family Planning Perspectives* 10 (January/February 1978): 11–20. The most recent Census Bureau figures on premarital pregnancy are for the period 1985–1988. During this period, 40 percent of all first-time mothers are reported to have conceived their babies out of wedlock. *Boston Globe*, 22 June 1989, 3.

9. For a fine study of the relationships between economic change, change in the family, and religious response in our early history, see

Mary P. Ryan, *Cradle of the Middle Class: The Family in Oneida County, New York, 1790–1865* (New York: Cambridge University Press, 1981).

10. For an excellent discussion of this in the context of early American history, see Daniel Scott Smith, "Parental Power and Marriage Patterns: An Analysis of Historical Trends in Hingham, Massachusetts," *Journal of Marriage and the Family* 35 (August 1973): 419–428.

11. William Goode argues that love is an essentially democratizing force in family life. See his "On the Theoretical Importance of Love," *American Sociological Review* 24 (February 1959): 37–48. Also see Philip Slater, "Short Circuits in Social Life," in his *Footholds* (Boston: Beacon Press, 1977), 114–140.

12. Lawrence Stone, *The Family, Sex, and Marriage in England 1500–1800* (New York: Harper & Row, 1977).

13. Many aspects of Stone's work remain hotly debated among historians of the family. There is little disagreement over the fact that there are crucial differences between the traditional and modern families. Most also agree that these differences center on the nature of the bonds between spouses and between parents and children. What is at issue are Stone's assertions that the changes began when they did and that the changes originated in the upper classes. Thompson's research in colonial Middlesex County, for example, clearly shows that affection between spouses was a widely established expectation by the 1650s for all classes. This debate is by no means merely technical haggling among experts but, for our purposes, we need only note the controversy. By relying on Stone as we do, it is not our intention to endorse his account. What matters for us is that the sentimentalization of family bonds steadily became a more prominent theme in family life from the seventeenth century to the present. Stone's account of the elements of this shift, if not of the shift itself, seems reasonable to us.

14. Burgess, for decades the leading figure in the sociology of the family, popularized the notion of the companionate family through his widely read textbook (with Harvey J. Locke), *The Family: From Institution to Companionship* (New York: American Book Company, 1953).

15. See Neil J. Smelser, *Social Change in the Industrial Revolution* (Chicago: University of Chicago Press, 1959), especially Chapters IX and X. Smelser's account of the industrial revolution has drawn substantial criticism but so far as we know, there is no reason to question his description of the relationship between family and factory.

16. For a detailed treatment of this, see Edmond S. Morgan, *The Puritan Family: Religion and Domestic Relations in Seventeenth Century New England* (New York: Harper & Row, 1966); and John Demos, *Little Commonwealth: Family Life in the Plymouth Colony* (New York: Oxford University Press, 1970).

17. For an account of Sewall's and his contemporaries' embeddedness in kinship, see Morgan, *The Puritan Family*, 150–160.

18. See Philip J. Greven, Jr., "Family Structure in Seventeenth-Century Andover, Massachusetts," *William and Mary Quarterly* 23 (1966): 234–256. Also see Morgan, *The Puritan Family*.

19. Benjamin Franklin, *The Autobiography of Benjamin Franklin*, ed. Leonard W. Labaree et al. (New Haven: Yale University Press, 1964).

20. Before the process we are sketching here went very far, the state also began to play a role. With such policies as the homestead acts, which made possible the acquisition of land without regard to kinship or inheritance, the state struck important blows for the independence of the young, just as, a century later, the G.I. Bill greatly reduced the role of parents in the life decisions of their sons and daughters. We shall explore this in greater detail in Chapter 2.

21. See Degler, *At Odds*, 3–25, for a synthesis of the historical research bearing on this.

22. Ellen K. Rothman, "Sex and Self-Control: Middle Class Courtship in America, 1770–1870," *Journal of Social History* 15 (Spring 1982): 409–425.

23. Quoted in Charles Strickland, "A Transcendentalist Father: The Child-Rearing Practices of Bronson Alcott," *Perspectives in American History*, vol. 3 (Cambridge: Harvard University Press, Charles Warren Center for Studies in American History, 1969), 5. Alcott is by no means typical, in this or any other respect; he was a curious mixture of traditional and modern. But however contradictory, he anticipates the intense concern for the psychic life of the child that would become commonplace in our own day.

24. Degler, *At Odds*, 84; 107.

25. See, for example, Barbara Welter, "The Cult of True Womanhood: 1820–1860," *The American Quarterly* (Summer 1966): 151–174.

26. See Howard Gadlin, "Private Lives and Public Order," *The Massachusetts Review* XVII, no. 2 (Summer 1976): 304–330.

27. By starting with a subjective factor, we do not mean to enter the long and heated debate over which is more important, subjective desire or objective necessity. For us, it is an arid debate, even when its heat makes interesting reading. It seems clear that a change in sentiment alone would not have carried the day. In the absence of structurally emergent possibilities, sentiment would wither or find other outlets. By the same token, as we will try to make clear in a later chapter, without significant changes in subjective expectations, many economic and political changes would necessarily have been different and some may even have been foregone. For us, then, it is arbitrary to signify one factor as preeminent.

Chapter 2

1. In the early stages of this process, the labor of children and young adults helped sustain the faltering household economy. Mill girls—mostly young single women from New England's farms—came to Lowell, Massachusetts, and other budding industrial centers to work, and sent home the bulk of their earnings. The classic insider account of this is Lucy Larcom's *A New England Girlhood* (New York: Corinth Books, 1964). Also see her volume *An Idyll of Work* (Boston: J. R. Osgood and Co., 1875).

2. To be sure, we are oversimplifying the matter here. Capital came from many sources other than extracting it from workers. For example, much of the capital that fueled the industrial revolution came from the profitable slave trade—that is, the selling of slaves as opposed to the labor of slaves. See Eric Williams, *Capitalism and Slavery* (New York: Capricorn Books, 1976). But the fact remains that investment funds ultimately derive from some people, through whatever processes, foregoing current consumption.

3. For a concise review of the economy's troubles at the turn of the century, see Walter LaFeber, *The New Empire: An Interpretation of American Expansion, 1860–1898* (Ithaca, NY: Cornell University Press, 1963), 1–61.

4. Merritt Roe Smith's work on the origins of mass production is interesting in this connection. Though he focuses on the emergence of the techniques, it is clear from what he writes that at least some of the contributing pressure that moved us toward mass production came as a result of employers having to cope with an undependable labor force. If replaceable parts could be produced by machines designed for that purpose, then workers, too, could become replaceable and employers would not be as disrupted by irresolute workers. See Merritt Roe Smith, "Military Entrepreneurship," in *Yankee Enterprise: The Rise of the American System of Manufactures*, ed. Otto Mayr and Robert C. Post (Washington, DC: Smithsonian Institution Press, 1981), 63–102.

5. Henry Lawson, *In The Days When the World Was Wide and Other Verses* (London: Angus & Robertson Ltd., 1913), 176–178. The work of Henry Lawson was brought to our attention by the folksinger Priscilla Herdman. She sets some of Lawson's poems, including "The Shame of Going Back," to music on her album *The Water Lily*, Flying Fish (1980).

6. For a summary of the way the recession of the early 1980s impacted on the nation's households, see U.S. Bureau of the Census, *Households, Families, Marital Status, and Living Arrangements: March, 1984*, series P–20, no. 391 (Washington, DC: U.S. Government Printing Office, August 1984).

7. For a classic presentation of this perspective see F. Hayek, *The Road to Serfdom* (Chicago: University of Chicago Press, 1944).

8. William L. O'Neill, "Divorce in the Progressive Era," *American Quarterly* (Summer 1965): 205–217.

9. This mixture of punitiveness and self-righteousness continues down to the present in conservative thought. Enthusiasm for Darwinian metaphor is more problematic. It can be found in the intellectual underpinnings of laissez-faire political economy, from Hayek to Friedman, but it is less commonly a part of popular conservatism. This is largely because popular conservatism is deeply rooted in fundamentalist religious belief, which is obviously inhospitable to even a hint of Darwinian thought.

10. This brief discussion of the history of feminism in the United States draws upon William L. O'Neill's *Everyone Was Brave: The Rise and Fall of Feminism in America* (Chicago: Quadrangle Books, 1969); and William H. Chafe, *Women and Equality: Changing Patterns in American Culture* (New York: Oxford University Press, 1977).

11. This view, greatly simplified and condensed here, is more a composite than the position of any given feminist. The writer who comes closest to fully articulating the perspective outlined here is Charlotte Perkins Gilman. See her *Women and Economics* (New York: Harper & Row, 1966), originally published in 1899. Gilman gives full expression to these thoughts in her utopian novel, *Moving the Mountain* (New York: Charlton, 1911).

12. See Barbara Leslie Epstein, *The Politics of Domesticity: Women, Evangelism, and Temperance in Nineteenth-Century America* (Middletown, CT: Wesleyan University Press, 1981).

13. The desire to modernize the home by educating the housewife was an important component in legitimizing women's colleges. Alice Freeman Palmer, president of Wellesley, extolled the virtues of a college education for women thusly:

> Little children under five years die in needless thousands because of the dull, unimaginative women on whom they depend. Such women have been satisfied with just getting along, instead of packing everything they do with brains, instead of studying the best way of doing everything small or large; for there is always a best way, whether of setting a table, of trimming a hat, or teaching a child to read. And this taste for perfection can be cultivated.

As cited in Burton Bledstein, *The Culture of Professionalism* (New York: W. W. Norton, 1976), 119.

14. Laura Shapiro's *Perfection Salad* (New York: Farrar, Straus, Giroux, 1986) contains a rich analysis of one aspect of this general development. She examines the ways cooking changed with the introduction

of standardized measures, cooking schools (and cooking courses in the public schools), cookbooks, and food magazines.

15. There is a profound irony in this. The people who were most preoccupied with Americanization also tended to be the people who were least open to policies intended to ease the burdens on the kin network of mutual aid. Insistence on disrupting the cultural continuities of ethnic groups meant, in effect, that immigrants had to abandon the close ties to kin that were the principal means of transmitting their ethnic culture and identity. Requiring the children of immigrants to attend public school and, thus, to master English also meant that these youngsters would learn to devalue their parents' knowledge and skills. We shall return to this in the next chapter.

16. There are several excellent analyses of the birth control-cum-family planning movement. Our brief overview derives from Madaline Gray's biography of Margaret Sanger, *Margaret Sanger* (New York: Richard Marek Publishers, 1979); from Linda Gordon, *Women's Body, Women's Right* (New York: Grossman, 1976); from James C. Mohr, *Abortion in America* (New York: Oxford University Press, 1978); and from David Kennedy, *Birth Control in America* (New Haven: Yale University Press, 1976).

17. Even now, there is considerable resistance to the implications of this feature of our economy. The desire among employers to drive wages down is, apparently, high on to irresistible even though it is in the long run self-defeating.

18. As quoted in Martin Nicolaus, "The Unknown Marx," *New Left Review* (March-April 1968): 56. Nicolaus is the English translator of Marx's *Grundrisse*, from which the above quotation is taken.

19. The idea that large numbers of people might be reluctant to spend their wages, preferring instead to reduce their total work time, sounds silly, given what happened. So thoroughly have we become accommodated to consumption, to a linkage between leisure and consumption, and to ever expanding appetites that, now, the constant expansion of desires is regarded matter-of-factly as human nature. Obviously, consumer demand is no more natural than are thrift and self-denial: each is a cultural product, a pattern of behavior that has to be shaped and constantly reinforced if it is to even begin to appear so commonplace as to be regarded as "natural."

20. See Stuart Ewen, *Captains of Consciousness* (New York: McGraw Hill, 1976). For a more comprehensive account of the rising fortunes of the advertising industry, see Roland Marchand, *Advertising the American Dream: Making Way for Modernity, 1920-1940* (Berkeley: University of California Press, 1985).

21. Ewen, *Captains of Consciousness*, 62.

22. Erving Goffman, *The Presentation of Self in Everyday Life* (Garden City, NY: Doubleday Anchor, 1959).

23. In fact, though the success of an ad campaign is typically measured in increased sales of the product being touted, research has shown that the effect of any given ad spills over onto other products as well. Even if an ad doesn't get an individual to buy any particular product, a good ad raises the propensity to purchase in general.

24. Delores Hayden, *Redesigning the American Dream* (New York: W. W. Norton, 1984).

25. Hayden, *Redesigning the American Dream*, 34.

26. Alfred Chandler, Jr., *The Visible Hand* (Cambridge: Harvard University Press, 1977), 303–305; 402–405.

27. See Emma Rothschild, *Paradise Lost: The Decline of the Auto-Industrial Age* (New York: Random House, 1983).

28. U.S. Bureau of the Census, *U.S. Statistical Abstract, 1976* (Washington, DC: U.S. Government Printing Office, 1977), 717.

29. After 1929, mortgage debt declined with the depression. It did not attain predepression levels until several years after the end of World War II, when it increased rapidly. By 1950, $72.9 billion in mortgages were outstanding and, by 1960, this nearly trebled, rising to $206.8 billion. U.S. Bureau of the Census, *Historical Statistics of the United States, Colonial Times to 1970* , Bicentennial Edition, Part 1 (Washington, DC: U.S. Government Printing Office, 1975), 254.

30. The following section depends on the work of James Weinstein, *The Corporate Ideal in the Liberal State, 1900–1918* (Boston: Beacon Press, 1968); Gabriel Kolko, *The Triumph of Conservatism, 1900–1916* (Glencoe, IL: Free Press, 1963); and Robert H. Wiebe, *Businessmen and Reform* (Cambridge: Harvard University Press, 1962).

31. Alfred D. Chandler, Jr., in his *Strategy and Structure* (Cambridge: MIT Press, 1962), provides a compelling account of the reasons why the scale of industry grew so rapidly after the Civil War.

32. For an interpretive history of the NCF, see Weinstein, *The Corporate Ideal in the Liberal State.*

33. Caroline Bird, *The Invisible Scar* (New York: David McKay, 1971). Also see Studs Terkel, *Hard Times: An Oral History of the Great Depression* (New York: Pantheon, 1970).

34. E. W. Baake, *The Unemployed Worker* (New Haven: Yale University Press, 1940).

35. Hayden, *Redesigning the American Dream*, 6.

36. There are numerous accounts of the active volunteerism of suburbanites. Whyte's account of Park Forest, a suburb of Chicago, is one of the most famous. See William F. Whyte, *The Organization Man* (New

York: Simon and Schuster, 1956). Another detailed study of the social organization of a new suburb can be found in Herbert Gans, *The Levittowners* (New York: Pantheon, 1967).

37. The most compelling of these criticisms is leveled by Richard Sennett in his provocative book, *The Uses of Disorder* (New York: Vintage Books, 1970).

38. It should go without saying that this was largely restricted to whites. Racism kept the vast majority of blacks well on the periphery of the consumer culture and far away from suburbs. This began to change somewhat in the late 1960s and early 1970s as civil rights legislation began to assist the black middle class in its efforts to enter the mainstream of work, home ownership, and consumption. For an account of how the broader trends we are describing here have played out amongst blacks, see Bart Landry, *The New Black Middle Class* (Berkeley: University of California Press, 1987).

39. Of course the opposite is true too. Once started, decline can become self-reinforcing.

40. Indeed, observers continue to be struck by the degree to which families remain networks for the circulation of cash gifts as well as goods and services. Some estimates indicate that if all such transactions were fully reported, the GNP would rise by as much as 10 percent. Much of the so-called underground economy is not so much underground as it is intrafamilial. But though the network of family ties has by no means disappeared, there can be little doubt that its loss of exclusivity in these regards has meant the steady weakening of these ties.

41. John R. Seeley, et al., *Crestwood Heights: A Study of the Culture of Suburban Life* (New York: Basic Books, 1956).

42. This reduction in desire for consumption derives from two related aspects of social life among networks of kin and tightly bound stable neighborhoods. First, the pleasures and intrigues of interaction make people less interested in seeking pleasure through consumption. Second, and probably more important, integration in networks means that sharing and borrowing reduce the need for each household to purchase all of the things a household requires. For an example of how a family-orientation reduces consumerism, see Herbert Gans's description of an Italo-American neighborhood in his book *The Urban Villagers* (Glencoe, IL: Free Press, 1962).

43. The figures are from "The Long-run Decline in Liquidity," an editorial appearing in *Monthly Review* 22 (September 1970): 6.

44. New York: Macfadden Books, 1962.

Chapter 3

1. This is not to say that people were passive. The anthropological and historical record is filled with myriad ways people have struggled to control human fertility and to prolong life. Clearly, the desire to control destiny is not a modern aspiration. This said, it is also worth repeating that our forebears were far more stoical, far more resigned to the fragility of their efforts, than we are.

2. Gerald M. Platt and Fred Weinstein, *The Wish to Be Free: Society, Psyche, and Value Change* (Berkeley: University of California Press, 1969).

3. Those who insist that parental discipline and authority must be bolstered if we are to avoid the pitfalls of permissive, secular decadence must also insist that schools and the media, the two principal contacts children have with adults not directly chosen by parents, ought to echo the views of the parents. Otherwise, their authority will be exposed, children will perceive options and choices, and many will come to resent the ironfisted approach of their parents. Current attempts to prevent sex education, to introduce prayer in schools, to teach "creation science" as an antidote to Darwinian biology, as well as efforts to censor libraries and media programming are efforts to prevent children from encountering ideas incompatible with the views of their parents. In this sense, the Luddites who attempted to stop the industrial revolution by smashing machines and burning factories are the precursors of the latter-day Luddites who wish to twist education and culture to be consistent with their particular views.

4. Philip Slater's essay "Changing the Family" was the initial source of this line of reasoning for us. See Philip Slater, *Footholds* (Boston: Beacon Press, 1977), 48–67.

5. Our generalizations regarding Italo-Americans are based on a number of fine studies. See Herbert Gans, *The Urban Villagers* (Glencoe, IL: Free Press, 1962); Elizabeth Yans-McLaughlin, *Family and Community: Italian Immigrants in Buffalo, 1880–1930* (Ithaca: Cornell University Press, 1977); Humbert Nelli, *The Italians of Chicago, 1880–1920* (New York: Oxford University Press, 1970); and Francis A. J. Ianni, *A Family Business: Kinship and Social Control in Organized Crime* (New York: Russell Sage Foundation, 1972).

6. The current dispute over bilingualism in our schools and in public facilities is a dispute that, similarly, has considerable implications for family life. To reject bilingualism is to insist that Hispanic children learn to derogate the language of their parents. That this will reduce the authority of parents can scarcely be doubted. In this sense, the contro-

versy is not only about language and assimilation; it is also about the integrity of a certain kind of relationship between parents and children.

7. We are drawing here upon the following studies of Jewish Americans: Marshall Sklare, *American Jews* (New York: Random House, 1971); Marshall Sklare, *Jewish Identity on the Suburban Frontier: A Study of Group Survival in the Open Society* (New York: Basic Books, 1967); Sidney Goldstein and Calvin Goldscheider, *Jewish Americans: Three Generations in a Jewish Community* (Englewood Cliffs, NJ: Prentice-Hall, 1968); and Judith R. Kramer and Seymour Leventman, *Children of the Gilded Ghetto* (New Haven: Yale University Press, 1961).

8. M. Wolfenstein, "The Emergence of Fun Morality," *Journal of Social Issues* 7 (1951): 15–23. Also see H. Gadlin, "Child Discipline and the Pursuit of Self: An Historical Interpretation," *Advances in Child Development and Behavior* 12 (1978): 231–265.

9. Of course this can be read several ways. Christopher Lasch, among others, has argued that the decline of parental authority has produced, in effect, perverse flexibility and bogus choices. Echoing David Reisman's notion of the "other directed personality," Lasch claims that current forms of childrearing produce adults who are essentially passive, ready to accommodate to whatever seems stylish or "in." The desire for approval overwhelms whatever willingness there might otherwise be to take chances or to resist convention. Needless to say, we do not agree— or better, as we shall make clear in our concluding chapter, we think Lasch captures only one piece of a much more complex process. See Christopher Lasch, *Haven in a Heartless World* (New York: Basic Books, 1977); *The Culture of Narcissism* (New York: W. W. Norton, 1979); *The Minimal Self* (New York: W. W. Norton, 1984).

10. David Hogan, *Class and Reform* (Philadelphia: University of Pennsylvania Press, 1985), 107.

11. For an elaboration of this, see Ellen Greenberger, "Children's Employment and Families," in *Families and Work*, ed. Naomi Gerstel and Harriet Engel (Philadelphia: Temple University Press, 1987), 396–406. Greenberger shows that at one time children's work was simply one more indication of their embeddedness within the family. Now, when adolescents work, it is often an attempt to achieve distance and autonomy from family. In a similar vein, a recent study has shown that though most children continue to be assigned household chores, the overwhelming reason parents give for asking their children to "help out" is a belief that it is good for children, not that they actually need the assistance or that it is the duty of children to help parents. See Lynn K. White and David Brinkerhoff, "Children's Work in the Family: Its Significance and Meaning," in *Families and Work*, 204–218. It bears not-

ing, though, that there may be a change in the offing. With the steady growth in the ranks of working couples and working single parents, children may be expected to make genuinely substantive contributions to the running of the home. Several recent articles in the *New York Times*, for example, report that advertisers for major consumer items have begun to pitch campaigns to latchkey children because they often have a decisive role to play in the consumer choices of their parent(s). See Andrew H. Malcolm, "Teen-Age Shoppers: Desperately Seeking Spinach," 29 November 1987, 3–10; and Randall Rothenberg, "Ad Scene: For Children Home Alone, A Word from the Sponsor," 9 May 1988, D 8.

12. See Daniel Stern, *The Interpersonal World of the Infant: A View from Psychoanalysis and Developmental Psychology* (New York: Basic Books, 1985). Also see Jessica Benjamin, *The Bonds of Love: Feminism, Psychoanalysis and the Problem of Domination* (New York: Pantheon, 1988).

13. Ralph Waldo Emerson, "Self-Reliance," in *The Collected Works of Ralph Waldo Emerson*, vol. 2, (Cambridge: Belknap Press of Harvard University Press, 1979), 41–42.

14. New York: Harper & Row, 1986.

15. Again, at the risk of being repetitive, it is worth noting that this may be changing as more and more parents, because of work demands, rely on their children for the performance of important household duties. It is too soon to be able to say with any assurance what, if any, effect this will have on the dynamic we are sketching here.

16. Dorothy Dinnerstein, in her powerfully provocative book, *The Mermaid and the Minotaur* (New York: Harper & Row, 1976), argues that this sense of vulnerability in the face of loved ones arises out of our prolonged helplessness as infants. In our helplessness, we want what we cannot possibly have: we want complete nurturence a la womb and, failing that, we want autonomy—freedom from dependence upon the whimsy of others. Torn between two mutually exclusive and impossible goals, Dinnerstein argues, we become furious at our caretaker. Unhappily, our caretaker is, typically, a woman. Hence the long, virtually unbroken, derogation of women. It may be that emotional dependency is, as Dinnerstein suggests, always a loaded issue. If this is the case, our analysis points to key reasons why dependencies have become increasingly problematic in recent generations.

17. To get a sense of the change *Fortune* has chronicled, see the following articles: "The Class of '49," *Fortune*, June 1949, 84 ff. This article reports that "The class of '49, patently, is a settling-down generation" (86). Daniel Seligman, "The Confident Twenty-Five Year Olds," *Fortune*, February 1955, 100 ff., describes many who are still single but who are all expecting marriage, three to four children, and a house in the sub-

urbs. Duncan Norton-Taylor, "The Private World of the Class of '66," *Fortune*, February 1966, 128, records youthful disaffection with routine, careerism, and conventional notions of "settling down." Judson Gooding, "The Accelerated Generation Moves into Management," *Fortune*, March 1971, 100 ff. Gooding reports that, unlike previous young executives, this cohort is committed to ". . . individuality, openness, humanism . . . and change" (101). They are also reported to be hostile to arbitrary tests of commitment or allegiance. Gwen Kinkead, "On a Fast Track to the Good Life," *Fortune*, 7 April 1980, 74–84. The rising stars Kinkead features are all preoccupied with career advancement, against which all is measured; private lives are adjunct to work.

18. *Youth 1976: Attitudes of Young Americans Fourteen through Twenty-five Towards Work, Life Insurance, Finances, Family, Marriage, Life Styles, Religion* (New York: American Council of Life Insurance, n.d.), 44–48.

19. Daniel Yankelovich has polled the nation's youth on a broad range of social and political values. His findings show dramatic shifts in attitudes toward marriage. It is not so much that marriage has gone out of style, though only slim majorities report "looking forward to marriage," as it is that ideas about commitment seem to be undergoing change. There appears to be greater tolerance of extramarital relationships as well as increased receptivity to divorce. See his *The New Morality: A Profile of American Youth in the 70's* (New York: McGraw-Hill, 1974), and *New Rules: Searching for Self-Fulfillment in a World Turned Upside Down* (New York: Random House, 1981).

20. The predominance of career considerations in structuring life choices is revealed in the upsurge of women who postponed pregnancies in their twenties, largely in order to pursue careers, and who are now, in their thirties, deciding to have a child. Census figures released in 1989 show a steady rise in the fertility rate of women in their thirties. The Census Bureau also reports that the number of childless wives in their late twenties who indicate plans to have a child "at some point" is rising. See the *Boston Globe*, 22 June 1989, 3. In Chapter 6 we will show how this accommodation to the dictates of career is a two-way street. As more women get solidly established in careers and *then* decide to have a child, employers will face steadily mounting pressure to accommodate to the needs of these women lest they lose valued employees.

21. Marion F. Solomon, *Narcissism and Intimacy* (New York: W.W. Norton, 1989), 4.

22. Barbara Ehrenreich, *The Hearts of Men* (Garden City, NY: Anchor Press, 1983).

23. Judith S. Wallerstein and Sandra Blakeslee, "Children After Divorce," *New York Times Magazine*, 22 January 1989, 19. For a fuller ac-

count of this important study, see their *Second Chances: Men, Women, and Children a Decade after Divorce* (New York: Ticknor and Fields, 1989).

24. Mel Krantzler, *Creative Divorce: A New Opportunity for Personal Growth* (New York: M. Evans, 1973); Melody Beattie, *Beyond Codependency and Getting Better All the Time* (San Francisco: Harper & Row, 1989).

25. See, for example, Rhona Rapoport, Robert Rapoport, and Ziona Streliz (with Stephen Kew), *Fathers, Mothers and Society* (New York: Basic Books, 1977). For a popularized summary of recent trends in this regard, see Vance Packard, *Our Endangered Children: Growing up in a Changing World* (Boston: Little, Brown, 1983), especially Chapter 3, "The Rise of Sentiment against Children."

26. This figure comes from the study "Raising Children in a Changing Society," commissioned by General Mills, as cited in Daniel Yankelovich, *New Rules*, 104. This change, as with so many others, is visible on the nation's bumpers—large recreation vehicles commonly sport the bumper sticker "We are spending our children's inheritance."

27. For men, the change was from 32 percent in 1960 to 16 percent in 1985. For women, the change was from 51 to 32 percent over this same period. These figures, and the ones cited above are taken from the Bureau of the Census, *Marital Status and Living Arrangements: March, 1985* , Current Population Reports, Series P- 20, No. 410 (Washington, DC: U.S. Government Printing Office, 1986).

28. *New York Times*, 14 July 1988, 4. The problem with such figures is that they do not track the number of families that experience this twist. Children leave, some return to stay, some return for a year or two, and others never return. It is likely that many more than the estimated 8 to 16 percent of families have been host to a returning son or daughter.

29. This complex set of issues is now beginning to be systematically explored. The most thorough study to date is by Allan Schnaiberg and Sheldon Goldenberg, "From Empty Nest to Crowded Nest: The Dynamics of Incompletely-Launched Young Adults," *Social Problems* 36 (June 1989): 251–269.

30. Marabel Morgan, *The Total Woman* (New York: Pocket Books, 1975), originally published in 1973 by Fleming H. Revell Company.

31. Joseph Veroff, Elizabeth Douvan, and Richard A. Kulka, *The Inner American: A Self-Portrait from 1957 to 1976* (New York: Basic Books, 1981).

32. Actually, this may be less a new development than it is a rediscovery of an older mode in which children and their putative needs were distinctly secondary to the needs of adults.

Chapter 4

1. See Chaya S. Piotrkowski, *Work and the Family System: A Naturalistic Study of Working-Class and Lower-Middle-Class Families* (New York: Free Press, 1978), for an insightful discussion of the impact of different ways of integrating or separating work life from family life. Our focus here is on how different types of families are organized in relation to different types of work and different degrees of affluence.

2. The phrase is Lewis Coser's. See his *Greedy Institutions: Patterns of Undivided Committment* (New York: Free Press, 1974).

3. For example, see Talcott Parsons and Robert F. Bales, *Family, Interaction, and Socialization Process* (Glencoe, IL: Free Press, 1955). Also see the following articles on the family by Parsons: "The Kinship System of the Contemporary United States," in *Essays in Sociological Theory* (Glencoe, IL: Free Press, 1949), 177–196; and "The Social Structure of the Family," in *The Family: Its Function and Destiny*, ed. Ruth N. Anshen (New York: Harper & Bros. 1949), 173–201.

4. William F. Whyte's classic, *The Organization Man* (New York: Simon & Schuster, 1956), is one such study. But from the standpoint of analyzing family life, none surpasses John R. Seeley et al., *Crestwood Heights* (New York: Basic Books, 1956).

5. Seeley et al., *Crestwood Heights*. See especially chapters nine and eleven. Seeley shows how parents are trapped between competing experts. Given the intrinsic ambiguities of childrearing (one cannot know the final effects of what one does until years later, when the child has grown at least to young adulthood), parents are continually alert to new theories or approaches. This gives rise to almost fad-like movements in what otherwise are supposed to be scholarly if not scientific professions. Seeley also shows how a wide variety of what he calls "arbiters of taste" arise because so many in the upper middle class have cut themselves off from webs of association that once defined the parameters of good taste.

6. See Gail Sheehy, *Passages: Predictable Crises of Adult Life* (New York: Dutton, 1976). It is interesting to observe our susceptibility to psychological explanations that suggest certain life problems are the inevitable outcome of the working out of a natural and universal developmental process rather than the result of faulty social arrangements. This is one of the ways we accommodate our personal life to social structure.

7. Betty Friedan, *The Feminine Mystique* (New York: W. W. Norton, 1963).

8. Much of the above draws on Annie Oakley's analysis of housework, *The Sociology of Housework* (New York: Pantheon Books, 1974).

9. There are now available a number of accounts of these complexities of mothering. See, for example, Jane Lazarre, *The Mother Knot* (New York: McGraw-Hill, 1976).

10. Daniel Bell, "The Great Back-to-Work Movement," *Fortune*, July 1956, cited in *Industrial Society and Social Welfare*, H. L. Wilensky and Charles N. Lebeaux (New York: Free Press of Glencoe, 1965), 127.

11. The term is Hanna Papanek's. See her essay, "Men, Women, and Work: Reflections on the Two-Person Career," in *Changing Women in a Changing Society*, ed. Joan Huber (Chicago: University of Chicago Press, 1973), 90–110. Also see Arlie Russell Hochschild, "Inside the Clockwork of Male Careers," in *Crisis in American Institutions*, 3rd ed., eds. Jerome H. Skolnick and Elliot Currie (Boston: Little, Brown, 1976), 251–266.

12. Martha R. Fowlkes, *Behind Every Successful Man: Wives of Medicine and Academe* (New York: Columbia University Press, 1980).

13. Kathleen Gerson's *Hard Choices: How Women Decide about Work, Career, and Motherhood* (Berkeley: University of California Press, 1985) is an insightful analysis of the ways both family life and work life interact to produce often dramatic shifts in women's commitments to both domesticity and work. Some women seek out work as compensation for marital or romantic disappointments, while others turn to marriage and childbearing in response to disenchanting experiences in the workplace.

14. See Paul L. Wachtel, *The Poverty of Affluence* (New York: Free Press, 1983).

15. Lee Rainwater, Richard P. Coleman, and Gerald Handel, *Workingman's Wife* (New York: Oceana Publications, 1959).

16. Greg J. Duncan, *Years of Poverty, Years of Plenty: The Changing Economic Fortunes of American Workers and Families* (Ann Arbor, MI: Institute for Social Research, University of Michigan, 1984), 40–69.

17. Lillian Rubin, *Worlds of Pain* (New York: Basic Books, 1976).

18. For example, Carol Stack cites an instance among the several expanded families she studied in which the female relatives of a new bride systematically undermined the young marriage in order to keep the young woman close to family of kin. Carol Stack, *All Our Kin* (New York: Harper & Row, 1974).

19. See, for example, John H. Scanzoni, *The Black Family in Modern Society: Patterns of Stability and Security* (Chicago: University of Chicago Press, 1977).

20. Frank Furstenberg, *Unplanned Parenthood: The Social Consequences of Teenage Childbearing* (New York: Free Press, 1976).

21. For an analysis of the baby boom in the context of long-term trends in marriage and birth rates, see Andrew J. Cherlin, *Marriage,*

Divorce, Remarriage: Social Trends in the United States (Cambridge: Harvard University Press, 1981).

22. For the figures on the growth in dispensing mood-altering drugs, see Henry L. Lennard et al., *Mystification and Drug Misuse* (San Francisco: Jossey-Bass, 1971). An article appearing in *McCall's* in the same year as Lennard's book came out reported on the ways pharmaceutical companies marketed their new psychoactive drugs to the doctors writing the prescriptions. Here are two examples of advertisements taken from medical journals, as reported in Roland H. Berg, "The Over-Medicated Woman," *McCall's*, September 1971:

> A full page photograph shows a woman in her mid-thirties, arms akimbo, a glum, somewhat defiant look on her face. The copy, in bold headlines, proclaims: THE COLLECTOR. AT 35 SHE'S COLLECTED, AMONG OTHER THINGS, A COLLEGE DEGREE SHE'S NEVER USED, TWO CHILDREN UNDERFOOT MOST OF THE DAY, A HUSBAND WHOSE CAREER TAKES HIM AWAY MOST OF THE TIME, A FOLDER OF UNPAID BILLS, AND VARIOUS SYMPTOMS—REAL OR IMAGINED. The copy closes by urging her physician to prescribe the particular tranquilizer the company is peddling.

> Another well-circulated ad pictures a nail-chewing young housewife gazing apprehensively through prison bars of mops, scrubbing brushes, and brooms. The clarion message to physicians announces: YOU CAN'T SET HER FREE. BUT YOU CAN HELP HER FEEL LESS ANXIOUS. YOU KNOW THIS WOMAN. SHE'S ANXIOUS, TENSE, IRRITABLE. SHE'S FELT THIS WAY FOR MONTHS. BESET BY THE SEEMINGLY INSURMOUNTABLE PROBLEMS OF RAISING A YOUNG FAMILY, AND CONFINED TO THE HOME MOST OF THE TIME, HER SYMPTOMS REFLECT A SENSE OF INADEQUACY AND ISOLATION. The answer: a magic tranquilizer the company manufactures.

23. Discussion of working wives has been going on for some time, but the literature that began to hold up couples in which both spouses worked as models, as an improvement on prevailing family arrangements, began in the late 1960s. One of the earliest, and still one of the most seminal, analyses of the dilemmas of conventional housewifery and the positive attractions of wives working was Alice Rossi's essay, "Equality between the Sexes: An Immodest Proposal," *Daedalus* 93 (1964): 607–652. Also see Robert and Rhona Rapoport, "Work and Family in Contemporary Society," *American Sociological Review* 30 (June 1965): 381–394; Jan E. Dizard, *Social Change and the Family* (Chicago: Community and Family Studies Center/University of Chicago, 1968); Rhona and Robert Rapoport, *Dual-Career Families* (Harmondsworth, England: Penguin Books, 1971). Michael Young and Peter Willmott, both British sociologists, were the first to put the dual-career family in broad historical perspective. See their book, *The Symmetrical Family* (New York: Pantheon, 1973).

24. This is a complex matter and one that we cannot even begin to resolve here. The fact that careers, on the average, pay far more than jobs makes a significant difference in the resources a couple has at its disposal, whether one or both are working. And this, as we have seen, shapes much of the character and dynamic of family life. But it is also true that an auto mechanic who is a workaholic may have family relationships that are very similar to those of an equally work-obsessed professional.

25. Rosanna Hertz, *More Equal Than Others: Women and Men in Dual-Career Marriages* (Berkeley: University of California Press, 1986). Hertz's study is one of the most probing of the studies of dual-career families. Though limited by the narrowness of her sample, the questions she raises are central to understanding emergent family forms. Many of our observations are indebted to her work. Noting the irony involved, Hertz discovers that those who have resorted to live-in help often get enmeshed in the complicated familial relationships of their domestic help. Given the low wages for such work, many are recent (and some illegal) immigrants with extensive ties to kin, many of whom are having difficulties with landlords, immigration (INS), or employers. Having rather deliberately cut ties to their own kin, those who hire domestic help can find themselves implicated in the personal lives of their domestic help. See her discussion, pp. 159–194.

26. In addition to the work on dual-career couples already cited, our discussion also draws upon the following sources: Caroline Bird, *The Two-Paycheck Marriage* (New York: Rawson, Wade Publishers, 1979); Rhona and Robert N. Rapoport, *Dual-Career Families Re-examined* (New York: Harper & Row, 1976); and Lynda Lytle Holmstrom, *The Two-Career Family* (Cambridge: Schenkman, 1973).

27. Hertz, *More Equal Than Others*, 13. The earlier study by Holmstrom, *The Two-Career Family*, had found couples still quite firmly embedded in traditional gender prescriptions. It is impossible to know if Hertz's findings represent a trend or if they are an artifact of her particular sample of affluent couples.

28. Arlie Russell Hochschild, with Anne Machung, *The Second Shift: Working Parents and the Revolution at Home* (New York: Viking, 1989). This deeply informative book came out just as this manuscript was about to be sent off to the typesetter. Our discussion of dual-career and working couples would have been amplified and made more concrete had we had the time to incorporate the analysis they present.

29. A recent study of dual-earner couples shows that they spend less time at home and less time together than do single-earner couples. The researchers conclude that "among dual-earner couples, more pressing work schedules mean losses in togetherness in every part of domestic

life. . . ." (399). See Paul William Kingston and Steven L. Nock, "Time Together among Dual-Earner Couples," *American Sociological Review* 52 (June 1987): 391–400.

30. See Janet G. Hunt and Larry L. Hunt, "The Dualities of Careers and Families: New Integrations or New Polarizations?" *Social Problems* 29 (June 1982): 499–510.

31. There is no study of contemporary divorce of the sort that Goode carried out in the 1950s. This is unfortunate because there are compelling reasons to believe that the meaning of divorce—and the reasons that lead people to seek divorce—have changed since Goode wrote his classic on the subject. When he wrote, it was still the case that divorce was uncommon among professionals and executives. This appears no longer to be the case. Similarly, it appears to be the case that the threshold of tolerance for aggravation has lowered substantially: people get divorced today for reasons that would not have been sufficient a generation ago. See William J. Goode, *After Divorce* (Glencoe, IL: Free Press, 1956).

32. In 1986 the Census Bureau reported that in roughly 18 percent of working couples the wife earned more than her husband. But for couples between the ages of 25–34, 34 percent of the wives earned more than their husbands. *Daily Hampshire Gazette*, 7 May 1986, 9.

33. See Louise Bernikow, *Alone in America* (New York: Harper & Row, 1986), 74.

34. Ever since Matina Horner's study of women's "fear of success," psychologists and others have been examining the myriad ways that women's participation in the public world has been made complicated by the legacy of patriarchy and the assumptions of gender differences. See Matina Horner, "FAIL: Bright Women," *Psychology Today* 3 (June 1969), 36 ff. Horner's work has received much critical scrutiny, the bulk of it indicating that there is no specific fear of success unique to women. For a review of this literature, see Michele A. Paludi, "Psychometric Properties and Underlying Assumptions of Four Objective Measures of Fear of Success," *Sex Roles* 10:9 / 10 (1984): 765–781.

35. Much of the rhetoric surrounding dual-career couples in general and childless couples in particular conveys the sense that such couples are flying in the face of all traditional values. In one sense this may be true. But as Gerson discovered, women who are career oriented largely accept the social definitions of what a good mother should be and do not think they can live up to such expectations. In effect, their desire to avoid maternity is not a rejection of the ideal. Revision of how mothers should act, Gerson discovered, comes from those women who are trying to juggle career and childbearing. It is these women who have been the source of ideas such as the distinction between the quantity of

time spent with a child versus the quality of time spent. See Gerson, *Hard Choices*, 177–184.

36. In 1983 the Census Bureau reported that in 1982, women between the ages of 30 and 34 gave birth to 73.5 children per 1000 women. In 1980, the number of births for the comparable age group was only 60. *Daily Hampshire Gazette*, 10 June 1983, 5.

37. See Doris R. Entwisle and Susan G. Doering, *The First Birth: A Family Turning Point* (Baltimore: Johns Hopkins University Press, 1981) for a thorough study of how couples adjust (or fail to adjust) to their first child.

38. As we shall see, the rapid increase in two-income families has begun to result in pressure on employers to introduce more flexible work schedules and other accommodations to the needs of working couples. But, for the most part, two-income families are still obliged to confront the need for child care and work schedule flexibility largely on their own, catch as catch can.

39. See E. Berman et al., "The Two-Professional Marriage: A New Conflict Syndrome," *Journal of Sex and Marriage Therapy* 1 (1975): 242–253.

40. Uma Sekaran, *Dual-Career Families* (San Francisco: Jossey-Bass, 1986).

41. See Hunt and Hunt, "Dualities of Careers and Families."

42. As with other family arrangements, it is important to distinguish between the ideal and the reality. Without doubt, there are many cohabiting relationships that suffer from the same inequalities and restrictions on autonomy as many marriages. And certainly there are cohabiting relationships where one or the other of the partners, usually the man, prefers cohabitation because it perpetuates an inequality grounded in the interpersonal dynamics of the relationship. But without denying these versions of cohabiting relationships, it is important to acknowledge the recent increase in the number and diversity of mainstream people for whom cohabitation is a self-conscious effort to avoid the pitfalls of marriage while maintaining companionship and autonomy.

43. This is not to say that if the divorce rate were to decline poverty would also decline. There is an important distinction, too often overlooked, between the causes of poverty and the reasons particular people wind up rich or poor. Large families, for example, are associated with poverty; but they are not the cause of poverty. Robert Kennedy's eleven children did not reduce him to squalor. The issue here is not the cause of poverty but rather the social dynamics by which we sort ourselves out. For a discussion of this, as well as an analysis of the relationship between family and poverty, see Duncan, *Years of Poverty*. Rising

divorce rates among whites and rising proportions of never-married mothers among blacks have, in the aggregate, altered the character of the poor: the ranks of the poor are rapidly swelling with women. For analyses of this, with particular reference to female-headed households, see, in addition to Duncan, Heather Ross and Isabel V. Sawhill, *Time of Transition: The Growth of Families Headed by Women* (Washington, DC: Urban Institute Press, 1975); Irwin Garfinkel and Sara S. McLanahan, *Single Mothers and Their Children* (Washington, DC: Urban Institute Press, 1986); Marion Wright Edelman, *Families in Peril* (Cambridge: Harvard University Press, 1987).

44. We say "apparently" here because we know of no studies that have been done on large, representative samples of single parents. There is, fortunately, a recent study that, while based on a narrow sample, systematically explores the attitudes toward remarriage among a group of divorced women. Our discussion is indebted to this study. See Terry Arendell, *Mothers and Divorce: Legal, Economic, and Social Dilemmas* (Berkeley: University of California Press, 1986).

45. As is so often the case, demographic processes do not affect all groups equally. Among blacks, the increase in never-married mothers has been a very important phenomenon. This has not been due to increases in the rates of out-of-wedlock pregnancies. In fact this rate has been declining. Rather, in the words of Garfinkel and McLanahan, *Single Mothers and Their Children*, "We conclude that the recent increase in families headed by unmarried women among blacks is due primarily to a decline in the propensity to marry on the part of young black men and women. In this sense the pattern for blacks and whites is similar: most of the growth in single parenthood is due to changes in marital behavior. The difference is that whites marry and increasingly divorce, whereas blacks are increasingly likely never to marry at all"(54).

46. See Arendell, *Mothers and Divorce*, 142, for a brief summary of these trends.

47. It would be misleading to think of all single people warmly embracing their independence. Roughly one-third of all single-person households are occupied by elderly women, many of whom live at or below the poverty level. Our discussion of singles obviously is not meant to describe people who are forced by circumstances into loneliness. Rather, we are describing those who intentionally desire to be on their own. We know of no data that allow us to separate out the willingly single from the unwillingly single. It is clear, though, that many singles, young and old, affluent and poor, are ambivalent at least some of the time. Suzanne Gordon's *Lonely in America* (New York: Simon & Schuster, 1976) explores the side of single life that is filled with pathos and fear.

48. It should be recalled that over the past fifteen years there has

been an increase in the proportion of 25–34 year olds living with their parents. While the economy may contribute to this, it is also quite probable that the autonomy that has attracted many has been intimidating to others. As we saw in the preceding chapter, our cultural emphasis on autonomy has left many people ill at ease, even debilitated. No doubt a number of these young adults had been on their own and in some way failed. The return home, however comforting, is not likely to be experienced by either the parents or the offspring as a triumphant return. Much more likely, the continuing dependence is a source of distress and worry all around.

49. See, for example, Linda Waite, Frances Goldscheider, and Christine Witsberger, "The Development of Individualism: Nonfamily Living and the Plans of Young Men and Women," *American Sociological Review* 51 (August 1986): 541–554. Also see Calvin Goldscheider and Frances K. Goldscheider, "Moving Out and Marriage: What Do Young Adults Expect?" *American Sociological Review* 52 (April 1987): 278–285.

50. The percentage is important because while the number of singles is at an all-time high, the percentage of the total population that is single is actually lower now than it was at the turn of the century, when 46 percent of the population was single. Indeed, the story through the twentieth century has been one of steady decreases in the proportion of single people. This trend was reversed beginning about 1960, when there was a relatively sharp increase, and it has continued at a somewhat slower pace up to the present.

51. Cited in Leonard Cargan and Matthew Melko, *Singles: Myths and Realities* (Beverly Hills, CA: Sage Publications, 1982), 281–282.

52. A similar process seems to be underway amid the elderly, many of whom are single and uninterested in living with their children. In retirement communities and congregate housing complexes for the elderly, there is a dense web of kin-like interaction, the creation, as it were, of intentional families. For one account of such a development, see Arlie Russell Hochschild's *Unexpected Community* (Englewood Cliffs, NJ: Prentice-Hall, 1973).

Chapter 5

1. The first of these critiques was David Reisman, Nathan Glazer, and Reuel Denney's, *The Lonely Crowd* (New Haven: Yale University Press, 1950). Vance Packard's *The Status Seekers* (New York: David McKay, 1959) was one of the better of the popularized critiques. But C. Wright Mills, first in *White Collar* (New York: Oxford University Press, 1951) and then in *The Power Elite* (New York: Oxford University Press, 1956),

was probably the most penetrating and systematic of the critics. The economist John Kenneth Galbraith, whose book *The Affluent Society* (Boston: Houghton Mifflin, 1958) provided the name for the new order, was also one of the most thoughtful of the critics, but it seems that people were so taken by the title of his book that they did not read on to encounter his misgivings.

2. The most sophisticated and compelling of the many critiques of affirmative action and related initiatives is Nathan Glazer's *Affirmative Discrimination: Ethnic Inequality and Public Policy* (New York: Basic Books, 1975). For a recent and telling analysis of the resurgence of racism under new guises, see David T. Wellman, "The New Political Linguistics of Race," *Socialist Review* 87–88 (1986): 43–62.

3. Ultimately, a tax revolt developed, led by the California ballot initiative Proposition 13, passed in the late 1970s. Mobilized around antipathy toward "big government," voters across the nation were urged to halt the expansion of government by restricting its revenue-generating capacities. Reagan, of course, was the master of this gambit, despite his record as governor of California and as president: in both offices he presided over steadily expanding budget outlays.

There is a deeply paradoxical element to this unwillingness to pay taxes. As we shall see later in this chapter, a broad expanse of state programs devoted to welfare of one sort or another enjoys majoritarian support. Leaders of tax revolts, including Reagan, garner support that is essentially racist by attacking welfare programs like Aid to Families with Dependent Children (AFDC), which are associated in the public's mind with black and Hispanic poor.

4. This portrait is heavily indebted to work of Richard Flacks. See his *Youth and Social Change* (Chicago: Markham, 1971). Also see Richard Flacks, "The Liberated Generation," *Journal of Social Issues* 23 (1967): 52–75; and Kenneth Keniston, *Young Radicals* (New York: Harcourt, Brace and World, 1968).

5. Louis Feuer's *The Conflict of Generations* (New York: Basic Books, 1969) is the most notable representative of this point of view.

6. The phrase is Daniel Bell's, but the sentiments conveyed were shared broadly by a new stratum of pragmatic cold-war liberals, many of whom, like Bell, had been communists or Trotskyists in their young adulthood.

7. For an account of the persistence of fundamentalism in the United States, see George Marsden, *Fundamentalism and American Culture* (New York: Oxford University Press, 1980). Also see Marsden's *Evangelicism and Modern America* (Grand Rapids, MI: W. B. Eerdmans, 1984); and James Davison Hunter's *American Evangelicism: Conservative Religion and*

the Quandary of Modernity (New Brunswick, NJ: Rutgers University Press, 1983). The authors are indebted to David Wills for guiding them to these analyses of fundamentalism and evangelicism.

8. Paul Weyrich, a new right leader, has pointed out that the conflicts that fundamentalists had with both state and federal governments over school curricula and tax exemptions for their private academies also contributed to the politicization of the religious right. He offered these observations on a PBS special, "The Conservatives," aired nationwide during the week of 18 January 1987.

9. There was anything but unanimity on this within the religious right. As we saw in Chapter 4, Marabel Morgan clearly rejects repressive or puritanical attitudes to *conjugal* sexuality. For a survey of the convolutions fundamentalists are going through over the issue of sexuality, see Barbara Ehrenreich, Elizabeth Hess, and Gloria Jacobs, "Unbuckling the Bible Belt," *Mother Jones*, July/August 1986, 46 ff.

10. This view of family life is consonant with the stereotypical imagery of what we have been calling the conventional family, particularly in lower-middle- and middle-class embodiments, which we described in the preceding chapter. One reason for this is revealed in Kristen Luker's study of pro- and anti-abortion activists, *Abortion and the Politics of Motherhood* (Berkeley: University of California Press, 1984). Luker found sharp class differences between the pro's and anti's. Anti-abortion activists were predominantly drawn from the lower middle class. They were women with little exposure to college and little experience in the labor force, whose husbands had stable blue-collar jobs or white-collar jobs on the lower rungs of large organizations. By contrast, pro-abortion activists predominantly came from the upper middle class. Also see Rosalind Pollack Petchesky, *Abortion and Woman's Choice: The State, Sexuality, and Reproductive Freedom* (Boston: Northeastern University Press, 1984).

11. See Gary Wills's brilliant study of Nixon, *Nixon Agonistes* (Boston: Houghton Mifflin, 1970).

12. No-fault divorce laws were enacted in several states in the early 1970s and began a significant—and by no means unambiguous—change in the legal understandings of marriage. See Lenore J. Weitzman and Ruth B. Dixon, "The Transformation of Legal Marriage Through No-Fault Divorce," in *Family in Transition*, 5th ed., ed. Arlene S. Skolnick and Jerome H. Skolnick (Boston: Little, Brown, 1986), 338–351. Lenore Weitzman has argued that the revisions in divorce law have contributed substantially to the economic woes of divorced mothers and to the rapid increase of single mothers in poverty. See her *The Divorce Revolution: The Unexpected Social and Economic Consequences for Women and Children in America* (New York: Free Press, 1985).

13. Though these themes were treated by a number of writers, none stressed them so vividly as George Gilder. In his book *Wealth and Poverty* (New York: Basic Books, 1981), he identifies the pursuit of wealth with a presumably innate masculine desire to protect and provide for loved ones. Anything that deflects this drive, whether it be welfare or feminist insistence upon equality between the sexes, will ultimately reduce a society's capacity to produce wealth. See Chapter 6, "The Nature of Poverty," for Gilder's views on the way family life and the economy are interwoven.

One of the most explicit expressions of this point of view recently appeared in a U.S. Office of Education report titled *The Family: Preserving America's Future* (December 1986). Quoting from the report, authored by Gary L. Bauer, then Undersecretary of Education (he was soon to be named the President's Chief Domestic Policy Advisor):

> *We must guard against abusing and misusing the pro-family label.* In the past, it has been used to cover an incredible array of political schemes. During the 1930s and 1940s, for instance, Social Democrats in several European nations purported to 'save' the family by socializing the costs of child rearing. State-funded day care, child allowances, national health systems, school feeding programs, and other welfare programs were put in place at tremendous expense. Government grew and taxed, pinching pocketbooks and forcing mothers into the workplace. Birth rates declined. All this has been done elsewhere in the name of the family. It must be avoided here (8). [emphasis in original.]

The report continues,

> This fabric of family life has been frayed by the abrasive experiments of two liberal decades. If by some terrible turn of events, it were to unravel, then both economic progress and personal liberty would disappear as well. Neither prosperity nor freedom can be sustained without a transfusion, from generation to generation, of family values: respect and discipline, restraint and self-sacrifice, interdependence and cooperation, loyalty and fidelity, and an ethical code that gives to individuals, however lowly, a transcendent import.
>
> The idols of our recent past were those who defied norms and shattered standards, and indeed there is always a place for 'rebels.' *But in a healthy society, heroes are the women and men who hold the world together one home at a time: the parent and grandparents who forego pleasures, delay purchases, foreclose options, and commit most of their lives to the noblest undertaking of citizenship: raising children who, resting on the shoulders of the previous generation, will see farther then we and reach higher* (9–10) [emphasis in original.]

14. Daniel Patrick Moynihan, *The Negro Family: The Case for National Action* (Washington, DC: Office of Policy Planning and Research, United States Department of Labor, U.S. Government Printing Office, March 1965).

15. Perhaps embittered by the reception his report received, or maybe hopeful that economic growth, by itself, would generate suffi-

cient opportunity for black men, Moynihan, as Nixon's chief domestic affairs advisor, came to urge "benign neglect" as the policy of choice. Now, as the senior senator from New York and chair of the Senate Finance Committee's Subcommittee on Social Security and Family Policy, Moynihan has announced his intention to promulgate sweeping welfare reforms specifically aimed at reducing welfare dependency of female-headed households. But Moynihan no longer believes in the necessity of the male breadwinner. Rather than attempting to bolster men's breadwinning capacities, Moynihan has declared the goal of helping single mothers become self-supporting. At the opening session of his subcommittee Moynihan observed: "A program (AFDC) that was designed for poor widows will not be supported in a world where mothers are poor because they are unsupported by their divorced husbands or because they are unwed." He continued, "A program that was designed to pay mothers to stay at home with their children cannot succeed when we now observe most mothers going out to work." *New York Times*, 24 January 1987, A 1.

16. Early in his administration, several of his most dedicated staffers, men who had literally worked night and day in his behalf, found themselves in divorce proceedings. Apart from the sympathy he no doubt felt for these close associates, Carter was also concerned lest he somehow appear to condone or even to contribute to the sundering of sacred vows. For a report on this episode see Laura Foreman's report, "Spend More Time with the Family? Carter's Aides Find They Can't," *New York Times*, 24 February 1977, C 30.

17. Obviously, the statistics on domestic violence are among the most unreliable. Much that goes on behind closed doors goes unreported. Estimates of abuse that are based on extrapolations from verified reports must be taken with more than a grain of salt. For a summary of some recent studies and some correlations to changes in unemployment rates, see Barry Bluestone and Bennett Harrison, *The Deindustrialization of America* (New York: Basic Books, 1982), 63–66.

18. It is almost impossible to determine whether the increased reports of family violence represent real increases or simply greater sensitivity and alertness to the problem. Hard, reliable numbers are virtually impossible to obtain, but estimates of wife battering range from a low of 2 million to a high of 6 million women beaten each year (*New York Times*, 1 July 1985, I 14). The incidence of child abuse appears to be even higher and, reflecting the tensions that arise when companionate couples are obliged to accommodate an elderly relative, rates of abuse of elderly relatives is also on the rise. In 1988, amid increasing reports of elderly abuse, The National Committee on the Prevention of Elder Abuse was founded and began publishing a journal, the *Journal*

of Elder Abuse and Neglect. For a brief overview of the steadily mounting incidence of reported child abuse through the eighties, see B. Kantrowitz, "And Thousands More," *Newsweek,* 12 December 1988, 58–59.

19. This is discussed more fully in Chapter 3. Allan Schnaiberg and Sheldon Goldenberg, "From Empty Nest to Crowded Nest: The Dynamics of Incompletely-Launched Young Adults," *Social Problems* 36 (June 1989): 251–269, review what little systematic data is available. There also have been numerous feature stories, columns, and vignettes that have derived from these circumstances. Some have been light-hearted; others have been quite somber indeed. For the somber side, see the story in the *New York Times,* 4 November 1985, II 11. In the former vein, a young woman wrote as follows to Ann Landers:

> Call me Mary. I am 26, single, have a master's in English and worked for a top-notch ad agency right out of college. I got pink-slipped in the crunch last September and have walked my feet off trying to find another job. No luck. Three weeks ago I was down to my last $100, so I called Mom and Dad and asked if I could have my room back until I got on my feet. They said "Of course." I've been trying to keep my mouth shut and my temper under control when Mom treats me like she did when I was in high school. I am expected to go with them to visit relatives who are bigots and bores. I cringe when I see Mom rewashing the tub because I didn't do it "right." I know it's hard on the folks to have me here, but it's harder on me to be here. My dignity and self-esteem are shot. My disposition is awful. I feel resentment growing by the day. Yet it is their home. They have a right to call the signals. If I don't find a job soon, I may move in with a semi-creep who has been pushing for the arrangement. What do you say, Ann?
>
> Ann responds: Don't trade bronchitis for lung cancer. Stay put. Follow every job lead possible. Good luck to you and your fellow clones.

20. Current estimates run as high as 1.5 million teenagers adrift in the nation. In a recent *U.S. News & World Report* story on "drifter teens," it was reported that a center for homeless teens turned away more than 16,000 youngsters in 1984 because their facilities were overcrowded. See "'Runaways,' 'Throwaways,' 'Bagkids'—An Army of Drifter Teens," 11 March 1985, 52–53.

21. Homelessness became a politicized issue during the Reagan administration because officials refused to admit that their policies were not working. Thus, the administration suggested that most of the nation's homeless *choose* to be on the streets. And HUD recently released a report with drastically lower estimates of homelessness than any of the estimates from other agencies, public and private, concerned with the problem. Whatever the actual numbers, it is clear that few of the "new homeless" are choosing life on the streets. Again, for illustrative purposes, see the *New York Times,* 22 January 1984, I 1; *New York Times,* 3 June 1984, I 42. In 1987, the U.S. Conference of Mayors issued a report that families seeking emergency shelter had increased by 31 per-

cent between 1985 and 1987 in a survey of 29 cities. Reported in the *Boston Sunday Globe*, 10 May 1987, 35.

22. These trends are derived from reports from the Census Bureau over the past few years in their series P–20, which chronicles changes in marital status, marriage rates, and household composition. See, for example, U.S. Bureau of the Census Current Population Reports, Series P– 20, No. 399, *Marital Status and Living Arrangements: March, 1984* (Washington, DC: U.S. Government Printing Office, 1985). In 1988, the last year for which data were available, the Census Bureau reported that the numbers of cohabiting heterosexual and homosexual couples was continuing to rise, the former nearing the 2.5 million mark and the latter passing the 1.5 million mark in 1987. *Boston Globe*, 13 May 1988, 3.

23. The data on birthrates is from U.S. Bureau of the Census, *Statistical Abstract of the U.S.: 1989* , 109th ed. (Washington, DC: Government Printing Office, 1989), 62. Gallup Poll results on desired family plans are reported in the *New York Times*, 21 March 1985, III 7. Also see Carin Rubenstein, "A Vanishing Way of Life: The Large American Family," the *New York Times*, 17 March 1988, C 1. The data on out-of-wedlock conceptions is from a summary of a Census Bureau report appearing in the *Boston Globe*, 22 June 1989, 3.

24. U.S. Bureau of the Census, *Statistical Abstract of the U.S.: 1989* , 109th ed. (Washington, DC: Government Printing Office, 1989), 399. For the data on mothers in the labor force, see the *New York Times*, 16 June 1988, A 19.

25. In a survey conducted in 1980, the National Commission on Social Security found only 17 percent of those surveyed favored ending Social Security, even though most, especially those between twenty-five and forty-four years of age, expressed fears that the system would be unable to pay them benefits when they retire. Indeed, when given the option of higher taxes or a three-year hike in the retirement age, 51 percent of the respondents preferred higher taxes. For a report on this survey, see *New York Times*, 28 May 1980, I 15.

26. For one of the most recent and comprehensive analyses of these polls and their bearing on the conservative tide, see Thomas Ferguson and Joel Rogers, "The Myth of America's Turn to the Right," *The Atlantic Monthly*, May 1986, 43–53. When the Supreme Court ruled in early July 1989 on the Webster case to return to the states the authority to restrict abortion, the anti-abortion advocates won an important victory. But the polls, with very few exceptions, continue to show a majority of Americans think the matter should remain the private decision of pregnant women. One week after the Webster decision was handed down,

the Gallup Poll recorded 53 percent of those polled disagreed with the ruling. *New York Times*, 10 July 1989, B 8.

27. It is ironic that Reagan may in fact have made his assault on the welfare state stick not by changing our values or character but, rather, by making it impossible to fund such programs because of the huge deficits his administration ran up. At least in the near term, any attempt to reinstitute or return severely constrained programs to their pre-Reagan levels of funding will have to contend with a massive tide of red ink and soaring interest payments on the national debt. Increased debt service charges on Reagan's deficits now exceed the total "savings" Reagan achieved by cutting human services programs. David Stockman, Reagan's first Director of the Office of Management and the Budget, indicates in his memoir of his years as Reagan's chief budget cutter that he thought the deficits that began to mount would provide added leverage in behalf of even more drastic cuts in domestic spending. See David Stockman, *The Triumph of Politics* (New York: Avon Books, 1987), 326–327. But Stockman admitted he misjudged the electorate and Congress. There was, Stockman realized, no extensive appetite for the kinds of reductions that he had in mind. He wrote: "The Republican quarrel with the American welfare state is over. The half-trillion-dollar budget which remains in 1986 after five years of sustained ideological challenge is there because the rank and file of GOP politicians want it for their constituents no less than the Democrats do" (435).

28. For an elaboration of this, see Samuel Bowles and Herbert Gintis, *Democracy and Capitalism* (New York: Basic Books, 1986).

29. We are using the term "alienating" here in its precise meaning: our culture rewards success in ways that systematically mystify social connectedness. Thus, success appears to be a product of the self (self-made man), not the result of social process.

Chapter 6

1. Our account of Morton's troubles is drawn from Michael Zuckerman's marvelously rich essay, "Pilgrims in the Wilderness: Community, Modernity, and the Maypole at Merry Mount," *The New England Quarterly* 1:2 (June 1977): 255–275.

2. Robert Bellah and associates have distinguished four variants of individualism that they argue have been formative of the American character (and the American predicament). Two, "biblical individualism" and "republican individualism," together resemble what we here are calling "repressive individualism." Their other two types, "utilitarian" and "expressive," are not so easily combined. We shall focus only

on the clearest antinomy to repressive individualism, viz., expressive individualism. See Bellah et al., *Habits of the Heart* (Berkeley: University of California Press, 1984).

3. For an elaboration on this, see Daniel Bell, *The Cultural Contradictions of Capitalism* (New York: Basic Books, 1976). Bell understands that the economy gives rise to the opposing tendencies we have called repressive and expressive individualism, but his primary concern is to show how this contradiction is fed by intellectuals and the dynamics of high culture.

4. The late historian Warren I. Susman captures this as nicely as anyone. Though we are necessarily oversimplifying matters here, Susman's *Culture as History* (New York: Pantheon, 1984) traces the ways the expressive self emerges and comes, by the late twentieth century, to predominate in the United States. Though fully cognizant of the manipulation and waste involved, Susman is one of the few critics who insists that expressivity has genuine emancipatory promise.

5. For a report of the hearings see the *New York Times*, 18 April 1985, A 25. The most controversial of the appointees, Eileen Gardner, had written, "There is no injustice in the universe. As unfair as it may seem, a person's external circumstances do fit his level of spiritual development." When asked to explain this view, Gardner responded ". . . [T]he circumstances a person is born into, the race, handicapping conditions, the sex—those circumstances are there to help the individual grow toward spiritual perfection." Gardner's appointment was withdrawn several days later. In so extreme a form as this, repressive individualism garners little broad sympathy. The wonder is that it still manages to get any support at all, much less appointment to high office.

6. Andrew Carnegie, *The Gospel of Wealth* (Cambridge: Harvard University Press, 1962). These essays were first published in 1900. See especially the essay, "The Advantages of Poverty,"50–77.

7. Charles Murray, *Losing Ground: American Social Policy 1950–1980* (New York: Basic Books, 1984). The success of Murray's book was carefully planned by the conservative think tank that commissioned the book. The irony of such manipulation of the market in the name of "free markets" is but another indication of how hard repressive individualists have to work in order to paper over the contradictory impulses to which their theory gives rise. For an account of the promotion of Murray's book see Chuck Lane, "The Manhattan Project," *The New Republic*, 25 March 1985, 14–15.

8. Among the many critics Murray's work has attracted, Christopher Jencks is most exacting. See his review essay "How Poor Are the Poor?" in *The New York Review of Books*, 9 May 1985, 41–49.

9. Researchers do, of course, find a relationship between marital in-

stability and reliance on welfare, but the causation is the reverse of what Murray claims. Because of marital breakup, many women find themselves in need of welfare support. Welfare, though, does not cause the breakup. See Greg J. Duncan, *Years of Poverty/Years of Plenty* (Ann Arbor, MI: Institute for Social Research, 1984), especially chapters 2 and 3. It is worth quoting Duncan on this matter.

> The fact that over a ten-year period the number of people who receive any welfare is considerably larger than over a one-year time span indicates that the current system does not foster large-scale dependency.... Thus the greater share of welfare recipients clearly did not come to rely on welfare as a longterm means of support. These temporary recipients represent a cross section of the American population. No broad demographic group in our society appears immune from shocks to their usual standard of living, shocks resulting from rapidly changing economic or personal conditions (90).

Duncan's research has been reaffirmed most recently by the General Accounting Office, the investigative agency of Congress. In a survey of all major research over the past twelve years and an analysis of 1,200 welfare family histories, the GAO concluded that welfare poses no disincentive to work; that welfare does not encourage otherwise stable families to break up; and that welfare has "little impact on the childbearing rates of unmarried women." *Boston Globe*, 21 March 1987, 3.

10. Some of Murray's critics, including Jencks, seem willing to accept his underlying assumptions that work, even at a degrading job, is better than unemployment and that welfare is inherently demoralizing. These assumptions are the bedrock of the conservative rejection of the welfare state. But it is by no means clear that all work gives dignity. Nor is it clear that it is more dignified to rely on kinfolk than on welfare. Both work and welfare have to be understood in historical and social context.

11. Again, Greg Duncan's work is instructive. He finds that even children from families heavily dependent upon welfare are unlikely themselves to become welfare dependent when they form households of their own. He also finds "no persuasive evidence" supporting the notion that "receiving welfare shapes individuals' characters to make them more likely to continue to need welfare." See Greg J. Duncan and Saul D. Hoffman, "The Use and Effects of Welfare: A Survey of Recent Evidence" (Ann Arbor, MI: Institute for Social Research, n.d.). The quotes above are from the ISR *Newsletter*, Winter 1986–87, 5.

12. As noted in Chapter 5, Bauer was with the Department of Education when he authored the report from which we are quoting here. *The Family: Preserving America's Future* (Washington, DC: U.S. Department of Education, November 1986), 13.

13. This may well be one of the reasons why recent immigrants from Asia have been willing to take jobs that urban blacks shun. Still re-

stricted in most avenues of upward mobility, blacks, especially the young who do not feel the weight of household responsibility, have little motivation to take deadend jobs that cannot even satisfy expressive needs. By contrast, though the origins are obviously not Protestant, Asians see work in other terms—even wretched work is connected to upward mobility, if not one's own then one's kin. For them, any link to the system they see as essentially open is something to be thankful for. Of course, blacks are not the only ones committed to expressivity even if it means unemployment. In the movie *Saturday Night Fever*, John Travolta plays a compelling character whose dull job as a clerk in a hardware store interferes with his passion for dancing. He quits his job. From the point of view of the young men and women depicted, there's little doubt that this is the rational decision for him to make. It's inconceivable that the hardware store is adequate to his persona.

14. The term "action seeking" comes from Herbert Gans. In his study of one of Boston's Italian communities, he found both "action seekers" and "routine seekers." The former had, from a middle-class point of view, chaotic lives—disrupted marriages, recurrent bouts of unemployment, scrapes with the law. See Herbert J. Gans, *The Urban Villagers* (New York: Free Press, 1962). Also see Joseph T. Howell, *Hard Living on Clay Street* (Garden City, NY: Anchor Books, 1973).

15. Studies of the lower class suggest ready formulations that work (superficially at least) to absolve the individual of guilt and remorse over a sundered relationship. Elliot Liebow, in his study of lower-class black men in Baltimore, *Tally's Corner* (Boston: Little, Brown, 1966), discusses how men excuse themselves for their betrayals of friends and lovers.

16. This worry, an echo of the concern employers had about declining incentives in the face of rising wages, was acute in the last decade, especially before inflation and unemployment began rising. It quickly became commonplace to observe that workers, whether white-collar or blue-collar, were no longer content with steady work and decent wages; they also needed stimulation, some reasonable sense that they and their work mattered, and some sense of accomplishment. See Lloyd Zimple, ed., *Man against Work* (Grand Rapids, MI: William B. Eerdmans, 1974) for an interesting collection of essays on this subject.

17. This is not to dismiss or disparage the work of many who endeavored to set up and run drug clinics, hostels for the down and out, soup kitchens, and the like. In these efforts to build and protect a community, albeit a community of free spirits, few of whom were "civic-minded," we can glimpse the essential tension between expressive and repressive individualism. See Mitchell Goodman's anthology *The Movement toward a New America* (New York: Knopf, 1970).

18. For a particularly compelling account of how one group of women came to terms with this, see Nora Harlow, *Sharing the Children: Village Child Rearing within the City* (New York: Harper & Row, 1975). For some, these tensions resolved into a rejection of motherhood for themselves and considerable hostility toward mothering. See Nancy Chodorow and Susan Contratto, "The Fantasy of the Perfect Mother," in *Rethinking the Family: Some Feminist Questions*, eds. Barrie Thorne and Marilyn Yalom (New York: Longman, 1982), 54–71.

19. See Friedan, *The Second Stage* (New York: Summit Books, 1981). Also see Alice S. Rossi, "A Biosocial Perspective of the Family," in *The Family*, eds. Alice S. Rossi et al. (New York: W. W. Norton, 1978), 1–31. An important critique of this development in the feminist movement can be found in an essay by Wini Breines, Margaret Cerullo, and Judith Stacey, "Social Biology, Family Studies, and Antifeminist Backlash," *Feminist Studies* 4 (February 1978): 43–67.

20. Jean Baker Miller, *Toward a New Psychology of Women* (Boston: Beacon Press, 1976), 94–95.

21. Edwin Schur, *The Awareness Trap* (New York: McGraw-Hill, 1976).

22. Bernard Farber, *Family Organization and Interaction* (San Francisco: Chandler, 1965).

23. Edward Shorter relates an anecdote that embodies precisely what we have in mind here. It seems that a couple in Toronto had come to grief. In the course of trying to resolve matters, each spouse had obtained an analyst and a lawyer. So far, not unusual. But their two children also each retained an analyst and lawyer. Presumably, the analysts helped each person to come to understand and acknowledge their self-interest, and it was then up to the lawyers to attempt a resolution that minimized the aggregate damage to the parties' respective interests. Unless one happens to be an analyst or a lawyer, this is a frightful specter.

24. This is not to suggest that all conservatives share a disdain for expressivity. For those conservatives who are verging on anarchism, the celebration of selfhood is as unmitigated as it is in Emerson or Whitman or any of the contemporary proponents of the self. Ayn Rand, for example, is clearly committed to a model of private life that is indistinct from the free market of which she is so enamored.

25. Fred Hirsch, *Social Limits to Growth* (Cambridge: Harvard University Press, 1976).

26. The main contours of Lasch's thinking on these matters can be traced through his last three books. The first, *Haven in a Heartless World* (New York: Basic Books, 1977), decried the decline of parental authority and the presumably related capacity of the family to instill in its members a capacity to resist social authority. In the second volume, *The*

Culture of Narcissism (New York: W. W. Norton, 1979), he traces the ways in which the collapse of the family produces individuals who are passive in the face of imminent danger and content to be preoccupied with the flimflam of commercial hucksterism, substituting sensation and experience for competence and control. In his most recent book, *The Minimal Self* (New York: W. W. Norton, 1984), Lasch draws the noose tighter. While parrying with critics he describes a trajectory of decline, both for society and the individual.

27. For a complementary analysis of the mixed blessings of private affluence see Staffan B. Linder, *The Harried Leisure Class* (New York: Columbia University Press, 1970).

28. Hirsch wrote in the early 1970s, well before the Reagan Revolution and the apparent restoration of confidence. But the confidence is more appearance than reality. Our economy is still plagued by high unemployment, low levels of savings and investment, steadily mounting debt—public and private—and declining productivity and competitiveness. And the polity is anything but a source of confidence. Polls indicate continuing low levels of trust in public officials, historic lows in voter participation, and widespread distrust of corporations. For an analysis of this see Seymour Martin Lipset and William Schneider, *The Confidence Gap: Business, Labor, and Government in the Public Mind* (New York: Free Press, 1983).

29. Edward Banfield, in his book *The Moral Basis of a Backward Society* (Glencoe, IL: Free Press, 1958), describes this as "amoral familism" and attributes to it the absence of civic-mindedness he alleges to be typical of the southern Italian peasants he is writing about. It is ironic, to say the least, that we may encounter more difficulty overcoming our own versions of privatized "amoral familism" than have Italian peasants who, while still venerating their families, nonetheless understand and acknowledge the centrality of the public sector in making the family life they desire an attainable and sustainable goal. For a rich account of how family life amongst Southern Italians has been interwoven with political and economic change, see Donald S. Pitkin's *The House that Giacomo Built* (New York: Cambridge University Press, 1986).

30. Nowhere is this design more apparent than in Harriet Beecher Stowe's classic *Uncle Tom's Cabin*. Her moving indictment of slavery, for which the book is justly remembered, is predicated upon the force of women's moral critique. Women are the bearers of civilization and the family is its crucible. The greatest wrong of slavery is that it destroys family—and thus familism.

31. In the growing debate about the looming crisis in medical malpractice (and all other forms of liability) insurance, far too much attention has been paid to lawyers who are presumed to be the predatory

instigators, colluding with equally predatory clients. Though there is no dearth of predatory impulse in our society, it seems to us that the rise in liability suits (against bars that sell to drinkers who are driving, against manufacturers of dangerous products, against employers who expose their workers to dangerous chemicals or processes, etc.) has far more to do with our expanding sense of rights than with increased venality.

32. It is estimated that nearly half of all those eligible for food stamps, for example, do not apply. Ironically, it is the more advantaged, one might even dare say "middle class," who are most persistent and successful in securing the benefits they are entitled to. Much of the hostility to welfare can be traced to the conviction that only families are appropriate agencies of succor. British socialist feminists Michele Barrett and Mary McIntosh, in their *The Anti-Social Family* (London: Verso, 1982), argue that this veneration of the family has made it possible for virtually all other social institutions to be far more callous and self-serving than would otherwise be possible. As they put it: "Caring, sharing and loving would be more widespread if the family did not claim them for its own" (80). Of course it is not that the family makes any such claim. Rather, as we are arguing here, it has been those able to play upon our attachments to family who have made other loci of familism seen illegitimate.

33. Ellen Galinsky's article "Family Life and Corporate Policies," in *In Support of Families*, eds. Michael W. Yogman and T. Barry Brazelton (Cambridge: Harvard University Press, 1986), 108–145, contains a very helpful overview of recent changes in corporate policy. She also reports on a survey of top managers' attitudes toward the intersections between work and family life. Not surprisingly, she finds management largely oblivious to the need to adapt worklife to family life. But whether or not it is unmindful of this, the labor force is demanding change. For example, the *Boston Globe* reported that part-time work even among professionals is spreading rapidly. Between 1983 and 1988 part-timers in the professions increased 12 percent, a rate of growth faster than that of part-time work in general. The same article reports that the number of firms with job-sharing policies is also growing rapidly. As of 1988, 17 percent of the banking and finance industry, 13 percent of education and government, and 10 percent of the insurance industry had such policies in place. *Boston Globe*, 25 June 1989, 85.

34. Sheila B. Kammerman, A. J. Kahn, and P. W. Kingston, *Maternity Policies and Working Women* (New York: Columbia University Press, 1983).

35. *New York Times*, 18 June 1987, A 20.

36. Galinsky, "Family Life and Corporate Policies," 132.

37. These programs ranged from on-site day-care centers to direct contributions to day-care expense. For a recent summary of corporate initiatives in the provision of day care, see Kirsten O. Lundberg, "A Tool to Keep Women in the Work Force," *New York Times*, 26 February 1989, D 13.

38. We base this on a summary of the report published in the *New York Times*, 22 June 1986, F 1. The Conference Board is an organization whose members are the top executives of the nation's largest corporations. The Board's staff functions to alert the nation's business leaders to changes in economic conditions as well as to trends in the broader society that have consequences for business.

39. San Francisco, of course, has a large and politically active gay population, and this makes the electoral defeat surprising. But, interestingly, columnist Ellen Goodman reports that heterosexual cohabitants have far outnumbered gay couples in availing themselves of such liberalizations of fringe benefit eligibility rules where they have been implemented. See her syndicated column, "A Test In Love(!) and Relationships," *Boston Globe*, 13 June 1989, 15.

40. For a review of these sorts of workplace initiatives, see T. J. St. Antoine, "Changing Concepts of Worker Rights in the Work Place," *Annals of the American Academy of Political and Social Science* 473 (May 1984): 108–115. See also John Simmons and William Mares, *Working Together: Employee Participation in Action* (New York: Knopf, 1983). For a more theoretical analysis of these changes, see S. Srivastva and D. L. Cooperrider, "The Emergence of the Egalitarian Organization," *Human Relations* 39 (August 1986): 683–724.

41. We know of no comprehensive survey of such programs, but reports from individual programs seem very encouraging. One highly touted program was implemented in York, Pennsylvania in the late 1970s. York had experienced a rash of teen pregnancies and the usual high dropout rate that ordinarily accompanies pregnancy. The school began to offer courses for pregnant mothers and in-school day care for the teens after their babies were born. The dropout rate was cut to a little over 9 percent compared to an 80 to 90 percent dropout rate nationally for pregnant teens. For an account of the York program, see Marjorie R. Geesey and Marion L. McAfee, "Meeting the Needs of the Teen-Age Pregnant Student: An In-School Program That Works," *Journal of School Health* 54:9 (October 1984): 274–352.

42. We are not claiming that these goals have been met. In fact, deinstitutionalization has probably contributed as much to the ranks of the nation's homeless as to the self-esteem of the mentally ill. But this seems more the result of our unwillingness to fund halfway houses and pay

for adequately trained staff than it is the result of a flaw in the basic idea behind the program.

43. For an account of Schroeder's campaign and her agenda, see her highly readable *Champion of the Great American Family* (New York: Random House, 1989). This book contains as good a detailed account of the many legislative initiatives, some already successful and others in various stages along the way to eventual legislative action, as any easily accessible book. The reader who wants more legislative history than we can provide here is encouraged to consult Schroeder's book.

44. This shows up in all sorts of interesting ways. Corporations have long been accustomed to moving their executives from one branch or operation to another. At one level this is justified as giving the executive broad familiarity with the firm's operations. At another level, the moves disrupt social bonds and the formation of commitments and loyalties that might compete with a central identification with the firm itself. Such moves, typically associated with a promotion, involve relocation. For the past decade or so, corporations have encountered growing resistance to these once routine moves. More executives now have wives who have careers and who do not want to relocate. Moreover, the husband's job no longer takes automatic priority. And as more families adopt highly egalitarian modes, the needs of children—their school attachments, etc.—figure importantly in decisions to move. The result of these changes is greater difficulty for corporate planners. For illustrative articles on this see "America's New Immobile Society," *Business Week*, 27 July 1981, 58–62; and L. D. Maloney, "Why the Nation Is Saying No to Moving Around," *U.S. News & World Report*, 9 August 1982, 64–67.

45. For a sober, and sobering, assessment of the recent changes in the workplace that have been heralded as steps toward a more humane work environment, see Robert Howard, *Brave New Workplace* (New York: Viking, 1985).

46. Of course it makes a difference whether the reform derives from popular agitation and political mobilization or from the anticipation of such mobilization by elites. In general, when reform comes by the latter method, the privilege of elites is maintained. For a discussion of this in historical terms, see Gabriel Kolko, *The Triumph of Conservatism* (New York: Free Press, 1963).

47. The stunning economic success of Japan has occasioned a flood of books endeavoring to unlock their secret and to draw from the Japanese experience applications to our own far less vigorous industrial sector. See for example Ezra F. Vogel, *Japan as Number One* (Cambridge: Harvard University Press, 1979). For a discussion of the origins of corporate paternalism in Japan, see Ronald P. Dore, *British Factory, Japanese*

Factory: Origins of National Diversity in Industrial Relations (Berkeley: University of California Press, 1973).

48. The so-called "Mommy Track," a distinct career path set aside for women who desire to be both employed and a parent, is another example of the risks of public familism in the service of narrow organizational ends. First put forward in an article by Felice N. Schwartz, the president of Catalyst, an organization she founded to promote the advancement of women in careers, the mommy track is based on the fact that the rigors of moving up the corporate ladder leave precious little time or energy for serious involvement in domesticity. Rather than forcing women who want to be mothers out of the corporate world, Schwartz recommends that firms establish two tracks—one for those who are willing to give their all to the firm and the other for those who wish to balance the demands of career with the raising of a family. See Felice N. Schwartz, "Management Women and the New Facts of Life," *Harvard Business Review* 89:1 (January–February 1989): 65–76.

Schwartz's proposal was quickly challenged by writers insisting that the prevailing structures of corporate careers are neither immutable nor particularly worthy of support. Rather than creating two tiers, why not restructure career demands so that parents can be both active parents and productive employees? Needless to say, mommy tracks are the opposite of what we mean by public familism. For an interesting reflection on the adjustments of corporations to women employees and to the growing involvement of men in the lives of their families, see an article sparked by the furor aroused by Felice Schwartz: "The Mommy Track: Juggling Kids and Careers in Corporate America Takes a Controversial Turn," *Business Week*, 20 March 1989, 126–134.

49 New York: Harper & Row, 1966.

50. *Disturbing the Nest: Family Change and Decline in Modern Societies* (New York: Aldine De Gruyter, 1988).

51. The recent bailout of the nation's savings and loan banks is only the most current example in a long chain of tax subsidies to irresponsibility and cupidity in the business world.

52. See Kathleen Gerson, *Hard Choices: How Women Decide about Work, Career, and Motherhood* (Berkeley: University of California Press, 1985), 132–157.

53. Philip Slater, *The Pursuit of Loneliness* (Boston: Beacon Press, 1970).

54. Jean Baker Miller, *Toward a New Psychology of Women* (Boston: Beacon Press, 1976); Carol Gilligan, *In a Different Voice* (Cambridge: Harvard University Press, 1987); Sara Ruddick, *Maternal Thinking: Toward a Politics of Peace* (Boston: Beacon Press, 1989). Also see Mary Belenky et al., *Women's Ways of Knowing* (New York: Basic Books, 1986)

and Jessica Benjamin, *The Bonds of Love: Feminism, Psychoanalysis and the Problem of Domination* (New York: Pantheon, 1988).

55. Weber distinguished between rationality that was employed to assess values or transcendent goals from the rationality that concentrated on perfecting means, irrespective of goals. Thus, one could be exceedingly rational in choosing the means for achieving an utterly irrational goal (the Nazi extermination of the Jews remains the most horrifying example). Emphasis on efficiency in production, independent of what is being produced and aside from the broader social costs of production, is another example of this sort of means-oriented rationality.

Bibliography

"America's New Immobile Society," *Business Week*, 27 July 1981, 58–62.

Arendell, Terry, *Mothers and Divorce: Legal, Economic, and Social Dilemmas* (Berkeley: University of California Press, 1986).

Baake, E. W., *The Unemployed Worker* (New Haven: Yale University Press, 1940).

Bane, Mary Jo, *Here To Stay* (New York: Basic Books, 1976).

Banfield, Edward, *The Moral Basis of a Backward Society* (Glencoe, IL: Free Press, 1958).

Barrett, Michele, and Mary McIntosh, *The Anti-Social Family* (London: Verso, 1982).

Bauer, Gary L., *The Family: Preserving America's Future* (Washington, DC: U.S. Office of Education: December 1986).

Beattie, Melody, *Beyond Codependency and Getting Better All the Time* (San Francisco: Harper & Row, 1989).

Belenky, Mary, et al., *Women's Ways of Knowing* (New York: Basic Books, 1986).

Bell, Daniel, "The Great Back-to-Work Movement," *Fortune*, July 1956, cited in *Industrial Society and Social Welfare*, eds. H. L. Wilensky and Charles N. Lebeaux (New York: Free Press of Glencoe, 1965).

———, *The Cultural Contradictions of Capitalism* (New York: Basic Books, 1976).

Bellah, Robert, et al., *Habits of the Heart* (Berkeley: University of California Press, 1984).

Benjamin, Jessica, *The Bonds of Love: Feminism, Psychoanalysis and the Problem of Domination* (New York: Pantheon, 1988).

Berg, Roland H., "The Over-Medicated Woman," *McCall's*, September 1971.

Berman, E., et al., "The Two-Professional Marriage: A New Conflict Syndrome," *Journal of Sex and Marriage Therapy* 1 (1975): 242–253.

Bernikow, Louise, *Alone in America* (New York: Harper & Row, 1986).

Bird, Caroline, *The Invisible Scar* (New York: David McKay, 1971).

———, *The Two-Paycheck Marriage* (New York: Rawson, Wade Publishers, 1979).

Bledstein, Burton, *The Culture of Professionalism* (New York: W. W. Norton, 1976).

Bluestone, Barry, and Bennett Harrison, *The Deindustrialization of America* (New York: Basic Books, 1982).

Bowles, Samuel, and Herbert Gintis, *Democracy and Capitalism* (New York: Basic Books, 1986).

Breines, Wini, Margaret Cerullo, and Judith Stacey, "Social Biology, Family Studies, and Antifeminist Backlash," *Feminist Studies*, 4 (February 1978): 43–67.

Burgess, Ernest W., and Harvey J. Locke, *The Family: From Institution to Companionship* (New York: American Book Company, 1953).

Caplow, Theodore, et al., *Middletown Families: Fifty Years of Change and Continuity* (Minneapolis: University of Minnesota Press, 1982).

Cargan, Leonard, and Matthew Melko, *Singles: Myths and Realities* (Beverly Hills, CA: Sage Publications, 1982).

Carnegie, Andrew, *The Gospel of Wealth* (Cambridge: Harvard University Press, 1962).

Chafe, William H., *Women and Equality: Changing Patterns in American Culture* (New York: Oxford University Press, 1977).

Chandler, Jr., Alfred D., *Strategy and Structure* (Cambridge: MIT Press, 1962).

———, *The Visible Hand* (Cambridge: Harvard University Press, 1977).

Cherlin, Andrew, *Marriage, Divorce, and Remarriage* (Cambridge: Harvard University Press, 1981).

Chodorow, Nancy, and Susan Contratto, "The Fantasy of the Perfect Mother," in *Rethinking the Family: Some Feminist Questions*, eds. Barrie Thorne and Marilyn Yalom (New York: Longman, 1982), 54–71.

"The Class of '49," *Fortune*, June 1949, 84 ff.

Coser, Lewis, *Greedy Institutions: Patterns of Undivided Commitment* (New York: Free Press, 1974).

Degler, Carl, *At Odds* (New York: Oxford University Press, 1980).

Demos, John, *Past, Present, and Personal: Family Life and the Life Course in American History* (New York: Oxford University Press, 1986).

———, *Little Commonwealth: Family Life in the Plymouth Colony* (New York: Oxford University Press, 1970).

Dinnerstein, Dorothy, *The Mermaid and the Minotaur* (New York: Harper & Row, 1976).

Dizard, Jan E., *Social Change and the Family* (Chicago: Community and Family Studies Center/University of Chicago, 1968).

Dore, Ronald P., *British Factory, Japanese Factory: Origins of National Diversity in Industrial Relations* (Berkeley: University of California Press, 1973).

Duncan, Greg J., *Years of Poverty, Years of Plenty: The Changing Economic Fortunes of American Workers and Families*, Ann Arbor, MI: Institute for Social Research, University of Michigan, (1984).

———, and Saul D. Hoffman, "The Use and Effects of Welfare: A Survey of Recent Evidence" (Ann Arbor, MI: Institute for Social Research, n.d.).

Edelman, Marion Wright, *Families in Peril* (Cambridge: Harvard University Press, 1987).

Ehrenreich, Barbara, *The Hearts of Men* (Garden City, NY: Anchor Press, 1983).

———, Elizabeth Hess, and Gloria Jacobs, "Unbuckling the Bible Belt," *Mother Jones*, July/August 1986, 46–51.

Emerson, Ralph Waldo, "Self-Reliance," in *The Collected Works of Ralph Waldo Emerson*, vol. 2 (Cambridge: Belknap Press of Harvard University Press, 1979).

Entwisle, Doris R., and Susan G. Doering, *The First Birth: A Family Turning Point* (Baltimore: Johns Hopkins University Press, 1981).

Epstein, Barbara Leslie, *The Politics of Domesticity: Women, Evangelism, and Temperance in Nineteenth-Century America* (Middletown, CT: Wesleyan University Press, 1981).

Ewen, Stuart, *Captains of Consciousness* (New York: McGraw Hill, 1976).

Farber, Bernard, *Family Organization and Interaction* (San Francisco: Chandler, 1965).

Ferguson, Thomas, and Joel Rogers, "The Myth of America's Turn to the Right," *The Atlantic Monthly*, May 1986, 43–53.

Feuer, Louis, *The Conflict of Generations* (New York: Basic Books, 1969).

Flacks, Richard, "The Liberated Generation," *Journal of Social Issues* 23 (1967): 52–75.

————, *Youth and Social Change* (Chicago: Markham, 1971).

Fowlkes, Martha R., *Behind Every Successful Man: Wives of Medicine and Academe* (New York: Columbia University Press, 1980).

Franklin, Benjamin, *The Autobiography of Benjamin Franklin*, eds. Leonard W. Labaree et al. (New Haven: Yale University Press, 1964).

Friedan, Betty, *The Feminine Mystique* (New York: W. W. Norton, 1963).

————, *The Second Stage* (New York: Summit Books, 1981).

Furstenberg, Frank, *Unplanned Parenthood: The Social Consequences of Teenage Childbearing* (New York: Free Press, 1976).

Gadlin, Howard, "Private Lives and Public Order," *The Massachusetts Review* XVII, no. 2 (Summer 1976): 304–330.

————, "Child Discipline and the Pursuit of Self: An Historical Interpretation," *Advances in Child Development and Behavior* 12 (1978): 231–265.

Galbraith, John Kenneth, *The Affluent Society* (Boston: Houghton Mifflin, 1958).

Galinsky, Ellen, "Family Life and Corporate Policies," in *In Support of Families*, eds. Michael W. Yogman and T. Barry Brazelton (Cambridge: Harvard University Press, 1986), 108–145.

Gans, Herbert, *The Urban Villagers* (Glencoe, IL: Free Press, 1962).

————, *The Levittowners* (New York: Pantheon, 1967).

Garfinkel, Irwin, and Sara S. McLanahan, *Single Mothers and Their Children* (Washington, DC: Urban Institute Press, 1986).

Geesey, Marjorie R., and Marion L. McAfee, "Meeting the Needs of the Teen-Age Pregnant Student: An In-School Program that Works," *Journal of School Health* 54:9 (October 1984): 274–352.

Gerson, Kathleen, *Hard Choices: How Women Decide about Work, Career, and Motherhood* (Berkeley: University of California Press, 1985).

Gilder, George, *Wealth and Poverty* (New York: Basic Books, 1981).

Gilligan, Carol, *In a Different Voice* (Cambridge: Harvard University Press, 1987).

Gilman, Charlotte Perkins, *Women and Economics* (New York: Harper & Row, 1966), originally published in 1899.

————, *Moving the Mountain* (New York: Charlton, 1911).

Glazer, Nathan, *Affirmative Discrimination: Ethnic Inequality and Public Policy* (New York: Basic Books, 1975).

Goffman, Erving, *The Presentation of Self in Everyday Life* (Garden City, NY: Doubleday Anchor, 1959).

Goldscheider, Calvin, and Frances K. Goldscheider, "Moving Out and Marriage: What Do Young Adults Expect?" *American Sociological Review* 52 (April 1987): 278–285.

Goldstein, Sidney, and Calvin Goldscheider, *Jewish Americans: Three Gen-

erations in a Jewish Community (Englewood Cliffs, NJ: Prentice-Hall, 1968).

Goode, William J., *After Divorce* (Glencoe, IL: Free Press, 1956).

————, "On the Theoretical Importance of Love," *American Sociological Review* 24 (February 1959): 37–48.

Gooding, Judson, "The Accelerated Generation Moves into Management," *Fortune*, March 1971, 100 ff.

Goodman, Ellen, "A Test In Love(!) and Relationships," *Boston Globe*, 13 June 1989, 15.

Goodman, Mitchell, ed., *The Movement toward a New America* (New York: Knopf, 1970).

Gordon, Linda, *Women's Body, Women's Right* (New York: Grossman, 1976).

Gordon, Suzanne, *Lonely in America* (New York: Simon & Schuster, 1976).

Gray, Madeline, *Margaret Sanger* (New York: Richard Marek Publishers, 1979).

Greenberger, Ellen, "Children's Employment and Families," in *Families and Work*, eds. Naomi Gerstel and Harriet Engel (Philadelphia: Temple University Press, 1987), 396–406.

Greven, Jr., Philip J., "Family Structure in Seventeenth-Century Andover, Massachusetts," *William and Mary Quarterly* 23 (1966): 234–256.

Harlow, Nora, *Sharing the Children: Village Child Rearing within the City* (New York: Harper & Row, 1975).

Hayden, Delores, *Redesigning the American Dream* (New York: W. W. Norton, 1984).

Hayek, F., *The Road to Serfdom* (Chicago: University of Chicago Press, 1944).

Herdman, Priscilla, *The Water Lily*, Flying Fish Records (1980).

Hertz, Rosanna, *More Equal Than Others: Women and Men in Dual-Career Marriages* (Berkeley: University of California Press, 1986).

Hirsch, Fred, *Social Limits to Growth* (Cambridge: Harvard University Press, 1976).

Hochschild, Arlie Russell, *Unexpected Community* (Englewood Cliffs, NJ: Prentice-Hall, 1973).

————, "Inside the Clockwork of Male Careers," in *Crisis in American Institutions*, 3rd ed., eds. Jerome H. Skolnick and Elliot Curie, (Boston: Little, Brown, 1976), 251–266.

————, (with Anne Machung), *The Second Shift: Working Parents and the Revolution at Home* (New York: Viking, 1989).

Hogan, David, *Class and Reform* (Philadelphia: University of Pennsylvania Press, 1985).

Holmstrom, Lynda Lytle, *The Two-Career Family* (Cambridge: Schenk-man, 1973).

Horner, Matina, "FAIL: Bright Women," *Psychology Today*, 3 (June 1969): 36 ff.

Howard, Robert, *Brave New Workplace* (New York: Viking, 1985).

Howell, Joseph T., *Hard Living on Clay Street* (Garden City, NY: Anchor Books, 1973).

Hunter, James Davison, *American Evangelicism: Conservative Religion and the Quandary of Modernity* (New Brunswick, NJ: Rutgers University Press, 1983).

Ianni, Francis A. J., *A Family Business: Kinship and Social Control in Organized Crime* (New York: Russell Sage Foundation, 1972).

Jencks, Christopher, "How Poor Are the Poor?" in *The New York Review of Books*, 9 May 1985, 41–49.

Kammerman, Sheila B., A. J. Kahn, and P. W. Kingston, *Maternity Policies and Working Women* (New York: Columbia University Press, 1983).

Kantrowitz, B., "And Thousands More," *Newsweek*, 12 December 1988, 58–59.

Keniston, Kenneth, *Young Radicals* (New York: Harcourt, Brace and World, 1968).

Kennedy, David M., *Birth Control in America* (New Haven: Yale University Press, 1976).

Kingston, Paul William, and Steven L. Nock, "Time Together Among Dual-Earner Couples," *American Sociological Review*, 52 (June 1987): 391–400.

Kinkead, Gwen, "On a Fast Track to the Good Life," *Fortune*, 7 April 1980, 74–84.

Kolko, Gabriel, *The Triumph of Conservatism, 1900–1916* (Glencoe, IL: Free Press, 1963).

Kramer, Judith R., and Seymour Leventman, *Children of the Gilded Ghetto* (New Haven: Yale University Press, 1961).

Krantzler, Mel, *Creative Divorce: A New Opportunity for Personal Growth* (New York: M. Evans, 1973).

LaFeber, Walter, *The New Empire: An Interpretation of American Expansion, 1860–1898* (Ithaca, NY: Cornell University Press, 1963).

Landry, Bart, *The New Black Middle Class* (Berkeley: University of California Press, 1987).

Lane, Chuck, "The Manhattan Project," *The New Republic*, 25 March 1985, 14–15.

Larcom, Lucy, *An Idyll of Work* (Boston: J. R. Osgood and Co., 1875).

———, *A New England Girlhood* (New York: Corinth Books, 1964).

Lasch, Christopher, *Haven in a Heartless World* (New York: Basic Books, 1977).

———, *The Culture of Narcissism* (New York: W. W. Norton, 1979).

———, *The Minimal Self* (New York: W. W. Norton, 1984).

Lawson, Henry, *In The Days When the World Was Wide and Other Verses* (London: Angus & Robertson Ltd., 1913), 176–178.

Lazarre, Jane, *The Mother Knot* (New York: McGraw-Hill, 1976).

Lennard, Henry L., et al., *Mystification and Drug Misuse* (San Francisco: Jossey-Bass, 1971).

Levitan, Sar, and Richard Belous, *What's Happening to the American Family?* (Baltimore: Johns Hopkins University Press, 1981).

Liebow, Elliot, *Tally's Corner* (Boston: Little, Brown, 1966).

Linder, Staffan B., *The Harried Leisure Class* (New York: Columbia University Press, 1970).

Lipset, Seymour Martin, and William Schneider, *The Confidence Gap: Business, Labor, and Government in the Public Mind* (New York: Free Press, 1983).

"The Long-run Decline in Liquidity," *Monthly Review* 22 (September 1970).

Luker, Kristen, *Abortion and the Politics of Motherhood* (Berkeley: University of California Press, 1984).

Lundberg, Kirsten O., "A Tool to Keep Women in the Work Force," *New York Times*, 26 February 1989, D13.

Malcolm, Andrew H., "Teen-Age Shoppers: Desperately Seeking Spinach," *New York Times*, 29 November 1987, 3–10.

Maloney, L. D., "Why the Nation Is Saying No to Moving Around," *U.S. News & World Report*, 9 August 1982, 64–67.

Marchand, Roland, *Advertising the American Dream: Making Way for Modernity, 1920–1940* (Berkeley: University of California Press, 1985).

Marsden, George, *Fundamentalism and American Culture* (New York: Oxford University Press, 1980).

———, *Evangelicism and Modern America* (Grand Rapids, MI: W. B. Eerdmans, 1984).

Miller, Jean Baker, *Toward a New Psychology of Women* (Boston: Beacon Press, 1976).

Miller, Sue, *The Good Mother* (New York: Harper & Row, 1986).

Mills, C. Wright, *White Collar* (New York: Oxford University Press, 1951).

———, *The Power Elite* (New York: Oxford University Press, 1956).

Mohr, James C., *Abortion in America* (New York: Oxford University Press, 1978).

"The Mommy Track: Juggling Kids and Careers in Corporate America Takes a Controversial Turn," *Business Week*, 20 March 1989, 126-134.

Morgan, Edmond S., *The Puritan Family: Religion and Domestic Relations in Seventeenth Century New England* (New York: Harper & Row, 1966).

Morgan, Marabel, *The Total Woman* (New York: Pocket Books, 1975).

Moynihan, Daniel Patrick, *The Negro Family: The Case for National Action* (Washington, DC: Office of Policy Planning and Research, United States Department of Labor, U.S. Government Printing Office, March 1965).

Murray, Charles, *Losing Ground: American Social Policy 1950–1980* (New York: Basic Books, 1984).

Nelli, Humbert, *The Italians of Chicago, 1880–1920* (New York: Oxford University Press, 1970).

Nicolaus, Martin, "The Unknown Marx," *New Left Review* (March–April 1968).

Norton-Taylor, Duncan, "The Private World of the Class of '66," *Fortune*, February 1966, 128.

Oakely, Annie, *The Sociology of Housework* (New York: Pantheon Books, 1974).

O'Neill, William L., "Divorce in the Progressive Era," *The American Quarterly* (Summer 1965): 205–217.

———, *Everyone Was Brave: The Rise and Fall of Feminism in America* (Chicago: Quadrangle Books, 1969).

Packard, Vance, *The Status Seekers* (New York: David McKay, 1959).

———, *Our Endangered Children: Growing up in a Changing World* (Boston: Little, Brown 1983).

Paludi, Michele A., "Psychometric Properties and Underlying Assumptions of Four Objective Measures of Fear of Success," *Sex Roles* 10:9/10 (1984) 765–781.

Papanek, Hanna, "Men, Women, and Work: Reflections on the Two-Person Career," in *Changing Women in a Changing Society*, ed. Joan Huber (Chicago: University of Chicago Press, 1973), 90–110.

Parsons, Talcott, "The Social Structure of the Family," in *The Family: Its Function and Destiny*, ed. Ruth N. Anshen (New York: Harper & Bros. 1949), 173–201.

———, "The Kinship System of the Contemporary United States," in *Essays in Sociological Theory* (Glencoe, IL: Free Press, 1949), 177–196.

———, and Robert F. Bales, *Family, Interaction, and Socialization Process* (Glencoe, IL: Free Press, 1955).

Petchesky, Rosalind Pollack, *Abortion and Woman's Choice: The State, Sex-*

uality, and Reproductive Freedom (Boston: Northeastern University Press, 1984).

Piotrkowski, Chaya S., *Work and the Family System: A Naturalistic Study of Working-Class and Lower-Middle-Class Families* (New York: Free Press, 1978).

Pitkin, Donald S., *The House that Giacomo Built* (New York: Cambridge University Press, 1986).

Platt, Gerald M., and Fred Weinstein, *The Wish to Be Free: Society, Psyche, and Value Change* (Berkeley: University of California Press, 1969).

Popenoe, David, *Disturbing the Nest: Family Change and Decline in Modern Societies* (New York: Aldine De Gruyter, 1988).

Rainwater, Lee, Richard P. Coleman, and Gerald Handel, *Workingman's Wife* (New York: Oceana Publications, 1959).

Rapoport, Rhona, and Robert Rapoport, *Dual-Career Families* (Harmondsworth, England: Penguin Books, 1971).

———, and Robert N. Rapoport, *Dual-Career Families Re-examined* (New York: Harper & Row, 1976).

———, Robert Rapoport, and Ziona Streliz (with Stephen Kew), *Fathers, Mothers and Society* (New York: Basic Books, 1977).

Rapoport, Robert, and Rhona Rapoport, "Work and Family in Contemporary Society," *American Sociological Review* 30 (June 1965): 381–94.

Reiff, Philip, *The Triumph of the Therapeutic*, (New York: Harper & Row, 1966).

Reisman, David, Nathan Glazer, and Reuel Denney, *The Lonely Crowd* (New Haven: Yale University Press, 1950).

Ross, Heather, and Isabel V. Sawhill, *Time of Transition: The Growth of Families Headed by Women* (Washington, DC: Urban Institute Press, 1975).

Rossi, Alice S., "Equality between the Sexes: An Immodest Proposal," *Daedalus* 93 (1964): 607–652.

———, "A Biosocial Perspective of the Family," in ed. Alice S. Rossi et al., *The Family*, (New York: W. W. Norton, 1978), 1–31.

Rothenberg, Randall, "Ad Scene: For Children Home Alone, A Word from the Sponsor," *New York Times*, 9 May 1988, D8.

Rothman, Ellen K., "Sex and Self-Control: Middle Class Courtship in America, 1770–1870," *Journal of Social History* 15 (Spring 1982): 409–425.

Rothschild, Emma, *Paradise Lost: The Decline of the Auto-Industrial Age* (New York: Random House, 1983).

Ruberstein, Carin, "A Vanishing Way of Life: The Large American Family," *New York Times*, 17 March 1988, C1.

Rubin, Lillian, *Worlds of Pain* (New York: Basic Books, 1976).

Ruddick, Sara, *Maternal Thinking: Toward a Politics of Peace* (Boston: Beacon Press, 1989).

"'Runaways,' 'Throwaways,' 'Bagkids'—An Army of Drifter Teens," *U.S. News and World Report*, 11 March 1985, 52–53.

Ryan, Mary P., *Cradle of the Middle Class: The Family in Oneida County, New York, 1790–1865* (New York: Cambridge University Press, 1981).

St. Antoine, T. J., "Changing Concepts of Worker Rights in the Work Place," *Annals of the American Academy of Political and Social Science* 473 (May 1984): 108–115.

Scanzoni, John H., *The Black Family in Modern Society: Patterns of Stability and Security* (Chicago: University of Chicago Press, 1977).

Schnaiberg, Allan, and Sheldon Goldenberg, "From Empty Nest to Crowded Nest: The Dynamics of Incompletely-Launched Young Adults," *Social Problems* 36 (June 1989): 251–269.

Schroeder, Patricia, *Champion of the Great American Family* (New York: Random House, 1989).

Schulz, William F., "Fostering Prejudice," *The Progressive*, January 1987, 15.

Schur, Edwin, *The Awareness Trap* (New York: McGraw-Hill, 1976).

Schwartz, Felice N., "Management Women and the New Facts of Life," *Harvard Business Review* 89:1 (January-February 1989): 65–76.

Seeley, John R., et al., *Crestwood Heights: A Study of the Culture of Suburban Life* (New York: Basic Books, 1956).

Sekaran, Uma, *Dual-Career Families* (San Francisco: Jossey-Bass, 1986).

Seligman, Daniel, "The Confident Twenty-Five Year Olds," *Fortune*, February 1955, 100ff.

Sennett, Richard, *The Uses of Disorder* (New York: Vintage Books, 1970).

Shapiro, Laura, *Perfection Salad* (New York: Farrar, Straus, Giroux, 1986).

Sheehy, Gail, *Passages: Predictable Crises of Adult Life* (New York: Dutton, 1976).

Simmons, John, and William Mares, *Working Together: Employee Participation in Action* (New York: Knopf, 1983).

Sklare, Marshall, *Jewish Identity on the Suburban Frontier: A Study of Group Survival in the Open Society* (New York: Basic Books, 1967).

———, *American Jews* (New York: Random House, 1971).

Slater, Philip, *The Pursuit of Loneliness* (Boston: Beacon Press, 1970).

———, *Footholds* (Boston: Beacon Press 1977).

Smelser, Neil J., *Social Change in the Industrial Revolution* (Chicago: University of Chicago Press, 1959).

Smith, Daniel Scott, "Parental Power and Marriage Patterns: An Analysis of Historical Trends in Hingham, Massachusetts," *Journal of Marriage and the Family* 35 (August 1973): 419–428.

Smith, Merritt Roe, "Military Entrepreneurship," in *Yankee Enterprise: The Rise of the American System of Manufactures*, eds. Otto Mayr and Robert C. Post (Washington, DC: Smithsonian Institution Press, 1981), 63–102.

Solomon, Marion F., *Narcissism and Intimacy* (New York, W. W. Norton, 1989).

Srivastva, S., and D. L. Cooperrider, "The Emergence of the Egalitarian Organization," *Human Relations* 39 (August 1986): 683-724.

Stack, Carol, *All Our Kin* (New York: Harper & Row, 1974).

Stern, Daniel, *The Interpersonal World of the Infant: A View from Psychoanalysis and Developmental Psychology* (New York: Basic Books, 1985).

Stockman, David, *The Triumph of Politics* (New York: Avon Books, 1987).

Stone, Lawrence, *The Family, Sex, and Marriage in England 1500-1800* (New York: Harper & Row 1977).

Strickland, Charles, "A Transcendentalist Father: The Child-Rearing Practices of Bronson Alcott," *Perspectives in American History*, vol. 3 (Cambridge: Harvard University Press, Charles Warren Center for Studies in American History, 1969).

Susman, Warren I., *Culture as History* (New York: Pantheon, 1984).

Terkel, Studs, *Hard Times: An Oral History of the Great Depression* (New York: Pantheon, 1970).

Thompson, Roger, *Sex in Middlesex: Popular Mores in a Massachusetts County, 1649–1699* (Amherst: University of Massachusetts Press, 1986).

U.S. Bureau of the Census, *Historical Statistics of the United States, Colonial Times to 1970*, Bicentennial Edition, Part 1 (Washington, DC: U.S. Government Printing Office, 1975).

——, *U.S. Statistical Abstract, 1976* (Washington, DC: U.S. Government Printing Office, 1977).

——, *Households, Families, Marital Status, and Living Arrangements: March, 1984*, Current Population Reports P–20, no. 391 (Washington, DC: U.S. Government Printing Office, August 1984).

——, *Marital Status and Living Arrangements: March, 1984*, Current Population Reports, Series P–20, no. 399, (Washington, DC: U.S. Government Printing Office, 1985).

——, *Marital Status and Living Arrangements: March, 1985*, Current Population Reports, Series P–20, no. 410 (Washington, DC: U.S. Government Printing Office, 1986).

Veroff, Joseph, Elizabeth Douvan, and Richard A. Kulka, *The Inner American: A Self-Portrait from 1957 to 1976* (New York: Basic Books, 1981).

Vogel, Ezra F., *Japan as Number One* (Cambridge: Harvard University Press, 1979).

Wachtel, Paul L., *The Poverty of Affluence* (New York: Free Press, 1983).

Waite, Linda, Frances Goldscheider, and Christine Witsberger, "The Development of Individualism: Nonfamily Living and the Plans of Young Men and Women, *American Sociological Review* 51 (August 1986): 541–554.

Wallerstein, Judith S., and Sandra Blakeslee, *Second Chances: Men, Women, and Children a Decade after Divorce* (New York: Ticknor and Fields, 1989).

———, "Children after Divorce," *New York Times Magazine*, 22 January 1989.

Weinstein, James, *The Corporate Ideal in the Liberal State, 1900- 1918* (Boston: Beacon Press, 1968).

Weitzman, Lenore J., *The Divorce Revolution: The Unexpected Social and Economic Consequences for Women and Children in America* (New York: Free Press, 1985).

———, and Ruth B. Dixon, "The Transformation of Legal Marriage Through No-Fault Divorce," in *Family in Transition*, 5th ed., eds. Arlene S. Skolnick and Jerome H. Skolnick (Boston: Little, Brown, 1986), 338–351.

Wellman, David T., "The New Political Linguistics of Race," *Socialist Review* 87–88 (1986): 43–62.

Welter, Barbara, "The Cult of True Womanhood: 1820–1860," *The American Quarterly* (Summer 1966): 151–174.

Weyrich, Paul, "The Conservatives," PBS, 18 January 1987.

White, Lynn K., and David Brinkerhoff, "Children's Work in the Family: Its Significance and Meaning," in *Families and Work*, eds. Naomi Gerstel and Harriet Engel (Philadelphia: Temple University Press, 1987), 204–218.

Whyte, William F., *The Organizational Man* (New York: Simon & Schuster, 1956).

Wiebe, Robert H., *Businessmen and Reform* (Cambridge: Harvard University Press, 1962).

Wilensky, Harold L., and Charles N. Lebeaux, *Industrial Society and Social Welfare* (New York: Free Press of Glencoe, 1965).

Williams, Eric, *Capitalism and Slavery* (New York: Capricorn Books, 1976).

Wills, Gary, *Nixon Agonistes* (Boston: Houghton Mifflin, 1970).

Wolfe, Alan, *Whose Keeper: Social Science and Moral Obligation* (Berkeley: University of California Press, 1989).

Wolfenstein, M., "The Emergence of Fun Morality" *Journal of Social Issues* 7 (1951): 15–23.

Yankelovich, Daniel, *The New Morality: A Profile of American Youth in the 70's* (New York: McGraw-Hill, 1974).

———, *New Rules: Searching for Self-Fulfillment in a World Turned Upside Down* (New York: Random House, 1981).

Yans-McLaughlin, Elizabeth, *Family and Community: Italian Immigrants in Buffalo, 1880–1930* (Ithaca: Cornell University Press, 1977).

Young, Michael, and Peter Willmott, *The Symmetrical Family* (New York: Pantheon, 1973).

Youth 1976: Attitudes of Young Americans Fourteen through Twenty-five towards Work, Life Insurance, Finances, Family, Marriage, Life Styles, Religion (New York: American Council of Life Insurance, n.d.).

Zelnik, Melvin, and John F. Kanter, "First Pregnancies to Women Aged 15–19: 1976 and 1971," *Family Planning Perspectives* 10 (January/February 1978): 11–20.

Zimple, Lloyd, ed., *Man against Work* (Grand Rapids, MI: W. B. Eerdmans, 1974).

Zuckerman, Michael, "Pilgrims in the Wilderness: Community, Modernity, and the Maypole at Merry Mount," *The New England Quarterly* 1:2 (June 1977): 255–275.

Index